P9-CBF-212

THE WALTER LYNWOOD FLEMING
LECTURES IN SOUTHERN HISTORY

LOUISIANA STATE UNIVERSITY

OTHER PUBLISHED LECTURES IN THIS SERIES:

Myths and Realities

Societies of the Colonial South

By

CARL BRIDENBAUGH

GREENWOOD PRESS, PUBLISHERS
WESTPORT, CONNECTICUT

Library of Congress Cataloging in Publication Data

Bridenbaugh, Carl.
    Myths and realities.

    Reprint 'of the ed. published by Louisiana State
University Press, Baton Rouge, in series: The
Walter Lynwood Fleming lectures in southern history.
    Includes bibliographical references and index.
    1.   Southern States--Social life and customs--
Colonial period, ca. 1600-1775--Addresses, essays,
lectures.   2.   Southern States--Intellectual
life--Addresses, essays, lectures.   I.   Title.
II.   Series: Walter Lynwood Fleming lectures in
southern history.
[F212.B75   1981]   975'.02   80-25280
ISBN 0-313-22770-5 (lib. bdg.)

Reprinted in 1981 by Greenwood Press
A division of Congressional Information Service, Inc.
88 Post Road West, Westport, Connecticut 06881

Printed in the United States of America

10 9 8 7 6 5 4 3 2 1

FOR
MARY HAINES HERRIOTT

PREFACE

In 1776 there was no South; there never had been a South. It was not even a geographical expression, as the members of the Federal Convention made evident when they spoke of "the Southern states." In the four and a half decades before the Revolution the vast domain of the King lying between Mason and Dixon's line and East Florida was the scene of three, possibly four, different modes of existence. There was the already old Chesapeake Society, erected on a tobacco base; there was the youthful Carolina Society, burgeoning on profits from rice and indigo; there was the lusty Back Country, as yet unformed but prospering in several stages from hunting to mixed farming. Christopher Crittenden has shown that on the economic side seaboard North Carolina was more than a variant from Virginia and South Carolina norms. That it also produced an individual social pattern could be readily demonstrated were there ample time and space.

I have said that when Independence came there was no South. Below Pennsylvania was a land of vast extent and of richly varied topography. Its people—white, black, and red, English, Scots, Scotch-Irish, Irish, Welsh, Palatine German, and Swiss—were as miscellaneous as the features of the terrain, constituting without question the least homogeneous human group in all America. There were as yet no Southerners; there was not even any Southern accent. Throughout the Southern colonies the one certain impression conveyed was that of diversity.

But, I am asked, were there any conditions of life in these societies that prefigured the South that was to be, the South as we have traditionally thought of it? Yes, two such conditions obtained. The Negro already supplied to each society its common and determining human element. Then as now, the essential condition of Southern social life was that it was overwhelmingly rural. Only against the rural background of these colonial Souths in which Negro slavery was a persistent factor can the land of Dixie, which the nineteenth century thought of as *The South,* be comprehended.

No sustained effort to analyze and depict the life of the Southern provinces has yet been made. Historians of the region have understandably concentrated their attention upon the ante-bellum or reconstruction eras, but in so doing they have unwittingly left their history open at both ends, with neither a beginning nor a conclusion. In this volume, which is designed to elucidate Southern life and culture, I shall be concerned with the first societies to develop, and in particular with the years from 1730 to 1776. The "Old South" was preceded in time by the "Old Souths."

One must go directly back to the sources in a study such as this because earlier writers concerned themselves almost exclusively with institutional and political history, with reactions against external criticism, and with celebrating uncritically the achievements of their friends and kin. Above all, these authors, stemming from the gentry, wrote essentially aristocratic narratives of the past, and such comments or asides bearing on economic, social, and intellectual matters as they indulged were usually *obiter dicta* or at the most defensive assertions not subject to proof. I do not for a moment claim that this approach to history is unique to the South, but it has been and still is rather more intensely cultivated there than in other parts of the country.

Before I could deal with realities I found that there were many myths to be swept away from my mind; hence the title, *Myths and Realities*. It will at once be evident to the reader that the entire social and cultural history of the Southern colonies must be investigated and retold. All I can hope to do is to draw aside the curtain for an instant to afford those interested a glimpse of the great unknown and unsuspected Southern historical heritage. I am painfully aware that each of a score of topics to which I have accorded a paragraph or merely a sentence deserves extended study.

Although I am not a Southerner, I have spent many delightful and instructive years in Dixie, and have traveled far and wide to its cities, villages, farms, fields, and mountains. I not only have read a substantial portion of its history but have plunged headlong into its literature. I have talked with and lived among Southerners of all ranks and backgrounds, and have come to have a deep affection for, and I hope an understanding of, them and their land. A distinguished Virginian recently agreed that no son of the Old Dominion can write its history with any degree of objectivity, because he himself is part of the myth. Be that as it may, I offer the following revisions of ideas about the colonial societies of the South in the belief that they provide a useful perspective, since they are sketched against the broad backdrop of all the colonies and, indeed, of the cosmopolitan Western World of the eighteenth century.

Above all, *Myths and Realities* is meant to be a call to historians of the nation as well as of the section to turn back and investigate the enlightening first half of Southern history, not only for itself but because such a study will readjust, amplify, and clarify our understanding and interpretation of the second half of Southern history. It will perform the greatest of all historical services by explaining the present to us.

The following chapters are printed as they were written for oral delivery.

Carl Bridenbaugh

Berkeley
August 16, 1951

ACKNOWLEDGMENTS

My debts are many, and they are all to Southerners, or to those who, like me, have been hospitably adopted by the South. I seem always beholden to Douglass Adair of Williamsburg, who clothes ruthless criticism in such a kind and learned guise that one hastens to accept it. Christopher C. Crittenden of Raleigh genially caused me to rethink some of my ideas, as did my former colleague, Margaret Kinard, and Roberta Bridenbaugh.

For generous grants of time and materials I want to thank James W. Foster of Baltimore; David J. Mays and William J. Van Schreeven of Richmond; the University of North Carolina Library; Frank L. Horton and Douglas L. Rights of the Moravian Archives at Salem; Chalmers Davidson of Davidson College; Anna Wells Rutledge and Granville Prior of Charleston; Robert L. Meriwether and J. H. Easterby of Columbia; E. Merton Coulter of Athens; William R. Hogan, Fred C. Cole, and Wendell H. Stephenson of New Orleans; J. Kimbrough Owen of Baton Rouge; and P. W. Turrentine of Arkadelphia.

That my researches appear in their present form is due to the generosity of the History faculty of Louisiana State University in inviting me to give the Walter Lynwood Fleming Lectures in Southern History, November 5–6, 1951, and to the University authorities and the Louisiana State University Press for bringing it promptly to publication.

Contents

I

The Chesapeake Society

THE beautiful and accurate *Map of the Inhabited part of Virginia containing the whole Province of Maryland with part of . . . North Carolina Drawn by Joshua Fry & Peter Jefferson in 1751* was the first delineation of that portion of the Chesapeake country that lay beyond the tidewaters. To those well-informed gentlemen the "settled parts" of the largest and most populous English society in America consisted of the shores washed by the Chesapeake Bay and the lands drained by its tributaries, and they evidently felt no need of making any distinction between Tidewater and Piedmont on their map. The omission is significant. In discussing what I call the "Chesapeake Society" I shall follow their lead.

By 1776 members of the Chesapeake Society had come to occupy a region whose northern limits commenced at the head of the Great Bay, then moved westward across Maryland to the confluence of the Monocacy and the Potomac. On the west, settlement stopped short of a line at the foot of the Blue Ridge, which ran from the Potomac southwest through Leesburg, Culpeper and Orange courthouses, and Charlottesville, then turned almost due south across the James and on to Occaneechee Island (near Clarksville) in the Roanoke River. The southern reaches followed that stream eastward along its course to Albemarle Sound, thereby bringing the Chowan, Perquimans, Pasquotank, and Currituck precincts of North Carolina within the confines of the Chesapeake Society.[1]

That this vast area exhibited within itself marked variations of climate, soil, and topography I will readily concede. But I also contend that the salient features of the civilization developed within these limits from 1730 to 1776 were those of the Chesapeake-Tidewater folk, extended, albeit often in modified forms, to embrace the whole country. Such, at least, was the avowed intent of the people. Indeed, demographically, economically, politically, and culturally, Thomas Jefferson's Albemarle County in the western Piedmont grew to resemble Hanover and New Kent far to the eastward much more than it did Augusta County which lay in the Great Valley only a few miles to the westward through Rockfish Gap. Although it was hardly true of western Maryland or of the Carolina Back Country, the society of the Virginia Piedmont must be regarded as a continuation of that of the Tidewater, for upon analysis the difference between the two seems artificial. In like fashion, provincial boundaries separating Lord Baltimore's province from the Old Dominion, or North Carolina's Albemarle settlements from Virginia, appear equally artificial when a whole society is under examination. Cultural and social uniformities prevail over political and environmental diversities, and the older distinctions have no great validity for the four decades preceding Independence. I shall, therefore, consider the Chesapeake Society as a complete unit.

*   *   *   *   *

[1] Morgan P. Robinson, "Virginia Counties," Virginia State Library, *Bulletin* (Richmond, 1916), IX, 124, 128–35, and maps; Stella H. Sutherland, *Population Distribution in Colonial America* (New York, 1936), 179–80, 199; Williamsburg *Virginia Gazette,* May 25, June 22, 1739.

Within this great territory of over 42,000 square miles lived some 235,000 people in 1735, and their number more than doubled by the eve of the Revolution. There was room for all, and more too. Travelers always noticed that much of the arable land in the Tidewater as well as in the Piedmont remained unoccupied, and their observations were borne out by a density of only twenty-three persons per square mile. Although some Scots, French Huguenots, and more Germans and Scotch-Irish settled on the fringes of the region, particularly in northern and western Maryland, the white population of the Chesapeake Society was almost as completely English in composition as that of Yankee Connecticut. This was scarcely a homogeneous people, however, since 45.5 per cent were Negro slaves descended from African tribesmen of many shades of color and of varied physical characteristics.[2]

Climate, soil, tradition, and current demands conspired to intensify and spread westward the fabled tobacco economy whose institutions had become fixed in the Tidewater before 1700 and which replaced the small farm as portions of the Piedmont passed rapidly through their frontier phase and became rural areas. There were, to be sure, noticeable sectional and time variations in this process, but sooner or later the familiar plantation pattern dictated the life of the entire society. Tobacco was king. The same need for a cash crop and the credit system evolved by English merchants in the previous century continued to bind the tobacco planters to the mother country.

The ruralness forced by tobacco culture was deepened

[2] By 1775 the population density of the Piedmont (21.5) almost equaled that of the Tidewater (24.5). For the entire Southern colonies the figure was 14.6 as compared with Rhode Island's 45.0. Sutherland, *Population Distribution*, 37, 202n., 203; Charles A. Barker, *Background of the Revolution in Maryland* (New Haven, 1940), 9; Margaret Armstrong, *Five Generations* (New York, 1930), 20.

by the geography of the Chesapeake region. Travel and communication by water up and down the Great Bay were both easy and rapid, but the principal rivers—the Potomac, Rappahannock, York, James, and Roanoke—flowed west to east, causing north and south traffic to proceed by ferries or to move inland beyond the falls where fords and bridges were available. At first roads were few and overland travel developed slowly. A weekly postal route running from Philadelphia to Williamsburg, and continuing as far south as Edenton once a month, was opened in 1738; but Maryland alone enjoyed quick and easy communication with the Northern colonies, either by land or by sea. Virginia and the Albemarle section of North Carolina, although in comparatively frequent touch with the British Isles, were far more isolated from their sister colonies than we have realized. New England's maritime peddlers found less occasion to call at Old Dominion river landings than at the ports of any of the other continental provinces, and this colony had allocated virtually none of its own merchant shipping to keep its people in contact with the rest of America.[3] Economic isolation from other parts of English America led to a significant social and cultural dwelling apart, and it is the consequences or ramifications of this condition that I wish to single out.

Tobacco planting—supplemented or replaced by 1750 by lumbering, production of naval stores or iron, and the increased cultivation of corn, wheat, and cotton—was an extractive agriculture requiring continual acquisition and clearing of new lands as soil exhaustion inexorably ren-

[3] *Va. Gaz.*, Apr. 28, 1738; Apr. 27, 1757. Local Virginia service to Fredericksburg, Hobbs's Hole, Hanover C. H., Petersburg, York, and Hampton commenced in 1766; for Maryland's much superior communications, see Annapolis *Maryland Gazette*, June 10, 1729; Oct. 18, 1745; *Maryland Historical Magazine*, VIII (1913), 170; and for a stage line from Philadelphia to Baltimore, *Va. Gaz.* (Rind), Jan. 14, 1772.

dered old regions less and less profitable. Great planter and small farmer alike eagerly sought better opportunities in the West until by the mid-century the economic center of gravity of the Chesapeake Society had shifted beyond the fall line to the Piedmont, where mansion house and small dwelling rose side by side.

The very scattering of the population over the country-side militated against urban development. Despite the rise of Norfolk and Baltimore as grain shipping centers toward the close of the colonial era, and the appearance at the heads of navigation of such little inland entrepôts as North East and Upper Marlboro, Alexandria, Dumfries, Fredericksburg, Richmond, and Petersburg, the fundamental ruralness of this society was undisturbed. Lacking urban focal centers it did not even produce the tiny villages that dotted the English colonies to the north, and the inevitable corollary was a fatal failure to give birth and support to a dearly needed middle class of artisans and tradesmen.

This rural society, produced by the interaction of geography and economy, also was buttressed by the traditions and inclination of the yeoman stock; when some of the members prospered and moved up into the lesser gentry, they sought with determination to preserve in Virginia what they fancied and recalled of the life of the English countryside. Sprung from necessity, it came to be dignified as an ideal; but this concept of English country life was almost as unreal as the European stereotype of the Noble Savage. How this sanction arose is best revealed by an examination of the social structure.

Like its government, society in the Chesapeake area seemed easy-going on first appearance, but it was stratified and had its hierarchy of ranks, from the many to the few. At the bottom were the "vast Shoals of Negroes" who constituted nearly half of the population in 1775 or about

170,000 souls. The slaves proved a potent force in the land despite their base status. The majority, especially in Maryland, were country-born. All affected the white man's habits and customs.[4] Their influence on their masters was not confined solely to producing tobacco, performing menial tasks, breeding, and increasing in value as slave prices mounted; their presence as the largest single element in the population started and held the Chesapeake civilization on its unique course—a course that forever prevented the possibility of its becoming the exact replica of the English rural society its votaries so eagerly sought to erect, and which their descendants often assume did come into being. Every aspect of life bore the impress of the slave, from the introduction of Africanisms into the language to the crystallization of social needs and customs in provincial legal codes. Without freedom, articulateness, leadership, property, status, or power, the blacks were nevertheless one of the determining factors of the Chesapeake Society.

"The number of Convicts and Indented servants imported" into the Chesapeake colonies is "amazing, besides the numbers of Dutch and German which is also Considerable," a French traveler reported in 1765. In theory the bound servant—if a free-willer—experienced a transitional state of servitude for five years, or seven if a transported convict; the longer term led most planters to prefer convicts, with the result that as a class, servants were frozen into a fixed status after 1750. Negro slave competition and diminishing opportunities to acquire cheap or free land further aggravated their condition. There is real poignancy in the announcement of Thomas Sparrow, An-

---

[4] Hugh Jones, *Present State of Virginia* (London, 1724), 36–38, 114; John Custis, Letter Book (typescript, Library of Congress), 164; Hunter D. Farish (ed.), *Journal & Letters of Philip Vickers Fithian* (Williamsburg, 1943), 80; William Eddis, *Letters from America* (London, 1792), 64–65.

napolis silversmith, in 1746 that no one is henceforth to deal with Robert Impey, because he "has indentured himself a Servant unto me . . . during the Term of his natural Life." On the other hand, there was David Benfield, physician and poacher of Oxford in Old England, who was transported for his crime and who, in 1772, proudly penned for his old gaoler a lively account of success in his profession in rural Maryland north of Baltimore. By eschewing former convict acquaintances, "I Keep the best Company as neare as I can," and will clear £100 this year. "I Lives Like a Ientleman." Between these extremes, but much nearer the former, fell the lot of the 8,846 convict servants transported to Maryland from 1745 to 1775 and of perhaps half as many more shipped to the Old Dominion.[5]

By far the largest number of servants sent to the Chesapeake from 1728 to 1768 were Irish. About 1750 many German redemptioners began to arrive, and after 1768 English immigration started again. When we realize that between one half and one third of the white immigrants before the Revolution were indentured servants, redemptioners, or convicts, and that more than 50 per cent were Irish or German, the ethnic and social consequences of their presence take on increased significance. More than any other class, these people, most of them males, bitterly hated the black slave and regarded him as a real competitor. That many committed crimes and more sought to break the shackles of status by running away is easily understood. Often overlooked, however, is the fact that

[5] "Journal of a French Traveller in the Colonies, 1765," *American Historical Review*, XXVI (1921), 744; *Md. Gaz.*, June 17, 1746; Oct. 5, 12, 1752; Barker, *Maryland*, 35; Eddis, *Letters*, 66–69; *Md. Hist. Mag.*, II (1907), 44; *ibid.*, XXXVIII (1943), 194–95; *Va. Gaz.*, May 8, 30, Dec. 5, 1751; *Va. Gaz.* (Purdie & Dixon), Mar. 26, 1767; *Va. Gaz.* (Rind), Mar. 3, 1768.

they and their descendants eventually became a sound and thrifty section of the new American people.[6]

The lower class, "who ever compose the bulk of mankind," were fewer in Virginia than perhaps anywhere in the world, according to J. F. D. Smyth, and his observation can be applied to Maryland and Albemarle as well. Landless folk like the lower orders of the mother country were never numerous, although in the late colonial period farm tenancy developed noticeably in Virginia's Northern Neck and in the western counties of Maryland, where land had been engrossed in large parcels and withheld from sale. Uncouth, noisy, turbulent, uneducated, and illiberal as were these poor whites, even their severest critics found them at the same time kindly and hospitable. In a country guaranteeing rude plenty to everyone who made an effort with the soil, they stood out by their avoidance of labor, by swinish consumption of the ever-present peach brandy or hard cider, and by a horrible brutality in frequent rough-and-tumble fights in which eye-gouging and "Abelarding" were more conspicuous than not. "It would almost seem as if the poor white man would rather starve than work, because the negro works," reported Elkanah Watson.[7]

A large percentage of those white inhabitants who were not in bondage comprised the smaller or lesser planters

[6] Abbot E. Smith, *Colonists in Bondage* (Chapel Hill, 1947), 328–36; Kate M. Rowland, *Charles Carroll of Carrollton* (New York, 1898), I, 52; *Va. Gaz.*, Mar. 11, 1736/7; *Va. Gaz.* (Purdie & Dixon), Nov. 26, 1767; *Md. Gaz.*, July 7, 1747.

[7] Thomas Anburey, *Travels through the Interior Parts of America* (London, 1789), II, 373–74; J. F. D. Smyth, *A Tour in the United States of America* (London, 1784), I, 68–71; Winslow C. Watson (ed.), *Men and Times of the Revolution; or the Memoirs of Elkanah Watson* (New York, 1856), 61; Willard F. Bliss, "The Rise of Tenancy in Virginia," *Virginia Magazine of History and Biography*, LVIII (1950), 427–41; Dieter Cunz, *Maryland Germans: A History* (Princeton, 1948), 114; Andrew J. Morrison (ed.), *Johann D. Schoepf's Travels in the Confederation* (Philadelphia, 1911), II, 31.

who cultivated their tobacco fields by their own labor or perhaps with the aid of from one to five or ten slaves. As new interior lands of the Chesapeake country came under the plantation system, this class steadily increased, made up as it was of younger sons of richer planters and, even more, of successful recruits from servant ranks. Within the group there was a wide range of wealth and social position. On the one hand there were simple, unpretentious farming families like the Irish Jarratts of New Kent County, whose son Devereux has left the only vivid record of the middling planters of Virginia. It tells of "poor people, but industrious and rather rough in their manners," who farmed rather than planted their tract without any slaves. In contrast to such "Lubbers," "thick-skulls," or "common buckskins,"—"them that are born in the coun-trie"—stood the comfortably prosperous planter owning 200 to 500 acres and a number of slaves. Such a man was Thomas Hall with his 230 acres and a four-room, story-and-a-half house with a brick chimney, storehouses, dairy, smokehouse, and stable situated in Prince George County; or George M'Murdo, who lived somewhat more luxur-iously at "Maycox" in a "commodious Brick Dwelling, . . . with Cellars," a brick kitchen, and convenient out-buildings situated in the same county near the James River Ferry to Westover.[8] Such establishments of course re-quired an investment in five to fifteen slaves for efficient operation.

The characteristics of the lesser planters varied as widely as their estates. Many proved ambitious and enter-prising and sought, often with noticeable success, to win a

[8] Evarts B. Greene, *The Revolutionary Generation, 1760–1790* (New York, 1943), 17; Devereux Jarratt, *The Life of the Reverend Devereux Jarratt* (Richmond, 1806), 13–25; *Md. Hist. Mag.*, I (1906), 351; Farish (ed.), *Fithian Journal*, 240.

foothold with the gentry. Respect as well as envy was the portion accorded them by less successful neighbors. Then there were also those planters who made up the "semi-barbarian population" described by Elkanah Watson, who was decently shocked at seeing naked adolescent boys waiting on table before white females.[9]

Conditions of living joined with the aspirations of the people to produce in the tobacco country a ruling class more nearly approaching European aristocracies than any other America has known. Membership among these F.F.C.'s (First Families of the Chesapeake) came naturally and exclusively to the richest planting families and to the Anglican clergy, native merchants, physicians, and lawyers (especially in Maryland) associated with them, who more often than not divided their time between their special interests and agriculture. Wealth, lavishly displayed in broad acres, imposing mansions, and many slaves, was the passport for admission to this patrician order, and its possession elevated such great families as the Burwells, Carters, Fitzhughs, Lees, and Randolphs of Virginia, the Carrolls, Dulanys, Galloways, Lloyds, and Taskers of Maryland, and the Corbins, Hewses, Johnstons, and Joneses of the Albemarle to something approximating an American nobility.

Riches could be amassed in several ways. Tobacco built the seventeenth-century fortunes. In the eighteenth century, wheat growing, iron and lumber manufacture, shipbuilding, and trade frequently proved lucrative additions to the activities of the Byrds, Carters, Spotswoods, and Taskers. Many Tidewater gentlemen successfully combined trade with planting, and a few, like Carter Braxton, found profits in the convict and slave traffic. But acquisition of new lands was always the quickest and surest way to

[9] Watson (ed.), *Men and Times,* 32.

affluence in an expanding agricultural economy, making virtually every gentleman a land speculator. Dr. Thomas Walker, George Washington, and Daniel Dulany the Elder are but the most obvious examples of a familiar type. Political influence rendered the procuring of large tracts easy for the aristocrats, who filled all offices from vestry to governor's council. In Maryland members of a small number of prominent families included among the 350 odd persons holding office by favor of the Calverts not. only enjoyed profitable and stable revenues from fees without much expense of time or labor but also had ready access to ample grants of land.[10]

There was, besides, one other avenue leading directly to "the top of the province." This was a successful marriage into one of the principal families. "Now all the pritty Fellows here have a good tast," declared the spinster sister of Governor Gooch in 1729; "they like Youth, Beauty and Money, but I can tell them, if I had either of the three, I should think it hard fortune not to have a Love." No scruples deterred Chesapeake fortune hunters, who could love a rich girl more than a poor one; and when they were successful, the local press always gave them an accolade by reporting the heiress as "a young Lady possessed of an independent Fortune of at least 6000£," or, more tersely, as having "an agreeable Fortune." Apparently age made no great difference to some, for Isaiah Thomas in faraway Boston inserted in the columns of his *Massachusetts Spy* the human-interest story from Henrico County of the marriage of handsome, twenty-three-year-old William Carter to Madam Sarah Ellyson, a widow of eighty-five, described in the communication as "a sprightly old Tit, with three thousand pounds fortune." So common did these announce-

[10] Donnell M. Owings, "His Lordship's Favour," Harvard University, *Summary of Theses, 1942* (Cambridge, 1946), 174–78.

ments equating the fortune with the lady become that "Corporal Trim, jr.," lampooned the practice in 1773: "However, if I can but once marry a rich Bride, as I hope soon to do, and get into the House of Burgesses, I shall think it a very fine thing to be a Member of Parliament." [11] Marriage, wealth, and preference—a Chesapeake trinity.

The high value the gentry "put upon posts of honour, and mental acquirements" facilitated the entrance of a young man of mean estate to their ranks if he but possessed the latter. "For example," wrote Philip Fithian to his successor as tutor to the Carters of Nomini Hall, "if you should travel through this Colony, with a well-confirmed testimonial of your having finished with Credit a Course of Studies at Nassau-Hall; you would be rated, without any more questions asked, either about your family, your Estate, your business, or your intention, at about 10,000£; and you might come, and go, and converse, and keep company, according to this value; and you would be dispised and slighted if you rated yourself a farthing cheaper." To be a Princeton man in eighteenth-century Virginia was really something, for Madam Carter did her very best to marry off Tutor Fithian to Betsy Lee, cousin of Richard Henry and an agreeable young lady with a share in the luxurious estate of Mount Pleasant in Westmoreland.[12]

The most significant feature of the Chesapeake aristocracy was its middle-class origin. Middle- and lower-class Englishmen had laid the foundations for it in the previous century, as is well known, and their descendants worked to give it luster in succeeding years. Notwithstanding the

[11] Letter Book of Governor William Gooch (typescript, Colonial Williamsburg, Inc.), 152; *Va. Gaz.*, Dec. 30, 1737; *William and Mary Quarterly*, XI (1902–1903), 240; *Va. Gaz.* (Rind), Feb. 16, 1769; Boston *Massachusetts Spy*, Apr. 19, 1771; *Va. Gaz.* (Purdie & Dixon), Dec. 2, 1773; *Md. Gaz.*, June 3, 1746.

[12] Farish (ed.), *Fithian Journal*, 211–12.

brilliance eventually attained, in every respect this society was conditioned by its beginnings; lacking the leaven of a few noblemen, it never entirely threw off its bourgeois trappings. Nicholas Cresswell, who was familiar with both English and American gentility, accurately described General Washington as the second son of "a creditable Virginia Tobacco Planter (which I suppose may, in point of rank, be equal to the better sort of Yeomanry in England)." He found Washington living like "a Country Gentleman, much noted for his hospitality, great knowledge in agriculture, and industry in carrying his various manufactories of Linen and Woollen to greater perfection than any man" in the region.[13] Modern critics have delighted in leveling the charge of puritan middle-class morbidity and concern with death at Samuel Sewall for rearranging the coffins in the Boston family vault on Christmas Day; but such preoccupation is mild when compared with the pathological state of mind of Virginia's first gentleman, William Byrd II, who recorded in his diary on January 24, 1710: "I had my father's grave opened to see him [six years after his death] but he was so wasted there was not anything to be distinguished. I ate fish for dinner."

Most commentators—colonial, English, and French— agreed in believing that this bourgeois aristocracy, wherein they found "the best families and fortunes," was more numerous and respectable than elsewhere on the continent. Its members possessed great wealth and appeared prosperous: one observed that "the very Slaves, in some families here, could not be bought under 30000£"; all marveled at the noble mansion houses with their elaborate and costly furnishings. But such great wealth, consisting principally of land and slaves, was not negotiable; the land was often

[13] Smyth, *Tour,* II, 148; Nicholas Cresswell, *Journal* (New York, 1924), 252–54.

entailed and therefore not subject to transfer. Moreover
—and this was crucial—"the general luxury and extravagant way of living . . . among the planters" obscured the
fact that virtually every one of them was so "immers'd over
Head and Ears in Debt" to English and Scottish merchants
that the income from the estates went more and more to
pay interest charges as the situation became almost hopeless. Thomas Jefferson tells us that debts had become
hereditary from father to son and that many Chesapeake
estates had become a "species of property annexed to certain mercantile houses in London." According to the
Reverend Jonathan Boucher, "shrewd planters" were convinced that "a Mercht serves no Deity but his own Interest." It was true, however, as one Londoner insisted, that
Chesapeake planters "over value their incomes, and live
up to their suppositions without providing against Calami-
ties and accidents," or, he might have added, being able to
do so.

By the sixties hard times had come and large numbers
of planters, in Virginia at least, were upon the brink of
failure. Few could satisfy their creditors, and Thomas
Nelson warned: "These are but Preludes to Vast Changes
of property among us, that must soon take place." A very
good case can be made for the view that Speaker John
Robinson's illegal loans of £100,000 of retired currency to
insolvent planters were a desperate attempt to save the
Virginia aristocracy from economic ruin, although this
first American legislative scandal cannot be defended.
Wealth was apparent rather than real. Economically the
Chesapeake had reached its peak at the mid-century and
by 1765 the Tidewater areas actually faced bankruptcy.
The new lands of the Piedmont alone were prosperous.[14]

[14] Farish (ed.), *Fithian Journal*, 211; Harry S. Carman (ed.), *American Husbandry* (New York, 1939), 162, 175; *Md. Hist. Mag.*, VII (1912), 18,

In an aristocracy wealth guarantees status; status conveys privilege; privilege ensures power. This was true of the Chesapeake Society, where provincial assemblies were but planters' clubs ordering affairs for a class and deeming that what was best for the class was also fit for all. By an almost hereditary right a gentleman usually succeeded to a seat on the vestry; by the governor's commission he became a justice of the county court; by the freemen he was chosen from among his equals for membership in the lower house of the assembly; or, by royal or proprietorial favor, he might be one of a select few to achieve the greatest prestige and power in the region by holding a seat on the governor's council. This process met with not only the acquiescence but the approval of the public, which customarily reasoned, as in the case of George William Fairfax, that "Family, Fortune and good sense all entitle him to a place there." [15]

Privilege and "such amazing property, no matter how deep it is involved, blows up the owners to an imagination, which is visible in all," commented a penetrating critic, "but in various degrees according to their respective virtue, that they are exalted as much above other Men in worth and precedency, as blind stupid fortune has made a difference in their property." Chesapeake bigwigs looked and acted the part, impressing all manner of folk from little Devereux Jarratt, who always ran away when one approached, to John Adams, who found them more forbidding than the nabobs of Boston. The most pleasing quality

296; W. P. Palmer (ed.), *Calendar of Virginia State Papers* (Richmond, 1875), I, 160; William Nelson, Letter Book, 1766–75 (Virginia State Library), 19; *Va. Gaz.* (Rind), Mar. 31, 1768; David J. Mays has a list of the debts owed to Robinson's estate in his forthcoming *Edmund Pendleton* (Cambridge, 1952); Paul L. Ford (ed.), *Writings of Thomas Jefferson* (New York, 1892–99), IV, 155; Carl Bridenbaugh, *Seat of Empire: The Political Role of Williamsburg* (Williamsburg, 1950), 68–69.
[15] Nelson, Letter Book, 37.

that Fithian found in Miss Betsy Lee was freedom from "Haughtiness, the Common foible here." Cultivated and witty Dr. Henry Potter from Cambridge and Leyden succeeded in his profession at Williamsburg under the patronage of Governor Gooch, who, however, cogently remarked that "the Country think him both too dear and too Proud, for they don't like those Qualities in any but themselves." Least praiseworthy of all their attitudes was that displayed towards persons who, like one Mr. Campbell, had lost a fortune, "on which Account," we are told, "his Family does not now meet with so great respect, as . . . they formerly did" from gentlefolk on the Northern Neck.[16]

Noblesse oblige was as much a part of the creed of the Chesapeake gentry as it was of the old regime in France. The inferior and middling sort of people generally found the owner of the big estate courteous, kind, and a fair and understanding judge on the quorum, ready to extend a helping hand before his aid was sought. A gentleman knew his neighbors of every rank and called them by name. Above all, the leading planters were imbued with the belief that they constituted a class whose obligations to serve and to govern well must be fulfilled in return for the privileges which were their birthright. This was a part of their code; this duty of service to the state was to be given without charge, as George Washington made clear to the Continental Congress when he accepted command of its army. There is no denying that aristocrats ruled in the interests of their class, but they brought to the political office a sound practical knowledge of the needs of their agricultural community, an understanding of how to deal with human beings learned on their estates, a habit of command that made

[16] Farish (ed.), *Fithian Journal,* 101, 211, 234; Gooch, Letter Book, 43–44.

them good leaders whether in politics or war, and a strong sense of justice. It was a responsible aristocracy.[17]

Historians often tell us that one of the really great advantages of the plantation system was the leisure it afforded the masters. Was this true? In the Chesapeake Society the exact opposite was actually the case. By its very nature the planter's task required virtually all of his waking hours. The proper conduct of a patriarchal domain with its commercial, agricultural, industrial, and legal obligations was a job requiring more time than the conscientious planter ever had at his disposal. Moreover, it was as confining and as hard as it was unremitting. Even a cursory investigation of the time which William Byrd II, Robert Carter, George Washington, and Charles Carroll of Carrollton allocated to various duties on their estates demonstrates the truth of my assertion. If many planters are known to have been indolent, this was not from lack of work to be performed on their part. Overseers were hard to get, and tobacco profits did not permit the absenteeism of the West Indian sugar nabobs. The Chesapeake planter's work was never done. In the oft-cited cases of Thomas Jefferson and James Madison we discover that they deeply resented the hours of reading and study that tobacco stole from them. Leisure was a myth; endless work was a reality quite as much for successful planter-gentlemen as for their lesser confreres—and the same held for their womenfolk as well.[18]

[17] Bridenbaugh, *Seat of Empire*, 2–18.

[18] See the diaries of William Byrd II, Landon Carter, Philip Fithian, and George Washington; Lewis Morton, *Robert Carter of Nomini Hall* (Williamsburg, 1941); Rowland, *Charles Carroll;* Irving Brant, *James Madison: The Virginia Revolutionist* (Indianapolis, 1941); Dumas Malone, *Jefferson the Virginian* (Boston, 1948); and Bridenbaugh, *Seat of Empire*. Douglass Adair will develop this subject in detail in a work on the intellectual origins of Jeffersonian democracy.

There was a beguiling casualness about the Chesapeake Society that tended to obscure the primary concern of each of its members with his or her status. The difference between it and that of England was that opportunities for white people to improve their status were far greater over here. A considerable amount of moving upward from servitude to the rank of the lower planter, and rather more from lesser to greater planter, occurred than might be expected. Life was ordered by and for the gentry, and because the road to prestige and property seemed open to all there was no seething social unrest that would develop into a revolutionary thrust for power as in Pennsylvania and New York where propertyless, unfranchised, urban groups pressed heavily against the aristocracy. In the tobacco country before the War for Independence, social classes were in equilibrium, and such questioning of the rule of gentlemen as there was came from the gentlemen themselves.

The one human institution common to and binding all ranks together was the family. Rural imperatives made large families desirable as well as possible, and the people of the Chesapeake gloried in a benevolent patriarchal regime, whether in the great houses or in humble cabins. Stemming directly from the importance of the family connection and greatly intensified by the conditions of rural life was the extent of intermarriage, which was naturally most discernible among patrician families, although eventually nearly every white person—and sometimes black—became kin to everyone else, and the degree of kinship was a vital matter. What Jonathan Boucher discovered of the Northern Neck applied equally to the whole region: "Certain districts come to be settled by certain families; and different places are there known and spoken of, not as here [in England], by any difference of dialect (for there is

no dialect in all North America) but by their being inhabited by the Fitzhughs, the Randolphs, Washingtons,
Carys, Grimeses, or Thorntons. This circumstance used to
furnish me with a scope for many remarks, such as do not
so often occur here. The family character both of body and
mind, may be traced thro' many generations: as for instance every Fitzhugh has bad eyes; every Thornton hears
badly; Winslows and Lees talk well; Carters are proud
and imperious; and Taliaferros mean and avaricious; and
Fowkeses cruel." [19]

Everywhere in the eighteenth century family arrangements were made for the benefit of what was definitely a
male society. Yet, as contrasted with their sisters in Old
England, the women of the Chesapeake possessed many
advantages and were marching forward to more. The
freedom of movement permitted them amazed most Englishmen, who generally praised their accomplishments,
gentility, animated conversation, and attention "to the
more important embellishments of the mind." But it was
their persons that never failed to catch the foreigner's eye
and excite his admiration: they were tall, often handsome,
and had unusually "fine shapes." "I think I have not seen
three crooked women in the country," insisted Nicholas
Cresswell, who thought such good figures developed naturally because the ladies refused to wear stays in the summer and seldom wore them in the winter. What with excessive child-bearing, however, and, for the poorer sort,
hard household labor, it is not surprising that the fair sex
faded early and that few had good teeth at twenty-five.[20]

Indulgence in the female passion for finery and fashion
was restricted only by purse, never by class lines or sumptu-

[19] Jonathan Bouchier (ed.), Jonathan Boucher's *Reminiscences of an
American Loyalist, 1738–1789* (Boston, 1925), 61; Barker, *Maryland,* 3.
[20] Eddis, *Letters,* 31–32, 113; Cresswell, *Journal,* 270–71.

ary laws. Concern about what to wear and the ability to acquire desired furbelows is reflected in a report of 1774 that "common Planter's Daughters here go every Day in finer Cloaths" than the people in the north of England save for Sunday display. Even in the Piedmont, where male finery was confined to buckskin fringe and nary a silk stocking was seen, Dr. Johann Schoepf relates that at cabins "about which all the evidences of negligence are to be remarked, it is nothing extraordinary to see the lady of the house, and women generally, clothed and adorned with great fastidiousness; for the fair sex in America cannot resist the propensity to make themselves fine, even when remotely situated they must forego the pleasure of being admired except by the casual traveller." But it paid dividends, for another tells us that "that great curiosity, an Old Maid, is seldom seen in this country. They generally marry before they are twenty-two, often before they are sixteen. In short this was a paradise in Earth for women." [21]

Family influence and discipline, coupled with universal celebration of some of the bourgeois virtues imparted a highly moral tone to society. Even at the highest level, the F.F.C.'s, who imitated nearly everything English, shrank from the loose and cynical morality of the nobility and suffered genuine shock when they encountered it on visits home. The one striking exception to this was the universal indulgence in profanity and rural earthy talk by both men and women of all ranks. Himself no prude, Jonathan Boucher could only occasionally "stop the Torrent of Ribaldry." He resented "their forward intrusion which subjects you to hear obscene Conceits and broad Expression; and from this, there are times when no sex, no Rank,

[21] *Md. Hist. Mag.*, VII (1912), 5; Morrison (ed.), Schoepf's *Travels*, II, 33; Cresswell, *Journal*, 271.

no Conduct can exempt you." In the "first Class of the Female Sex," Fithian was quick to place sixteen-year-old Priscilla Carter, because she "never swears, which is here a distinguished virtue." [22]

Between 1735 and 1750 the Chesapeake Society attained its greatest prosperity. We have just examined the countryside, the economy that flourished in it, and the people living there or moving into it for nearly a century and a half. Now the greatest test of a society is the kind of civilization that it produces—the state of its public mind, taste, and manners, when it is at its peak. What kind of a culture did this society nourish and what was its achievement? As we seek the answer in the remainder of this chapter, it will be well to keep three facts prominently in mind: first, that cultures vary widely and what is accomplished by one people may not be accomplished by another; second, that we can expect to find cultural development only in the aristocracy, only among a relatively small number of the people; and third, that we are dealing with a rural region, a region without stimulating urban centers and whose metropolis was London, three thousand miles across the sea.

The loneliness endemic in a rural existence was heightened by the plantation system, which forced the master's family to live far removed from the nearest neighbor in a sort of fearful isolation among its Negro slaves. Desire for companionship induced a gregariousness and eager search for sociability, and the agricultural way of life and a mild climate combined to develop an out-of-door folk whose leisure called for nearly as much activity as their labors. No one can deny that many were indolent and, taking advantage of a bounteous nature, passed an inordinate amount of time in ease and pleasure; but the fact remains

[22] *Md. Hist. Mag.*, VII (1912), 22, 23; Farish (ed.), *Fithian Journal*, 65.

that the better planters, of whom George Washington was the archetype, worked very hard and, when they found the time, played just as hard. There was often a hectic flush to their gaiety, and it almost seems as if they felt they must seize the moment and make the most of it. Whether hard-working or lazy, rich or poor, these people responded with energy and vivacity to any proposal of a sociable nature and were seldom restrained by religious codes.[23]

Most outdoor recreations revolved around the horse. Throughout the area riding was the principal form of exercise for both men and women, and every great planter maintained a large stable and a carriage house full of chaises and chairs, plus a coach for long-distance travel. Many young gentlemen, like the fourth Landon Carter, hunted foxes on horseback with their dogs, although there was no chase of the pink-coat variety in this part of America before 1776. Always popular, horse racing was the leading sport after 1730, becoming formalized with the founding in 1750 of the Jockey Club of Annapolis. In Virginia, by 1774 Dumfries, Fredericksburg, and Portsmouth sported similar associations, whose four-day fall meetings attracted "a prodigious concourse of spectators." Under the aegis of such fanciers of horseflesh as John Tayloe of Mount Airy, Benjamin Tasker of Belair, Samuel Galloway of Tulip Hill, and William Byrd III of Westover, the local breed was steadily improved by imported stallions, which sometimes earned their owners between £20 and £300 a year. Such noble steeds as Yorick, Nonpareil, Traveller, Selim, and Merry Tom sired an equine aristocracy paralleling the F.F.C.'s, and today they tell at Mount Airy that the young descendants of the Tayloe family take more interest and pride in the pictures and pedigrees of the estate's horses, whose scions have won every Kentucky

---

[23] Andrew Burnaby, *Travels through the Middle Settlements in North America, in the Years 1759 and 1760* (London, 1798), 25.

Derby up to Gallant Fox, than they do in the famed Tayloe portraits and genealogy.[24]

The middling and inferior sorts customarily enjoyed the same outdoor amusements as their superiors. They hunted on horseback or afoot and swelled the turbulent crowds that watched, bet, and drank at the racecourse. In each village, at every courthouse, and at intervals along the King's highway were literally hundreds of ordinaries or taverns—the "Bacchanalian Mansions" of the average man—to which the commonalty resorted day and night to hear the news, talk politics and horses, swap yarns, gossip, get away from work and their wives, and enjoy the crude conviviality of the vicinity. Here rum, toddy, flip, and other potations generated uproarious laughter and, not infrequently, blind anger that ended in a rough-and-tumble fight. Such places were the "Race-Horse Tavern," commonly known as the "Long-Ordinary," at Fredericksburg, which boasted a billiard table, and the groggery at Cumberland Court House, where in 1766 Colonel John Chiswell, haughty and sober, murdered besotted Robert Routledge in cold blood for a fancied insult. In the yards of establishments like Seayre's at Hobbs's Hole or Avery's in Prince George County, Virginia, the excitement of bloody cockfights tended to bring sporting men of all ranks together in the same ironic manner that the turf did.[25]

Annual fairs always drew large crowds, as did election

[24] E. S. Riley, *The Ancient City* (Annapolis, 1887), 158; Eddis, *Letters,* 106–107; *Md. Gaz.,* Mar. 8, 1770; Rowland, *Charles Carroll,* I, 52, 67; *Md. Hist. Mag.,* VII (1912), 13; *ibid.,* XXXV (1940), 200; *Va. Gaz.* (Royle), sup. ex., Oct. 25, 1765; *Va. Gaz.* (Purdie & Dixon), Apr. 25, 1766; *Va. Gaz.* (Rind), May 30, 1766; Aug. 4, 1768; July 21, Aug. 25, 1774; *W. & M. Quart.,* XIV (1906), 253; Fairfax Harrison, *The Equine F F V's* (Richmond, 1928), 43, 46, 51; conversation of author with the Misses Tayloe at Mount Airy, Aug. 29, 1950.

[25] *Va. Gaz.,* Mar. 7, 1750/1; Apr. 11, 1751; Feb. 27, 1752; *Va. Gaz.,* Jan. 2, 1752; *Va. Gaz.* (Rind), Apr. 8, 1773; Jones, *Present State of Virginia,* 48.

days and the regularly scheduled meetings of county courts, which were the occasion not only for much extra-legal business but also for merriment of all kinds. Frequent court days were needed, for, as William Eddis found, litigation was a major sport. In 1774 aristocratic Nicholas Cresswell reported attending a Maryland "reaping frolic. This is a Harvest Feast. The people very merry, Dancing without either Shoes or Stockings, and the Girls without stays, but I cannot partake of these diversions." Two weeks later he witnessed a barbecue given by a number of young Roman Catholics, who alternatively drank "Plenty of Toddy" and danced until the small hours. Even lowly slaves were permitted lighter moments on Sunday, when they gathered and danced to the music of the banjo. "Some of them sing to it, which is very droll music indeed." [26]

Of course there were times when this "pleasurable people" could not be outside and had to seek amusement indoors. The lower and middle classes, as we have seen, sought out the ordinary, leaving their women at home to work and watch the brood. The superior sort had just such exigencies in mind when they built their great houses, which were designed as much for periodic ostentatious entertainment as for comfortable day-to-day living. I must emphasize the fact that the renowned open hospitality practiced by the gentry sprang initially from the social needs of their isolated existence and only secondarily from the conscious imitation of customs and courtesy of the gentlefolk of all ages and countries. It was this very fact of its being called out by the necessities of the people that made the habit of hospitality of such lasting importance and that in time elevated it to a code.

Spontaneity characterized most of the hospitality of the Chesapeake Society, but when it assumed the form of extended visiting it became almost the only kind of group life the region afforded. At holiday times and as often in between as circumstances permitted, the week-end party that frequently stretched out to ten days or two weeks bred a "universal Mirth and Glee" and provided numerous outlets requiring participation by everyone, young and old. Elaborately prepared dinners of many courses served by troops of slaves in livery were always concluded with a long round of toasts to each lady present and many that were not. William Byrd II was only one of many planters whose billiard table saw constant use by both ladies and gentlemen seeking a respite from card games that went on endlessly. Leisurely conversation enabled the older guests to pass away the time, and although one heard stimulating talk about current literature, politics, and agriculture, serious listeners regretted that "instead of manly instructive Discourse, subjects of Gaiety and Levity are always started and always attended to." And sooner or later, notwithstanding many successful sallies of wit and elegant repartee, gentlemen of all ages would get around to tobacco prices and move on to animated discussions of horseflesh and fighting cocks—at which point we may assume that the ladies sought a change at playing cards, the spinet, or the guitar, in walks in the formal garden, and in gossip in the gazebo. Young couples had meanwhile seized the long-anticipated opportunity and stolen off for courting, since matchmaking among tobacco dynasties was a prime reason why many a planter invited the neighborhood gentry to his board.[27]

The Chesapeake "Grandees" found the most complete expression of their social instincts in dancing. "Not a bad dancer in my government," bragged William Gooch. From

[27] Eddis, *Letters*, 28; *Md. Hist. Mag.*, VII (1912), 4, 13; Farish (ed.), *Fithian Journal*, 47, 56, 107, 225.

early childhood boys and girls were taught their steps by
expert masters like Francis Christian. His strict discipline
made him a valued adjunct to Northern Neck society, although crusty old Landon Carter always resented the two
days a week his boys lost from school when Christian was
in the neighborhood. Get a good dancing master, was
Charles Carroll's advice to his son in London, "for nothing
contributes more to give a gentleman a graceful and easy
carriage." Writers have made much of the "stately minuet," which few could execute perfectly; nearly everyone
regarded it as something to be put up with when the ball
began and eagerly awaited the chance to cut "vulgar Ca-
pers." Listen to an English spark describe "a Reel or
Country-dance," when it was at last announced at a Satur-
day night ball at Alexandria in 1774. There were thirty-
seven ladies present, "dressed and powdered to the life,
some of them very handsome and as much vanity as is necessary. All of them are fond of dancing, but I do not . . .
think they perform it with the greatest elegance. Betwixt
the Country dances they have what I call everlasting jigs.
A couple gets up and begins to dance a jig (to some Negro
tune) others comes up and cuts them out, and these dances
always last as long as the fiddler can play. This is sociable,
but I think it looks more like a Bacchanalian dance than a
polite assembly." Providing an excuse to gather a company and to get exercise, a chance to excel in grace and
poise, to wear new clothes, and to find a mate for life or
merely to flirt, and a spectacle for the very young and very
old, Terpsichore was the favorite muse of the Chesapeake
country. "Virginians are of genuine Blood," says Fithian,
"They will dance or die." [28]

[28] *Md. Hist. Mag.*, VII (1912), 13; *W. & M. Quart.*, XIV (1906), 182,
249; Farish (ed.), *Fithian Journal*, 44, 163, 232; Rowland, *Charles Carroll*, I, 20; Cresswell, *Journal*, 53; *Va. Gaz.*, Nov. 25, 1737; Apr. 14, 1738.

The highly developed—yea institutionalized—custom of visiting by families bred a social ease for which the gentry grew famous. "Being early introduc'd into Company, and soon commencing ripe, they are a livelier, readier wit than we in England, in a general Way, may boast of," was the comment of a Briton in 1759. "But here where we find it more Easy to introduce ourselves into large and mixed Companies we imagine we perceive in the stiff and formal Cast w'ch a recluse and studious Life generally give us, a Capacity for Action, w'ch being therefore tempted to exert We discover various latent Talents, w'ch neither ourselves nor others had suspected us to be possess'd of." [29]

Not all diversion was beneficial. We cannot overlook the predilection of many gentlemen for gambling, which became a fashionable vice and a part of the extravagance that characterized the aristocracy. It even attracted a warning homily from a South Carolinian that was published in the *Virginia Gazette* in 1751. "I am no Enemy to Recreation," wrote Robert Crichton, but it should not be "made a Trade." He who is "a Cully to a Gaming Table, may as well be one to a Harlot." When he thought of the reckless gaming of the third William Byrd, Parson Isaac Giberne, and his own son John, Landon Carter echoed this sentiment: "They play away and play it all away. . . . I hate such vulgarity." [30]

Amusements and recreation of an organized nature naturally did not develop as widely as in the urban and village centers of the northern colonies; yet certain of these social activities did take root. Commencing with the theater built by William Levingston at Williamsburg in 1716—the

[29] *Md. Hist. Mag.,* VII (1912), 21–22; Eddis, *Letters,* 112–13.
[30] *Va. Gaz.,* Sept. 5, 1751; *W. & M. Quart.,* XI (1902–1903), 243; *ibid.,* XIV (1906), 248, 250; *Va. Mag.,* XX (1912), 413.

earliest of which there is any record in the colonies—
theatricals offered by local talent and, after 1750, by the
New York and American Companies of Comedians earned
popular support and applause in the provincial capitals
during "publick times." At such times plays, dancing assemblies, and horse races were scheduled to coincide with
meetings of the courts and legislative bodies. Towards the
close of the era occasional performances were given at
Norfolk and smaller communities like Petersburg, Hobbs's
Hole, Fredericksburg, Upper Marlboro, and Chester
Town on the Eastern Shore.[31]

Gentlemen's clubs, which achieved such a prominence in
colonial life, for some reason failed to develop in Albemarle or Virginia, save in the case of a few Masonic lodges
in larger towns, and the forming of several national societies at Norfolk.[32] Provincial club life seems to have had
its inception in Maryland with the founding of the Ancient
South River Club (still extant) in the 1720's and to have
reached its apogee at Annapolis and its environs. The
fraternal Scot George Neilson and his Royalist Club appear to have inaugurated a trend toward societies featuring
good fellowship, witty conversation, heavy drinking, and
hilarity of all sorts. Most famous of these bodies, probably
because of the literary talents of its historian Dr. Alexander Hamilton, was the Tuesday Club of Annapolis,
which boasted among its offshoots the Thursday Club of
Hickory Hill, the Old Dominion's sole social club to leave
a record. Possibly the presence of diverse national elements

[31] *W. & M. Quart.*, 3d ser., V (1948), 359–74; *Md. Gaz.*, June 18, July
2, 1752; Feb. 7, 1760; Eddis, *Letters*, 93, 108; *Va. Gaz.*, Sept. 10, 1736;
Aug. 29, Nov. 14, Dec. 19, 1751; Apr. 30, June 12, 1752; *Va. Gaz.* (Purdie
& Dixon), May 16, 1771; Helen Hill, *George Mason* (Cambridge, 1938),
27, lists a theater at Dumfries in 1771.
[32] *Va. Gaz.*, Dec. 15, 1738; Dec. 14, 1739; Apr. 18, 1751; Cresswell,
Journal, 58.

among the gentry, as well as greater ease of communication and nearness to Philadelphia, brought the spawning of clubs in Maryland. At any rate, as early as 1729 reports had it that "there are settled clubs in every County, where they talk over affairs." In 1747 the secretary of the Tuesday Club was solicited by a harried clubman of Chester Town for a means of ridding his group of a "Medley of disagreeable Members who rather spoil than improve Conversation." In addition to the regular "set clubs," English, Scottish, Welsh, and Irish gentlemen met on the anniversaries of their titular saints to celebrate common origins; and about 1770 native Americans wearing bucktails in their hats were foregathering at Norfolk as well as in Maryland to whoop it up with an Indian dance followed by a ball for the ladies in the honor of St. Tammany. So important did associational activity become that in 1771 "Laudator" published a set of six rules for forming a club in the *Maryland Gazette*.[33]

In an age of increasing intercolonial travel by members of all classes, it is notable that tobacco planters seldom journeyed out of their own region. Only those Marylanders who lived around the head of the Great Bay and regarded Philadelphia as their metropolis proved exceptions to this statement. It is also true that navigable waterways and good highways within the area facilitated a large amount of local travel to and from plantations and colonial capitals, or from estate to estate for visits; and after the last French war, many made long journeys across the Blue Ridge or to the North Carolina line to the mineral springs.[34] Yet though the planters of the Chesapeake

[33] *Md. Gaz.*, Mar. 24, 1747; Dec. 26, 1771; Tuesday Club, Minutes, Feb. 18, 1751 (Md. Hist. Soc.) ; Henry Darnall, *Account of the Transactions of the Merchants of London* (Annapolis, 1729), 12; Eddis, *Letters*, 114–15; *Va. Gaz.* (Rind), May 19, 1774.
[34] Carl Bridenbaugh, "Baths and Watering Places of Colonial America,"

managed to see one another, and many of their most affluent and venturesome spirits made the long voyage to the
British Isles or France, the fact remains that this gentry
and their fellow countrymen enjoyed less contact economically and socially with other planters to the south or with
mercantile aristocrats of the North than any other colonial
Americans.

It may seem odd to switch suddenly from recreation
to religion, but upon consideration the transition is really
natural, for it was as a social rather than as a religious
institution that the church served the Chesapeake Society
of these years. In all three colonies the Church of England
was established by law and supported by taxation, and its
vestry existed as the primary agency of local government
in each. From Anglican pulpits each Sunday, provincial
laws and news were officially published; to church doors
notices of all kinds were nailed; the local rates were set
and all taxes collected by the vestry. There were reasons
aplenty other than worship of the Deity that drew country-
folk to church. Once each week it provided an occasion to
see one's neighbors and to be seen, to transact business, and
to hear the latest news and local gossip. It was a social
gathering enjoyed by all, for it suited all tastes.

Latitudinarian breezes blew through the Anglican
church in the eighteenth century ventilating it of much of
the puritanism it had shown in the seventeenth. Clergy and
worshipers alike slipped into an easy formalism that for
a time cloaked dissent and irreligion along with orthodoxy.
Of spiritual nurture the Church had little enough to give,
and it gave less. Recent clerical scholarship to the contrary,
it is abundantly evident that the ethical and pastoral be-

W. & M. Quart., 3d ser., III (1946), 160–64; Va. Gaz., Oct. 28, 1737;
Wyndham B. Blanton, Medicine in Virginia in the Eighteenth Century
(Richmond, 1931), 9.

havior of Anglican ministers, even with the fine salaries paid in Maryland, was never very high; for every learned and cultured clergyman like the poetic James Sterling or the scholarly Thomas Brown, there was a worldly cleric like Commissary James Blair of William and Mary or a time-serving gamester like Parson Isaac Giberne, whose taste for fine wines and backgammon excelled his desire to minister to even "the polite part of the Parish." On one occasion at least, after a public notice that services would be held at 11 o'clock, the latter came to church "about 10, read prayers and was gone before any body but a few was there," and all an irate church warden could say was: "I am content. The Gent. entertains when he pleases to go into his Pulpit, and I said nothing." Several times in Loudoun County, Cresswell was disgusted upon coming to service to find "The Parson is drunk and can't perform the duties of his office." Some remembered the Reverend Peter Waggoner more "as a bad Painter, than as a Divine," and honest old Andrew Sprowle of Norfolk was once heard to say: "The Parsons do nothing well, unless they are paid for it." There are many "worthless ones here" among the clergy, said the Reverend Jonathan Boucher in 1760, "who, generally speaking, are the most despis'd and neglected Body," and to do the people "Justice, Candor I'm afraid w'd be obliged to confess, that none have less reason than they to complain of Injustice." [35]

Parishes were large, distances were great, and the serious parson found his work very hard. Rich vestries did build such beautiful edifices as Christ Church, Pohick, and St. Peter's, and that of St. Barnabas in Maryland even

[35] Letters of Alexander Spotswood (Colonial Williamsburg, Inc.), I, 27; Gooch, Letters, 5; Va. Gaz., Oct. 29, 1736; Va. Mag., XXXIII (1925), 56; Md. Hist. Mag., VII (1912), 13–14, 17–18, 340; Nelson, Letter Book, 99; W. & M. Quart., XIV (1906), 40; Cresswell, Journal, 52; Farish (ed.), Fithian Journal, 89, 91.

commissioned the first ecclesiastical art of the English colonies when Gustavus Hesselius painted his *Crucifixion* in 1721; but by the middle of the century the established church was in a precarious state. Infidelity and deism made inroads among the faithful, while dissenters lured them away from the "one true church." "Religion among us," the Reverend Thomas Bacon sadly but shrewdly opined, "seems to wear the face of the country, part moderately cultivated, the greater part wild and savage." [36]

Nothing so completely revealed the indifference and ineptitude of the Church of England and the starved spiritual condition of the people as the unprecedented success of the Great Awakening. From the day in 1739 at Williamsburg when George Whitefield thundered at the congregation from Bruton's pulpit, "What think ye of Christ?", strange and illegal bodies took to gathering stray lambs in such numbers that by the outbreak of the Revolution, although the Anglicans still held a bare majority in Maryland, a very large minority of Virginia's people were dissenters, and the Albemarle district contained even more than the Old Dominion. Presbyterians, led by the great Samuel Davies, Quakers, and Baptists won adherents throughout the Piedmont and made daring inroads in such Tidewater-Anglican strongholds as the Northern Neck and Nansemond, as well as on the Eastern Shore. Denounced by the clergy as whimsical enthusiasts and coerced by the civil authorities, the newer denominations nevertheless steadily poached upon Episcopal preserves and challenged with increasing insistence the laws requiring them to pay parish levies and their ministers to take out licenses to preach. Taxation without representation was no newfangled idea

[36] William S. Perry, *Historical Collections relating to the American Colonial Church: Maryland* (Hartford, 1870–78), IV, 324; *Va. Gaz.*, Mar. 2, 1753; *Va. Gaz.* (Rind), Sept. 8, 1774; Barker, *Maryland*, 48–49.

to Chesapeake dissenters in 1765 when their Anglican fellows were protesting to Parliament about its practice. Many a Presbyterian had left Ulster to avoid this very thing only to encounter it upon American shores. Conditions eventually forced some toleration in fact, if not in theory, for most sects save the harshly treated Roman Catholics of Maryland. Also, many Anglican gentlemen became more rationalistic than orthodox in their thinking. "The Experience we have had of them is sufficient to convince us that tho' they are Dissenters, they have as much Religion as renders them good Subjects, and entitles them to an extensive Toleration," wrote Philo-Virginica of the Presbyterians in 1752.[37]

The amazing spread of dissent inculcated a neopuritan attitude toward personal behavior that had important and lasting social as well as moral effects. All along the line from the educated Presbyterian to the unlettered Baptist, preachers stood for a strict Calvinistic code which implied censure of the gay and easy life of the Anglican gentry. At a Maryland ferry Thomas Chalkley found "the people were fiddling and dancing" and asked if they thought Luther a good man. When they said yea, the Quaker preacher quoted the great reformer at them: "That as many paces as the man takes in his dance, so many steps he takes towards hell." This, he added, "spoiled their sport." Anglican condescension further aroused the social resentment that, merged with bitterness over taxes and the difficulty of procuring cheap lands, determined many of the smaller planters to move southward into the more hospitable Carolinas. The vestry, most important bulwark of the

[37] Saul K. Padover (ed.), *The Complete Jefferson* (New York, 1943), 674; *Va. Gaz.*, Dec. 21, 1739; Oct. 10, 31, 1745; Mar. 5, Apr. 3, 10, 1752; Franklin B. Dexter (ed.), *Literary Diary of Ezra Stiles* (New York, 1901), I, 330; *Va. Gaz.* (Rind), July 21, 1768; Farish (ed.), *Fithian Journal*, 96; Eddis, *Letters*, 46, 49; *Md. Gaz.*, Mar. 25, Dec. 2, 1746; Mar. 3, 1747.

established church, now came under a more serious attack than that launched by the dissenters, as some of the eastern gentry used the *Virginia Gazette* as a vehicle to denounce it as the worn-out institution of a special class that had failed in political responsibility. By 1774 many orthodox, thinking gentlemen were alarmed about the "prevailing ignorance and impiety among the bulk of the people, that bold spirit of infidelity that has seized the minds of the fashionable and opulent, and that defection from the established religion so much complained of in many parts" and attributed its origin to the failure of the clergy. Under the combined pressures of the revivalists and the deists, the Church of England stood like the ass of the tribe of Issachar, bound down between two burdens. Establishment was tottering, and religious, if not social, democracy was on its way.[38]

In a country of widely dispersed plantations served by a weak and indifferent church, provisions for education fell largely upon parents, although the government of Virginia accepted responsibility for the orphan and the very poor. In the Old Dominion some schooling in the three R's must have been given to most of the middling and inferior sorts, since the large majority of people could read and write a little; but in Maryland, where the law of 1723 calling for a school in every county failed of its purpose, and in North Carolina, where public efforts went for nought, illiteracy was high. Facilities for secondary training under such a dispensation were consequently even more scanty. Although the Old Dominion had here and there an endowed free school, Governor Horatio Sharpe's admission in 1763 that there was not "even one good grammar school" in Maryland was a pretty accurate report for the

[38] Thomas Chalkley, *Journal* (New York, 1808), 93; *Va. Gaz.* (Rind), Dec. 22, 1768; Sept. 8, 1774; James K. Owen, "The Virginia Vestry" (Thesis, Princeton University, quoted by permission).

entire area. In 1773 a fair-minded Boston gentleman making a survey of the colonies found that "the commonalty and farmers through this province were a vastly more ignorant and illiterate kind of people than with us; . . . a spirit of inquiry and literature . . . is manifestly subordinate to a spirit of gaming, horse-racing and jockeying of all kinds." [39]

Tobacco planters, eagerly creating a privileged aristocracy in the Chesapeake country, sought to transplant from England the Renaissance education for an ideal gentleman without ever seriously considering whether or not it was valid in a new world. Many sent their sons back to England for training in the academy at Leeds in Yorkshire, or to the universities of England and Scotland, and frequently on to the Inns of Court at London. Maryland Roman Catholics like the Carrolls patronized the English Jesuit school at St. Omer in Flanders. Despite polish acquired overseas, however, many gentlemen came increasingly to believe that education at home was less dangerous and more useful as well. Tutors, recruited from servant and convict ranks, brought over from Scotland, or employed from Northern colleges, instructed the children of the great plantation families. Not infrequently they prepared boys for entrance to the Grammar School at the College of William and Mary; for private schools conducted in Virginia by such well-known pedagogues as Donald Robertson of King and Queen County, James Maury in Albemarle County, and Jonathan Boucher at Port Royal (and later Annapolis); or for Samuel Wilson's excellent Somerset Academy on the Eastern Shore of Maryland. [40]

[39] Marcus W. Jernegan, *Laboring and Dependent Classes in Colonial America* (Chicago, 1931), 131–71; Jarratt, *Life,* 19–20; *Md. Gaz.,* July 30, Nov. 5, 1772; *Correspondence of Governor Horatio Sharpe* (*Archives of Maryland,* Baltimore, 1895), III, 115; "Journal of Josiah Quincy," Massachusetts Historical Society, *Proceedings,* XLIX, 466.

[40] *Va. Mag.,* XXXIII (1925), 194–97, 288–92; *Md. Hist. Mag.,* VII

The College of William and Mary at Williamsburg was
the region's only institution of higher learning. Managed
by the Anglican clergy and enjoying better financial support
than any other in America, this seminary, consisting of a
grammar school, Indian school, and a college, was attended
by over four hundred students from the area between
1699 and 1776, although many Marylanders went to the
College of Philadelphia after 1750. Because they desired
only to pass some time agreeably in a collegiate way of
living as their brethren did at Oxford and Cambridge, and
also because the families of most planters could ill afford
to keep their sons long at Williamsburg, very few students
remained in residence more than a year or so. If degrees
in course were ever awarded at William and Mary, it was
in the years immediately before the Revolution when the
institution was under fire by "Academicus" and others because it did not conform to the curriculum and discipline
of Nassau Hall and Northern colleges. Yet, ironically,
when young Thomas Jefferson came down from James
Maury's Piedmont school in 1760, he acquired at the college from the conversation of Professor William Small
his "first views of the expansion of science" and an insight
into the nature of the Enlightenment that inspired him to
the end of his life. Through his introduction to the "attic
society" of Governor Francis Fauquier, F.R.S., of George
Wythe, and of Small, he was able to indulge his "passion"
for music and conversation and be initiated into the mysteries of the social graces and the law, as well as some of
the devious politics that went on down at the Capitol.
No American undergraduate has ever gotten so much
from his alma mater and the community in which it was

(1912), 5, 19, 23, 292–93, 299, 314, 339; *ibid.,* XLIV (1949), 200–3; Bouchier
(ed.), *Reminiscences,* 49; Rowland, *Charles Carroll,* I, 18–19, 53–54; *Md.
Gaz.,* Apr. 26, 1745; *Va. Gaz.* (Rind), Feb. 23, 1769.

located as Thomas Jefferson, whose memory is so curi-
ously neglected there in these latter days. The very criticism he was to level against the college, that it did not
produce scholars, proved it admirably adapted to the
needs of the country, which it answered perhaps better
than did any of its sister institutions. It did train gentlemen who rendered vital public service in the hour of
need.[41]

The education available in the Chesapeake Society was
probably suitable and adequate for the sons of the wealthiest planters who intended to enter the law, the ministry,
or the practice of medicine. But very few families of actual
wealth existed, as the Reverend James Maury had the
wit to see and point out in 1762 when he wrote "A Treatise
on Education" for his friend Jonathan Boucher. This is
the most significant cultural document dealing with the
colonial society of the Chesapeake and forces us to dis-
card many hitherto cherished ideas. Since "Few Men of
Fortune will expend on their Son's Education the Sums
requisite to carry them thro' a regular Course of Studies,
proper to qualify them for shining in . . . Professions,"
the clergyman asserts that the study of Latin and Greek
should be discarded. For this heresy he gives reasons based
on a sound understanding of the wants of young men ",who,
when they shall settle in the World, are to be masters of
competent Fortunes, which they are to improve, either by
the Culture of our Staple, by Merchandise, or by some
other Method, than either of the Learned Professions.
And such are most of those among us, who class with
the Gentry. . . . The Business, which these are usually
obliged to pursue;—the Variety of Cares, insep'able from

[41] *Provisional List of Alumni . . . of the College of William and Mary*
(Richmond, 1941) ; *Md. Gaz.*, Mar. 21, 1754; Farish (ed.), *Fithian Journal,*
86; *Va. Gaz.* (Rind), May 19, 26, June 2, 9, July 7, 1774; Herbert L. Gant-
ner, "William Small," *W. & M. Quart.*, 3d ser., IV (1947), 505-11.

their Situation and Way of Life; render it quite obvious, they can have little Opportunity or Leisure, after they launch out into the busy World, to apply to the study of the Languages.—Moreover, few, very few of them prosecute their Studies, either in private or public Schools, so long as their twentieth Year. Besides, they commonly marry very Young, and are thence in the early Stages of Life encumbered with Families. And tho' you suppose them born to the greatest Fortunes, yet the prudent Management of a large Virginia Estate requires so frequent and close an Inspection, in Order, not only to improve but preserve it, that the Possessor, when once he comes to be charged with the Care of it, can expect but little of that Leisure and Repose, which are requisite for a pleasurable or successful Engagement in such Parts of Literature, as the Languages, Criticism, and curious and deep Researches into Antiquity."

To succeed in his calling and also in his public status as justice and assemblyman, the affluent young gentleman ought to substitute history, geography, and "at least a general Knowledge of the Laws, Constitution, Interests and Religion of his Country" for the ancient tongues.[42]

But, warns Mr. Maury, not many are born to affluence, and the average planter "will be obliged to call in the Assistance of some lucrative Business to help out his little Patrimony to support himself and Family." At fourteen or fifteen he should have been apprenticed to some merchant to learn business methods and gain such a general knowledge of affairs as is "necessary for every Gentleman."

This "Man of genius, well acquainted with Books and

[42] Helen D. Bullock (ed.), "A Dissertation on Education," Albemarle County Historical Society, *Papers*, II (1941–42), 42–44; Burnaby, *Travels*, 20.

not vulgarly with Men," saw what has often escaped historians, that training "in the most necessar[y] Branches of useful, practical knowledge," is "much more than can . . . be, or than is usually effected by the present Mode of educating our Youth : of which, perhaps, no favourable Opinion will be formed, if we are to judge from Proficiency in Literature, that has been made by the Generality, either of those, who have received their Education here, or of others, who have been sent to Great Britain for that Purpose. . . . For *our Youth,* I repeat it again; because the Genius of our People, their Way of Life, their Circumstances in Point of Fortune, the Customs and Manners and Humors of the Country, difference us in so many important Respects from Europeans, that a Plan of Education, however judiciously adapted to these last, would no more fit us, than an Almanac, calculated for the Latitude of London, would that of Williamsburg." [43]

Thus was educational achievement circumscribed by the nature and the demands of the country. It is idle to compare it with the urban accomplishment of Boston or Philadelphia, where an ambitious middle class demanded schooling better suited to its needs and got it. Society was not responsive to the requirements of common folk, who, if they really wanted more education than they had, were inarticulate. For a few of the wealthiest aristocrats—a very few indeed—the ideal of a "balanced education" was achieved. Such were Thomas Jefferson and James Madison, who synthesized learning and culture with the active life of planting and politics; but their preoccupation with intellectual pursuits proved them to be biological sports in the Chesapeake Society. George Washington, Speaker John Robinson, the elder Daniel Dulany, and Samuel Gal-

[43] *Md. Hist. Mag.,* VII (1912), 295; Bullock (ed.), "A Dissertation," 45, 57–58.

loway—planter-soldier, planter-politician, planter-lawyer, and planter-merchant—came nearer to the norm of their age and place. In the school of life, of men, and of measures, they were educated by participation; but it cannot be said that even the tobacco aristocrats were possessed of either a wide or a profound literary culture.

The denizens of the Chesapeake country were not a reading people. From what we have just learned of their life and training this does not surprise us; yet much time and learning have been dissipated by devoted local scholars to prove that exactly the reverse must have been true. Unfortunately, although they have uncovered many lists of books and evidence of a few very large libraries, they have not asked the right questions of their materials. Out of a gentry numbering at the most about three hundred families, only a few were actually bookish and accumulated large collections. Books, it must be remembered, were comparatively more costly in colonial days than now. We must not be misled by the impressiveness of the libraries of William Byrd II, Robert Carter, Jonathan Boucher, Charles Carroll of Carrollton, and Thomas Bacon, which ranged from several hundred to four thousand volumes. These were so rare as to excite comment. In truth, the average planter owned only a few books, and those were confined largely to religious and devotional works, or to subjects related to his immediate concerns, such as books on farming, commerce, surveying, law, and household medicine. In other words, the planter read for practical reasons rather than for entertainment or self-improvement, and such literary culture as he possessed came, as Patrick Henry and George Gilmer readily admitted, from conversation, not from reading. George Washington's small collection of treatises on useful knowledge, which studied faithfully, or Lord Thomas Fairfax's 108 volumes at

Greenway, were larger libraries, if I may so dignify them, than most plantations afforded.[44]

Possession of a Bible, a prayer book or a Westminster catechism, possibly a *Pilgrim's Progress,* and a printed sermon or two about completed the literary furniture of the homes of the yeomanry, who spelled out their sentences with difficulty. The lower classes, being unlettered, had no need for books, for the rich traditional balladry of Old England transformed by endless repetition in America nourished the folk culture of plain people. Devereux Jarratt recalled in after years that he once could recite over a hundred verses of "Chevy Chase" and other "paltry songs, as most of those were, which then took my attention." Like many of their leaders, the lower classes got their larnin' by ear.[45]

After 1750 more and more people of all classes took to what was to become America's standard reading matter—newspapers. These were first supplied to the area by William Park, the printer, when he established successively the *Maryland Gazette* in 1727 and the *Virginia Gazette* in 1736. On the eve of Independence, Williamsburg had three journals called the *Virginia Gazette,* Norfolk had another, and rising Baltimore boasted the *Maryland Journal* and *Dunlap's Maryland Gazette.* These little newspapers served the cultural as well as the political and commercial needs of their readers by printing quantities of verse and essays on literary and moral subjects. There

---

[44] George K. Smart, "Private Libraries in Colonial Virginia," *American Literature,* X (1938), 24–52; articles by Joseph T. Wheeler in *Md. Hist. Mag.,* XXXIV–XXXVI (1939–41); Stephen B. Weeks, "Libraries and Literature of North Carolina in the Eighteenth Century," Amer. Hist. Assn., *Annual Report* (Washington, 1895); *Va. Mag.,* VII (1900), 299–303; *ibid.,* VIII (1901), 12; Rowland, *Charles Carroll,* I, 59; *Va. Gaz.,* June 23, 1738; *Va. Gaz.* (Rind), Dec. 15, 1768; *Md. Gaz.,* Dec. 23, 1746.

[45] Duc de la Rochefoucauld-Liancourt, *Travels through the United States of America* (London, 1800), III, 232; Jarratt, *Life,* 19.

was no freedom of discussion in the press until 1766, when
William Rind was brought to Williamsburg to set up a
rival to the established gazette, which Jefferson and others
claimed was too subservient to the royal governor. The
gentry were placed on parade immediately by a full discussion of the scandalous Chiswell-Routledge murder case
and the question of separating the offices of Speaker and
Treasurer; and, for the first time, their fellow Virginians
had the opportunity to examine both sides of a public issue.
Probably the newspapers published in Virginia and Maryland did not exceed fifteen hundred copies a week, but so
widely did they circulate in the region to ordinaries and
other public houses that they were read *by* many thousands
and *to* countless others also. Not only did the Tidewater
journals compare favorably with those of the great urban
centers, but their printers also occasionally published books
—pirated or written locally—and in their bookstores occasionally carried nearly as wide a selection of volumes for
sale as any on the continent. But it was government and
job printing that ensured them a living. Save at Annapolis
and Baltimore, where several short-lived circulating libraries undertaken by printers made the "Means of Knowledge . . . accessible to Men of Middling Fortunes,"
rural conditions forestalled any such development of public
or social libraries as took place to the northward.[46]

Literary achievement is not to be expected from an
aristocracy whose members are concerned with politics and
the extroverted life of a rural people. Such writers as it produces will be dilettantes who take up their pens for the
amusement or instruction of a small coterie at the most.

---

[46] Clarence S. Brigham, *History and Bibliography of American Newspapers* (Worcester, 1947), 218–19, 229, 240, 1158–62; Lawrence C. Wroth,
History of Printing in Colonial Maryland (Baltimore, 1922), 83; Colonial
Office 5: 1331 (Library of Congress Transcripts), 333; *Va. Gaz.*, May 24,
1751; *Va. Gaz.* (Rind), July 9, July 21, 1768; *Md. Hist. Mag.*, XXXIV
(1939), 111–37.

The second William Byrd of Westover, Dr. Alexander
Hamilton of Annapolis, and Colonel Robert Munford of
Mecklenburg were men of this type, amateurs in the best
sense. One was born and educated in Scotland; the other
two received their schooling in England and sought in the
Old Dominion to recapture the literary life they had tasted
at London. Urbane, witty, and instructive, their personal
narratives and plays are the best writing produced in the
Chesapeake Society, and indeed stood high among all
colonial literary efforts in their genres; yet as closet performances undertaken solely for self-satisfaction and never
given to the press during the colonial era they cannot be
considered typical of the tobacco gentry, among whom
literary effort was a great rarity.[47]

Although this was a versifying age, nothing of permanent merit or even of much temporary importance was
produced by the handful of poetasters. Three clergymen,
William Dawson, James Sterling, and Samuel Davies, were
perhaps the most gifted and, be it observed, were not
natives of the country. Recent efforts to inflate our concept
of the Chesapeake literary output have centered on the
relatively large quantities of occasional light verse and
moral essays to be found in Virginia and Maryland newspapers; but alas, I am forced to report that an inordinate
proportion of the lines addressed to young ladies by amor-
ous swains, and pieces on virtue, constancy, and manners
prove upon investigation to have come from contemporary
issues of the *London* and *Gentleman's* magazines and were
either plagiarized or used by printers as filler without

[47] John S. Bassett (ed.), *Writings of Colonel William Byrd of Westover*
(New York, 1901); Carl Bridenbaugh (ed.), *Gentleman's Progress: The
Itinerarium of Dr. Alexander Hamilton, 1744* (Chapel Hill, 1948); Alex-
ander Hamilton, History of the Tuesday Club (MS, Md. Hist. Soc.);
Robert Munford, *The Candidates, or the Humours of a Virginia Election*
(Williamsburg, 1948); Munford, "The Patriots," *W. & M. Quart.*, 3d ser.,
VI (1949), 436–503.

credit. Dull, conventional, and often banal as most of these effusions are, we need shed no tears that they were not signs of a native genius. Local doggerel that did make the press, such as the second "Sot-Weed Factor," at least possessed vigor and gave sure if halting and crude evidence of an emerging American humor. When Nathaniel Tucker visited Williamsburg in 1773, his brother St. George paraded him as a literary personage. When Purdie brought out *The Bermudian*—a bit of sentimental nostalgia pallidly penned at Charleston after a saturation in *The Deserted Village*—the President of the College, in a fawning sonnet, found him superior to Waller. The family were more perspicacious; they called him "Poor Natty." [48]

Mundane considerations and local aspirations brought forth a few literary works of considerable vitality. In a great epistolary age, many planters remote from one another and from London correspondents wrote letters that still make entertaining and instructive reading. "The General is remarked for writing a most elegant letter," said an admiring Englishman of George Washington. And the same was true of many a planter from the time of John Custis and William Byrd II to that of Thomas Jefferson and the brothers Lee. Although they are few when compared with the issues of other colonial presses, vigorous and often effective prose is to be found in the medical tracts that John Tennent wrote to advocate "Virginia Snake-Root" as a universal specific, and in the political pamphlet-

---

[48] *Va. Gaz.*, Oct. 22, 29, Dec. 3, 10, 1736; Apr. 14, 1738; Aug. 24, 1751; Jan. 17, 1752; *D.A.B.*, XVII, 587; Ralph L. Rusk (ed.), *Poems on Several Occasions* (New York, 1930); *Va. Gaz.* (Rind), Feb. 4, 1768; *Md. Gaz.*, Nov. 1, 1749; Percival W. Turrentine "Nathaniel Beverley Tucker" (MS Thesis, Harvard University, quoted by permission), I, 26; Bouchier (ed.), *Reminiscences*, 66–67; Hamilton, History of the Tuesday Club. Compare, however, Elizabeth C. Cook, *Literary Influences in Colonial Newspapers* (New York, 1912); Courtlandt Canby, "Robert Munford's *The Patriots*," *W. & M. Quart.*, 3d ser., VI (1949), especially 442–43; and Lewis Leary, *The Literary Career of Nathaniel Tucker* (Durham, 1951).

eering of Bland, Dulany, and Jefferson. Nevertheless Jonathan Boucher's complaint was substantially true: "There was not a literary man, for aught I could find nearer than the country I had just left [England]; nor were literary attainments, beyond merely reading or writing, at all in vogue or repute." [49]

In many ways the *Memoirs of Lieut. Henry Timberlake* (London, 1765) is the most readable of the writings published from 1735 to the Revolution, and like those of Byrd and Hamilton it is good action literature. In order to bare his deeds, the young soldier tells us he put aside the sword for the pen, "that I wield as a soldier, who never dreamt of the beauties of stile, or propriety of expression. Excuse then, gentle reader, all the faults that may occur, in consideration of that these are not my weapons, and that tho' I received almost as good an education as Virginia could bestow on me, it only sufficed to fit me for a soldier, and not for a scholar." His chronicle of frontier fighting is clear, sparing of phrase, fair-minded, and interesting. Especially happy is Timberlake's ability to render an Indian war song into fairer verse than the gazettes printed; at the same time he diffidently called it "loose poetry." The *Memoirs* were published in German in 1769 and in French in 1796; and Robert Southey drew heavily on them in 1806 for his epic *Madoc*. With a timely subject and full knowledge of what he was writing about, this scion of Hanover County's lesser gentry had risen admirably to the occasion.[50]

Among this busy people who, by force and by preference, favored conversation to reading and scribbling, there de-

[49] Louis B. Wright and Marion Tinling (eds.), *Quebec to Carolina* (San Marino, 1943), 193; Custis, Letter Book; *Va. Gaz.*, June 30, 1738; Bouchier (ed.), *Reminiscences*, 27, 42, 52; *Md. Hist. Mag.*, VII (1912), 161, 174; "Quincy Journal," 466.
[50] Samuel C. Williams (ed.), *Memoirs of Lieut. Henry Timberlake* (Johnson City, 1927); *Gentleman's Magazine*, XXXIV (1768), 142.

veloped significant qualities of speech, which immediately caught the ear of Englishmen accustomed to a "peculiar dialect" in each county of the mother country. With William Eddis, they seldom failed to notice "that a striking similarity of speech universally prevails; and it is strictly true, that the pronounciation of the generality of people has an accuracy and elegance, that cannot fail of gratifying the most judicious ear." Apparently, pronounced Southern accents were a thing of the future. One traveler reported that even household slaves spoke good English, and Robert Carter preferred an American to an English or Scottish tutor for his children "on account of pronounciation in the English Language," in which he declared colonials excelled. "Eminently endowed with a Knack of talking," the Chesapeake gentry developed public speaking into a fine art. To shine among one's fellows in provincial assemblies and to present the issues of politics to an unlettered electorate at the hustings required that the gentleman cultivate this talent so as to be able to pour forth a wealth of classical allusions and bring the subject to the point where he could "harangue plausibly and Handsomely round a Period." This was "Generally speaking, the Sum of their Literature," and the Reverend Samuel Davies, Patrick Henry, Richard Henry Lee, and their fellows did excel on the rostrum at a time when great orators influenced the course of history.[51]

The love of luxury and display that so definitely characterized the planting gentry would naturally be expected to find vent in an interest in the arts. As aristocrats they could be patrons, not practitioners; and a reverence for all

[51] Eddis, *Letters,* 59–60; Farish (ed.), *Fithian Journal,* 125; Alexander Hamilton, Letter Book, 1739–43 (Dulany Papers, Md. Hist. Soc.), 17; Edmund C. Burnett (ed.), *Letters of the Members of the Continental Congress* (Washington, 1921–), I, 66; Bridenbaugh, *Seat of Empire,* 38.

things English led them to seek their arts across the water rather than at home. We are familiar with the great Tidewater mansions, but it is well to recall that they seem to have been erected by local master-builders from plans made either professionally in England or in the colony by gentlemen working in conjunction with master-builders from imported English manuals of architecture and carpentry. Not until William Buckland came over under indenture in 1755 to work on Gunston Hall do we have evidence of the emergence of a bona fide professional architect, nor at any time before 1776 of a native practitioner. Perhaps it was because custom approved the gentleman amateur designer and because he could achieve acceptable solutions that architecture became the most successful art form in the region.[52]

Interest in the other arts was far more desultory, and such was the attitude toward music. Many young ladies learned to play the harpsichord or guitar under the tutelage of Charles Langford, John Stadley, and other music masters; and now and then a concert, followed by a ball, was held at Williamsburg or Annapolis. Less frequently the Carter family and some gentlemen of King William diverted themselves with chamber music. Occasionally one runs across gems in a newspaper like the lines "On Miss Anne Geddy singing and playing the Spinnet," penned, no doubt, by a lovesick youth for whom

[52] No serious scholar can accept as anything but highly speculative the conclusions of Thomas T. Waterman about Richard Taliaferro and John Ariss drawn from the scanty evidence presented in his *Mansions of Colonial Virginia* (Chapel Hill, 1945), 107, 214, 217–18, 244–45. *Md. Gaz.*, May 15, 1751; Sept. 30, Oct. 28, Dec. 16, 1773; Mar. 17, Apr. 21, 1774; Rosamond R. Beirne, "William Buckland, Architect of Virginia and Maryland," *Md. Hist. Mag.*, XLI (1946), 199–218; James Bordley, Jr., "New Light on William Buckland," *ibid.*, XLVI (1951), 153–55; *ibid.*, I (1906), 325, and *ibid.*, XXXVII (1942), 62–63.

Corelli, Handel, Felton, Nares,
With their concerts, solos, airs,
Are far less sweet to me.

Notwithstanding that music was "the favorite passion" of his soul, Thomas Jefferson had to admit his lot was cast "in a country where it is in a state of deplorable barbarism." [53]

Every gentleman and gentlewoman aspired to sit for a portrait in England; when this proved impossible, the next best thing was to pose for an English face painter at home. Those Virginians who did not have Kneller take their likenesses had to be content with the efforts of Charles Bridges and John Wollaston from England. The latter became court painter to the Chesapeake, executing portraits of thirty-five Randolphs among others, and the first American nude. Local limners met with little encouragement below the Potomac, and no native dauber ever appeared. Maryland, on the other hand, patronized Swedish Gustavus Hesselius and German Justus Engelhardt Kuhn, and eventually it produced John Hesselius and Charles Willson Peale (although it must be said that the latter won his success in Philadelphia). John Beale Bordley and other gentlemen of the Eastern Shore dabbled in painting. Probably more portraits were painted of worthies of the Chesapeake society than in any other section of America, but there is a world of difference between acquiring a likeness as a badge of gentility and appreciation of art. This gentry wanted portraits, not landscapes or still life; and they insisted when possible that their features be preserved for posterity by English limners whether or not they were the best available painters.[54]

[53] *Va. Gaz.*, Jan. 7, 1736/7; June 12, Oct. 12, 1752; *Va. Gaz.* (Rind), Dec. 24, 1767; Oct. 27, Dec. 22, 1768; Julian P. Boyd, *et al.* (eds.), *Writings of Thomas Jefferson* (Princeton, 1950), II, 196; *Md. Gaz.*, Feb. 25, 1773; Farish (ed.), *Fithian Journal*, 39, 76, 159, 200.
[54] Gooch, Letter Book, 43; *Va. Mag.*, IX (1902), 236-37; *Va. Gaz.*

The burgeoning interest of the English colonies in science expressed itself in two forms most congenial to an out-of-door people. Many know of the botanical work of John Mitchell of Urbanna on the Rappahannock, and of John Clayton, who employed the leisure of a sinecure clerkship in Gloucester County to plant a botanical garden and assemble the herbarium specimens which J. F. Gronovius of Leyden systematized and described in the *Flora Virginica* (1743, 1762). These two scientists acquired their initial impulse in England, where they were born. Among natives, John Custis of Williamsburg was the most active; he carried on an extensive amateur correspondence about seeds and plants with the famous Peter Collinson of London from 1734 to 1746. William Byrd II and Isham Randolph were others among Collinson's "Brothers of the Spade." In 1763, while he was a student in medicine at the University of Edinburgh, Arthur Lee was awarded Dr. John Hope's gold medal for promoting botany.[55]

More useful but nonetheless significant contributions were made by two F.F.C.'s to cartographical science. Joshua Fry and Peter Jefferson's *Map of the Inhabited Part of Virginia,* first published in 1754, went through four more English and three French editions by 1776. At London in 1755 Dr. Mitchell brought out his *Map of the British and French Dominions in North America,* which immediately became the standard, saw seventeen reprints in four countries, and was complimented by being widely plagiarized before 1776. The most important map in all

(Rind), Apr. 21, 1769, suppl.; *Md. Hist. Mag.,* XLIII (1948), cover, 96; *ibid.,* XXXVI (1941), 341–43; *Md. Gaz.,* Mar. 17, 1753; *Boston Chronicle,* May 11, 1769.

[55] *D.A.B.,* IV, 184; *ibid.,* XII, 50–51; *Va. Gaz.,* Nov. 21, 1745; Blanton, *Medicine in Virginia,* 142; Earl G. Swem, "Brothers of the Spade," Amer. Antiquarian Soc., *Proceedings,* LVIII (1949), 17–185; *Providence Gazette,* Aug. 11, 1764.

American history, it was used as late as 1932 in the New Jersey–Delaware boundary case. Colonel John Henry, father of Patrick, in 1770 issued a *Map of Virginia,* but because it was not based on accurate surveys it elicited considerable ironic comments from the local press.[56]

In 1773 "Academicus" wrote in Purdie and Dixon's *Virginia Gazette* that he had "often reflected with Concern on the slow Progress which Science had made amongst us. . . . This I have always imputed to the Want of the Intercourse and Association which is necessary to the Perfection of every Power of Man." Had he known that although Clayton and Mitchell lived only forty miles apart they had never met he would not have been surprised. I suspect that Thomas Jefferson was the driving force behind The Society for Promoting Useful Knowledge, which was established at Williamsburg this same year by his intimate John Page, and of which John Clayton became the first president. Despite its claims to a membership of one hundred, this body never rivaled the American Philosophical Society of Philadelphia and soon languished. Up in the Northern Neck within a year Landon Carter of Sabine Hall confided bitterly to his diary that, although his careful study of the "wevil fly" was scarcely noticed in Rind's paper in 1772, Colonel Lee was able to procure its publication in the first volume of the *Transactions* of the American Philosophical Society; and that Dr. Phineas Bond wrote to him upon returning from abroad that the paper "has immortalized me and all Europe have agreed" with the findings. Similarly, John Beale Bordley of Maryland, leading colonial student of agriculture, turned to Philadelphia in 1776 for publication of his *Necessaries:*

[56] A facsimile of the 1751 edition of the Fry and Jefferson *Map* was published at Charlottesville in 1950; *D.A.B.,* XIII, 51; *Va. Gaz.,* Jan. 5, 1738/9; *Va. Gaz.* (Purdie & Dixon), June 25, 1767; Aug. 30, Oct. 4, 1770; *Va. Gaz.* (Rind), Sept. 27, 1770; *W. & M. Quart.,* XIV (1906), 83–86.

Best Product of Land, Best Staple of Commerce. Professor Small might reveal the wonders of nature at the College, and George Wythe peer through his new microscope,
but Chesapeake planters were no votaries of science,
which, as Jefferson was to remark, demanded "a patient
pursuit of facts and cautious combination and comparison
of them"—a drudgery for which few had either the time
or the taste.[57]

* * * * *

As we come to a final estimate of the Chesapeake Society, I think it is clear that there have been many long-
held misconceptions of its character. Consider well the following facts: Virginia was first settled in 1607, Maryland
in 1634, the Albemarle in 1653; settlers moved into the
Piedmont by 1690. Here, then, is the spectacle of what in
American terms was an old civilization, the parts of which
ranged from 169 down to 85 years of age in 1776. It had
matured by 1700 and passed its economic peak a quarter
of a century before the Revolution. Whatever its attri-
butes, they cannot be ascribed to youth. More-or-less isolated from the rest of the colonies by the facts of geography, its people succeeded in achieving a stable agrarian
society in which there was no unrest. Equilibrium based on
a widely recognized and quietly accepted class structure
in which the aristocracy was completely dominant was
evident to all observers. As yet the internal strains and external pressures that would cause the migration of thousands of Virginians and Marylanders from the Chesapeake
country southward and westward had not been felt.

Those who have appointed themselves custodians of the

[57] *Va Gaz.* (Purdie & Dixon), Nov. 19, 1772; May 13, Aug. 5, 1773;
June 16, 1774; *Va. Gaz.* (Rind), Oct. 28, 1773; Nov. 19, 1772; *W. & M.
Quart.*, XIV (1906), 252; John Beale Bordley, *Necessaries: Best Product of
Land, Best Staple of Commerce* (Philadelphia, 1776), 1–15; Padover (ed.),
"Notes on Virginia," *The Complete Jefferson*, 612n.

historical reputation of this fascinating region have generally insisted that it produced that which, by its very nature, it could not produce—a developed intellectual and
artistic culture rivaling that of any other part of the colonies. A rural aristocracy reigned unchallenged by an alert,
ambitious, hard-working, imaginative middle class such as
emerged and contended for power in colonial cities. "Academicus" deeply regretted that "among the necessary
Means of Association, whose Influence we have attempted
to establish, are *populous* Cities, where Men of Genius,
from Motives of Amusement or Business, reside together;
of these we have a very distant Prospect Indeed." [58]

An active, hospitable country life, sometimes approaching the idyllic, as at Nomini Hall under the Carters, was
the outward sign of that stable order attained by the tobacco planters. Thomas Jefferson and James Madison
were as nearly unique in 1776 as was William Byrd in
1720. For each of them there were dozens of gentlemen
by whom, as a contemporary perceived, "the ingenuity of
a Locke or the discoveries of a Newton were considered as
infinitely inferior to the accomplishments of him who knew
when to shoulder a blind cock or to start a fleet horse. . . .
It is really affecting to consider what a prodigious number
of men have not the least spark of taste, have no relish for
the fine arts." They led a gracious but not a cultured life.[59]

In their own milieu, however, the Chesapeake gentlemen
did excel. Nowhere in the Western World did the rural
phase of the Enlightenment evoke such active responses
as among certain of this responsible aristocracy. To them
political and religious liberalism seemed indeed to stem
directly from the law of Nature and Nature's God; to
attain this liberalism they fearlessly changed from mon-

[58] *Va. Gaz.* (Purdie & Dixon), Aug. 5, 1773.
[59] "Quincy Journal," 466–67, 469–70.

archical to republican principles (with their democratic implications for the future), and devoted all their political, oratorical, and military wisdom and talents. This society gave to the world cause of liberty the magnificent group of planter-politician-statesmen of the Revolutionary era —the selfless public servants and men on horseback who yearned most of all to get the business over with and go back to their beloved acres. It accepted Jefferson and Madison as scholars and theorists because of the political exigencies of the age; yet it never wholly trusted their ideas. George Washington and Lighthorse Harry Lee, men of action, and the Carrolls, Howards, Mercers, and Smallwoods, these are the men typical of the Chesapeake Society at its best. To be fair we must evaluate a society in its own and not by borrowed terms.

The genius of this people lay in agriculture and politics; it displayed itself to the world as *noblesse oblige,* gracious hospitality, zest for living, effortless courtesy—all forms of action befitting their way of life. The Chesapeake Society produced a unique bourgeois aristocracy with more than its share of great and noble men; they were, however, men of intellect, not intellectuals.

II

The Carolina Society

THERE is an old saw which probably every one has heard that at Charleston the Ashley and Cooper rivers join to form the Atlantic Ocean. Historically there is much more significance to it than in most old sayings, for since the earliest days of the colony some Carolinians, at least, have thought and acted as if the adage were actually true. What was there about the Carolina Society of the late colonial period that lent color to such a quaint conceit? Or is it merely a misreading of their society's past by fond historians that is responsible? I hope to provide some answers in this essay on the Carolina Society.

In extent, age, numbers and kinds of people, as well as in provincial characteristics, the Carolina Society presented far-reaching contrasts with that of the Chesapeake. Although territorially it was always much smaller and more compact, with the passage of time its influence spread over great distances, and its limits became less clearly defined. But the heartland was always that area lying along the South Carolina seacoast from a few miles north of Winyah Bay to the Savannah, and stretching inland sixty miles at the most to the western boundaries of Georgetown, Charles Town, and Beaufort precincts, which actually encompassed the entire region. This was and is the celebrated Carolina Low Country.

For half a century after the first settlement of 1670,

South Carolina was a buffer province. It was walled in on the south and west by redskins and Latins; but during this time an unusually slow-growing population rendered any extension of its boundaries needless. Concurrent with the establishment of Georgia as a barrier against the Spaniard and a decided spurt in the rice culture after 1732, the Carolina Society came out of its infancy, began to assume a definite regional form, and to expand along all lines of human endeavor—territorially, economically, culturally. Eventually it took in the plantation country on either side of the Savannah River and on the Georgia Sea Islands as far south as St. Simon's; it also spread northward along the coast past the mouth of the Pedee after 1735. About this time, too, newly arrived immigrants pushed inland from Charles Town up the courses of the Santee and Edisto into the Middle Country, where they founded the townships of Williamsburg and Amelia, and the district of Orangeburg. Filling rapidly, these areas by 1750 had come to be regarded as part of the Low Country. Finally, the addition of East and West Florida to the English colonies in 1763 opened new commercial and agricultural opportunities by way of St. Augustine, Pensacola, and distant Mobile.[1]

The unique sea-island formation and the well-watered coastal lands formed a region of sounds, inlets, rivers, and creeks—sheltered waterways navigable for small boats in any season. All avenues in this country, by sea or by land, led not directly to London—as in the Chesapeake—but to the southern metropolis of Charles Town.[2]

[1] Henry Mouzon, *An Accurate Map of North and South Carolina, with their Indian Frontiers,* . . . *from Actual Surveys* (London, 1775); Public Records of South Carolina (MS, Columbia, S.C.), XIV, 147, 214; *ibid.,* XV, 198–203; Bartholomew R. Carroll (ed.), *Historical Collections of South Carolina* (New York, 1836), II, 467.

[2] John Drayton, *A View of South Carolina* (Charleston, 1802), 30–36; William A. Schaper, "Sectionalism and Representation in South Carolina,"

It is a truism that production of a cash crop which can readily find its way into world markets is essential to the prosperity of any colonial economy. At the opening of the eighteenth century the Carolinians had "found out the true way of raising and husking rice," and by 1730 began to realize its possibilities for bringing prosperity on a large scale. Rice culture, utilizing the swamplands so widespread in the new country, first inland and then tidal, caused a real and continuous expansion of the Carolina Society save in a serious depression during the years 1744–1749. Success in producing marketable indigo came during King George's War when rice prices were low, and, after the granting of a Parliamentary bounty in 1748, indigo culture was exceedingly profitable. This source of blue dye proved to be an ideal complement to rice because it grew best on high, loose, fairly rich, and dry soils unsuited for rice and not hitherto cultivated—especially on tracts in the eastern sections of the Middle Country. Also, indigo required no winter work, so that slave labor was released for cutting timber, caring for rice, and performing other needful tasks.[3]

Once the Low Country felt the stimulus of the new staples its growth was assured. In general, the period 1740 to 1776 showed a strong upward trend of prices that encouraged planters to improve more land. Rice exports trebled, and indigo multiplied fourfold, while the annual sterling value of Carolina produce rose from £100,000 in 1734 to more than a half a million pounds on the eve of the Revolution. A certain proof of accumulating wealth,

in Amer. Hist. Assn., *Annual Report,* 1900, I, 253–55; Mouzon, *Map of North and South Carolina.*

[3] Lewis C. Gray, *History of Agriculture in the Southern United States to 1860* (Washington, 1933), I, 277–78; Carman (ed.), *American Husbandry,* 281–87; George Chalmers, Papers relating to South Carolina (MS, New York Public Library), I, 121, 138, 173.

and one rarely found elsewhere in the colonies, was the appearance in the *South Carolina Gazette* of many advertisements by individuals and organizations of money to let at interest in sums from £100 to £6,000. Men were prospering. Robert Wells, Charles Town printer, told a friend in 1765 that "the Planters here all get rich, which you need not wonder at when you see this small province export about 120,000 barrels of Rice worth 35/ Ster on average, and upwards of 500,000 wt. of Indigo worth 3/ sterling round, besides many other articles as Corn, Lumber, Naval Stores, Pork, Hemp, &c." Contemporary opinion held that careful planters could recover initial investments in land and slaves with the proceeds of three or four good indigo crops.[4]

Each of these staples was better suited to a large rather than to a small farm economy, and as a result the plantation system with slave labor firmly rooted itself in the Low Country. Plantations varied greatly in size, however. On Edisto Island in 1732, for example, units ranged from 27 to 1,610 acres and averaged between 300 and 500 acres; the usual number of slaves was twelve. Estates of richer planters often ran to several thousand acres, consisting of rice swamps, indigo fields, and woodlands for producing lumber and pitch. Governor James Glen wrote in 1751 that "they reckon thirty Slaves a proper number for a Rice Plantation . . . tended with one [white] Overseer," and calculated to produce 2,250 pounds of rice for "each good working hand." Paul Hamilton's Edisto Island plantation consisted of 4,804 acres; and in the new Georgia

[4] George R. Taylor, "Wholesale Commodity Prices at Charleston, South Carolina," *Journal of Economic and Business History*, IV (1932), 358; Charles Town *South Carolina Gazette*, Oct. 8, Dec. 10, 1744; Aug. 23, 1746; Aug. 10, 1752; Feb. 19, June 18, 1753; Mar. 30, 1765; June 6, 1768; Robert Wells to ———, Aug. 13, 1765, South Carolina, Counties (MS, New York Public Library); David Ramsay, *History of South Carolina* (Charleston, 1809), II, 211.

area, Governor James Wright possessed eleven plantations on which over 500 slaves farmed cleared portions of
19,000 acres, while his friend John Graham owned 26,000
acres.[5]

By the middle of the century the inhabitants frankly
admitted that "the valuable land is chiefly engrossed by
the wealthy." In 1773 the region experienced a real estate
boom and Josiah Quincy recorded that the tales he had
heard of "the rise in value of lands seems romantic, but I
was assured they were fact." Although engrossed in large
parcels, much of the Low Country land remained un-
cleared, leaving South Carolina and Georgia with an even
less cultivated appearance than the Chesapeake country.[6]

Carolina's network of inland waterways did not have
sufficient depth to permit ocean-going vessels to ride up
to the plantation wharves, but it did provide easy avenues
for conveying rice, indigo, and other produce in decked
periaugers to ready markets at Charles Town or Savannah. "No roads is finer to travel than the Carolinas," said
John Bartram in 1765, and he was not alone in this belief.
Along highways "shaded with lofty pines" and across the
many streams on bridges or by good ferries, passed peddlers, carriers, and an occasional stage wagon from Charles
Town to supply the plantation country with notions or to
deliver mail and parcels. By the seventies a carriage road
ran from Savannah to St. Augustine, and regularly scheduled packet boats connected Charles Town with Georgia
and East Florida and with Pensacola. So avid was interest

[5] Assessment of St. Paul's Parish, Edisto Island, 1732 (MS, New York
Public Library); Guion G. Johnson, *Social History of the Sea Islands*
(Chapel Hill, 1930), 38–42; Plowden C. J. Weston (ed.), *Documents Con-
nected with the History of South Carolina* (London, 1856), 70–71; Carroll
(ed.), *Historical Collections*, II, 202; Gray, *Southern Agriculture*, I, 403;
S.C. Gaz., Jan. 7, 29, suppl., Feb. 5, 26, 1756; E. Merton Coulter, *History of
Georgia* (2d ed., Chapel Hill, 1947), 103, 105.

[6] Ramsay, *South Carolina*, II, 413; "Quincy Journal," 456.

in internal improvements that at the close of the colonial
period the Commons House of Assembly took under consideration the practicability of digging a twelve-mile canal
to connect the Santee with the headwaters of the Cooper
and thereby provide a protected inland route to Charles
Town.[7]

As I have just suggested, it was Charles Town that gave
the Carolina Society its commercial connections with the
rest of the world. This hub of the Low Country universe
was the only large urban center south of Philadelphia. A
population which grew from 6,800 to about 12,000 by the
end of the era developed nearly every business facility
needed to serve a rich agricultural hinterland. Hundreds
of small craft unladed barrels of rice and indigo at commodious wharves, where local merchants or factors representing English houses purchased them at the market prices
and stored them until they assembled cargoes for the rice
fleets that sailed periodically for European ports. These
same men also paid the insurance, handling charges, and
freight rates for shipping the rice and indigo. At their
warehouses, at other points along the Bay, and on nearby
side streets, overseers and planters found wholesale and
retail establishments containing the foodstuffs, hardware,
cheap New England furniture, clothing, and shoes needed
for their slaves, besides all manner of "European Goods
fit for the Season" to delight plantation womenfolk. Here

[7] John Bartram, "Diary of a Journey through the Carolinas, Georgia,
and Florida," Amer. Philos. Soc., Transactions, N.S., XXXIII, 23; Adelaide
L. Fries (ed.), Records of the Moravians of North Carolina (Raleigh,
1925), II, 918; John Tobler, South Carolina Almanack (Charles Town,
1756); S.C. Gaz., Mar. 2, Sept. 7, 14, Oct. 31, suppl., 1765; Oct. 13, 1766;
Aug. 17, 1767; Oct. 24, 1768; May 4, 1769; Jan. 18, Feb. 15, 1770; June
28, 1773; New York Gazette, or Weekly Post Boy, May 14, 1767; Savannah
Georgia Gazette, May 30, Oct. 24, 1765; Philadelphia Pennsylvania Chron-
icle, July 20, 1767; Journal of the Commons House of Assembly, S.C. (MS,
Columbia, S.C.), XXXVIII, 263–64; John Tobler, South Carolina and
Georgia Almanack (Charles Town, 1774).

and there they also patronized shops of artisans, whose livelihood derived largely from repair work, since even more than Virginians and Marylanders did these people value things English and imported.[8]

In addition to handling the plantation trade, which was its principal function as a community, Charles Town was also the center of an Indian traffic in deerskins, which always made up an important and profitable share of its exports. In return the Indian traders took off quantities of blankets, strouds, rum, guns, and trinkets. After 1750, too, an extensive wagon trade developed between the back country and Charles Town and brought increasing exchanges of wheat, flour, and pork for manufactured goods. The city was also the southern terminus of the colonial post, which connected there with provincial and private routes of growing importance. As the capital of South Carolina, its military headquarters, and the sole seat of provincial justice before 1769, the bustling little town was the focus of the entire economic and political life of the Carolina Society. After 1763 Savannah, St. Augustine, Pensacola, and Mobile prospered as entrepôts for their particular areas and for certain commodities, but always their commercial life was connected with and subsidiary to that of the Low Country metropolis. No wonder that as provincial planters looked out at the world through the Charles Town window their little rivers appeared to be the sources of a great sea.[9]

[8] Carl Bridenbaugh, *Cities in the Wilderness* (New York, 1938), 332–33, 335–36, 344, 347–48, 362; Leila Sellers, *Charleston Business on the Eve of the American Revolution* (Chapel Hill, 1934); Charles Town *South Carolina and American General Gazette*, Feb. 5, 1771; *S.C. Gaz.*, Dec. 5, 1771.

[9] *S.C. Gaz.*, July 29, 1756, suppl.; *Ga. Gaz.*, 1763–75, *passim; Boston Chronicle*, Apr. 18, 1768; Cecil Johnson, *British West Florida* (New Haven, 1943), 153–54, 156, 158; Charles L. Mowat, *East Florida as a British Province, 1763–1784* (Berkeley, 1943), 75–76; Sutherland, *Population Distribution*, 308.

If this attitude seems brash, one must bear constantly in mind that throughout the colonial period the Carolina Society was young and immature. Virginia had been an established, thriving colony for over sixty years when the first permanent settlement was made in South Carolina, which as late as 1730 had only twelve thousand inhabitants at the most. Before the American Revolution by far the greatest number of Low Country residents belonged to the first and second generations over here, and therefore naturally exhibited all of the qualities of a new people.

The salient characteristics of the Carolina Society stemmed in large part from the breed of people which composed it, although they were, of course, strongly influenced by the environment and economy just described. The Low Country embraced about 11,000 square miles, or about one-fourth the area of the Chesapeake Country. Over 110,000 people lived in it by the outbreak of the Revolution. Of these some 14,000 (half white, half colored) comprised the urban populations of Charles Town and Savannah. There were approximately 97,000 rural dwellers, only 26 per cent of whom were white; in the three Low Country precincts of South Carolina (omitting Charles Town) there were fifty-three slaves to each three whites! For the entire region the density of population was only nine per square mile. Although in Charles Town it boasted a thriving urban center, the Carolina Society was destined to develop under predominantly rural conditions.[10]

The white inhabitants, who made up scarcely a quarter of the population, were themselves not as homogeneous a group as the Chesapeake Society. Originally based on English immigrant stock from Barbados, they experienced frequent significant increments of French Huguenots,

[10] Federal Writers' Program, *South Carolina: A Guide to the Palmetto State* (New York, 1941), 8–91; Sutherland, *Population Distribution*, 240, 258–60.

Scots, Welsh, Swiss, Germans, and some Scotch-Irish throughout the period. Since many immigrants settled in groups and tended to cling to their national customs, they did not wholly coalesce into a unified Low Country folk. Especially was this true of inferior planters and their families, among whom such an amalgamation took much longer than the years between 1730 and 1776.

The region soon developed the familiar hierarchy of classes. Lowest, of course, stood the great mass of Negroes, who cannot be bypassed with the nod formerly accorded by historians. Cultivation of rice in miasmic swamps under the burning sun was more than the white man could, or would, endure. A source of labor was found in the black African slave, who, whether or not he could better withstand the trying climate and monotonous routine of rice growing, at least seemed to be better suited to the needs of the planter whose profits enabled him to invest in a parcel of slaves. Authorities differ about figures, but mortality among Negroes was high, and the importation of slaves mounted until in the seventies three to four thousand a year were brought in.[11]

Among the slaves themselves three classes or categories gradually evolved. Most coveted was membership in the "intra-plantation slave aristocracy" as a personal or house servant, a station that elevated the slave from the general run of his fellows, and assured him better food and clothing, lighter work, and many special privileges springing from intimate association with the planter's family. A second status was that of plantation artisan. Intelligent slaves received training from white craftsmen and became carpenters, smiths, coopers, bricklayers, and wheelwrights.

[11] Schaper, "Sectionalism in South Carolina," 301; *S.C. & A.G. Gaz.*, Mar. 16, 1772, suppl.; Chalmers, Papers relating to South Carolina, II, 15; Elizabeth Donnan, "Slave Trade into Carolina before the Revolution," *American Historical Review*, XXXIII (1928), 804–28.

Such craftsmen enjoyed a considerable measure of freedom on plantation premises, and now and then their services were hired out by their masters for periods of from one week to a year. Those living near Charles Town were occasionally allowed to dispose of their own time when there was no work for them at the plantation. The lot of the ordinary slave who toiled in the rice swamps or indigo fields to produce the great wealth of the Low Country was pitiful and hopeless in the extreme. An able prime field hand might rise to the hated role of driver of a gang; that was about all. Although most of them were much better off than the slaves of the Caribbean sugar colonies, at best their days were one dull round of hard work, often under brutal and unscrupulous overseers, with poor and insufficient clothing, inadequate shelter, and not infrequently bad food.[12]

Africans and their descendants usually proved a tractable people when well treated, but they were never actually happy in their servile state. One observer of country slaves described them as "contented, sober, modest, humble, civil and obliging," in contrast to the "rude, unmannerly, insolent, and shameless" Negroes of Charles Town. "They are as 'twere a Nation within a Nation, in all Country Settlements," Commissary Alexander Garden pointed out; "they live in Contiguous houses, and often 2, 3, and 4 Families of them in one house Slightly partitioned into so many Apartments, they labour together and converse almost wholly among themselves." Life offered them little except the festivities of the Christmas season, when no work was demanded. Many a slave ran away to seek refuge with the Spanish near St. Augustine, and others, freshly arrived from the Guinea coast, still retained their warlike tribal

[12] Samuel G. Stoney, *Plantations of the Carolina Low Country* (Charleston, 1938), 21; Carl Bridenbaugh, *The Colonial Craftsman* (New York, 1950), 138–41; *S.C. Gaz.*, Oct. 3, 1754; Jan. 29, suppl., Feb. 26, Apr. 1, 1756; *S.C. & A.G. Gaz.*, May 6, 1771.

attitudes. Fear of revolts, more real than fancied, led the vastly outnumbered whites to impose harsh penalties for even minor deviations from the path of rectitude and to enforce a rigorous and cruel slave code borrowed from Barbados. All Negroes traveling off the plantation had to carry passes from their masters or be taken up by the slave patrol, which preserved to the country a military character long after threats of external danger had passed. When half of the males from sixteen to sixty in Charles Town precinct went off to fight the Cherokees in 1759, the other half of the militia was called out to "guard against the Insurrections of their numerous Negro slaves." In the final analysis, therefore, the oft-repeated statement that the country Negro was contented is a myth; it is perhaps one of the greatest historical delusions; and of all human factors determining the nature of the Carolina Society, the silent influence of the black African was the most subtle, the most forceful, the most pervading, and the most lasting.[13]

The activities of this large servile population were inexorably directed toward the twin goals of prosperity and security for a comparatively small number of favored free whites and their families. "The inhabitants may well be divided into opulent and lordly planters, poor and spiritless whites and vile slaves," concluded Josiah Quincy in 1773. He was struck, as are we, by the absence of a considerable vigorous middle class in the Low Country; even those in the capital he judged "odious characters." Ambitious nonslaveholders either rose to planter status or sought opportunity elsewhere. Listless "cottagers," whom

[13] Schaper, "Sectionalism in South Carolina," 309; "Quincy Journal," 452; Journal of Commons House, XXIII, 14; Gertrude Foster, "Documentary History of Education in South Carolina" (Dissertation, Univ. So. Carolina, 1932), VIII, 8: 47; IX, 14: 19; *S.C. Gaz.*, Apr. 28, 1759; Aug. 27, Sept. 17, 1772; *Boston Post Boy*, Mar. 25, 1771.

Eliza Lucas looked upon with a mixture of pity and dis-
dain, also incurred the contempt of favored slaves, who
fastened on them the West Indian Negro label of "bock-
orau" (buccaneer), which with time became "po' buckra."
Yet somehow these people got along; there was no pauper
class in the area. Contemporaries estimated that rice and
indigo planters made up approximately 70 per cent of the
free white population of the Low Country, and urban
artisans, traders, and rural poor whites made up the other
30 per cent.[14]

"Some say the Number of Rice and Indigo planters in
the whole province does not exceed two thousand," declared Robert Wells in 1765; nevertheless, the Carolina
Society took its pattern from this gentry exclusively. Newness was the distinctive feature of the aristocracy. Beginning with a handful of Barbadian Goose Creek gentlemen
such as the Draytons and the Middletons in 1670, it developed slowly with English and Huguenot accessions until
about 1730, then flowered in wealth, prestige, and numbers with great rapidity, notably after 1763. As in all
pioneer communities, a career was open—almost guaranteed—to men of talent. Ambition, vision, and energy, re-
warded as a rule first in commerce, then in planting, stimulated the growth of a plutocracy fed by prosperous people
of middle-class English or European origins. Families of
actual gentle birth were even fewer than in the Chesapeake
country; the bourgeois grown rich and seeking gentility
set the style. At the beginning of the Revolutionary War,
the Carolina gentry had not, as Burke might have put it,
hardened from the gristle into the bone of manhood. Visitors noted "the rapid ascendancy of families which in less

[14] "Quincy Journal," 454–55; *S.C. Gaz.,* Apr. 23, 1737; Carroll (ed.),
Historical Collections, II, 260; Schaper, "Sectionalism in South Carolina,"
273–79; Ramsay, *South Carolina,* II, 413–15.

than ten years have risen from the lowest rank, have acquired upward of £100,000, and have, moreover, gained this wealth in a simple and easy manner." One who knew them well and resented the pretensions of *nouveaux riches* flung a searing taunt at them in 1771: "Pray . . . look back to your own Origin and Draw the Curtain up but for one twenty Years only, and View Persons as then and now. It is a strange Succession of fortuitous Causes that has lifted up many of your Heads. . . . But step back only to the beginning of this Century. What then was Carolina? What Charlestown?" [15]

Among these people, however, there was "a class of citizens who by natural gifts, useful acquirements, or wealth," were "plainly enough superior to the rest." They knew how to make themselves influential and secure in society, and, in many respects, appeared to Dr. Schoepf to "think and act precisely as do the nobility in other countries." Thus, while the economy and the presence of the Negro served to place all planters in one class, a real gap opened between the "inferior" or lesser, and the lavishly rich or "better," planters. Carolinians were slowly beginning to emerge from their plutocratic phase by 1776, but we must not expect them, after only forty-five years of development as a class, to display the maturity or mellowness that a century and a half and the onset of decadence brought to the Chesapeake Society. [16]

The Carolina Society offered magnificent vistas of opportunity for men of enterprise to grow up with a new country. There, after 1730, prosperity seemed endemic as

[15] Robert Wells to ———, Aug. 13, 1765, S.C., Counties; Rev. Charles Woodmason to John Rutledge, 1771, Fulham Palace MSS, South Carolina, No. 60 (Library of Congress Transcripts).

[16] Edward McCrady, *History of South Carolina under the Royal Government* (New York, 1899), 399, 513–14; David D. Wallace, *Henry Laurens* (New York, 1915), 7–8, 33; Schaper, "Sectionalism in South Carolina," 274, 296; Morrison (ed.), Schoepf's *Travels*, II, 205.

riches amassed in trade were plowed back into profit-yielding rice and indigo fields, and further profits laid out in more and more "black ivory." The union of merchant and planter, of countinghouse and field, was the rule rather than the exception. Here and there estates were consolidated by shrewdly arranged marriages, as in the case of Thomas Bee, who, in 1773, took as his second spouse Sarah Mackenzie, "a young widow of about twenty with eight or nine thousand guineas independent fortune in specie, and daughter to Mr. Thomas Smith," one of the richest men in the South. In addition, the increasing worth of slaves and the real estate boom produced by engrossing land added a measurable unearned increment to plantation values—and the whole was buttressed by the law of primogeniture. As if to compensate for the rawness of a youthful society, the size of the fortunes accumulated exceeded those known elsewhere in English America. "The planters," said Henry Laurens in 1750, "are full of money." Henry Middleton, for example, possessed an estate of 50,000 acres and 800 slaves; in 1748 Commissary Garden described Middleton and Henry Izard "as Gentlemen of great Integrity and large Estates, each of them at Least £1500 Sterlg Income pr. Annum." The British House of Commons was told in 1751 that Daniel Huger "is now, and long has been, possessed of eight thousand pounds old South Sea annuities." There is no doubt that in per capita wealth and income, Low Country whites led all Americans.[17]

Much truth is contained in Governor James Glen's assertion of 1753 that the proportion of "men and women

[17] "Quincy Journal," 448, 456; *D.A.B.*, XII, 598–99; Foster, "Documentary History of Education," V, 766a; Leo F. Stock, *Proceedings and Debates of the British Parliament respecting North America* (Washington, 1924–), V, 447; Wallace, *Henry Laurens*, 21, 123; Answers to M. Marbois' Questions, S.C., Counties, Misc. (N.Y.P.L.).

who have a right to the class of gentry" was greater there
than in any other colony in North America. Capacity to
exploit the resources of a virgin country enabled men, no
matter what their antecedents, to join in the plutocracy.
Some began well up in the social scale, like Joseph Allston
of the well-known planting family of All Saint's Parish on
Winyah Bay, who was nevertheless "a gentleman of im-
mense income all of his own acquisition." Josiah Quincy
learned in 1773 that but a "few years ago" at the age of
forty, Allston had started "with only five negroes"; since
then he had acquired five plantations and over five hundred
slaves, which netted between five and six thousand pounds
sterling a year, and "he is reputed much richer." Prospects
of quick riches lured many a man of humbler birth away
from his trade. Among those who fared well was Henry
Laurens, son of a saddler. Laurens commenced in a mercantile way and in the "Guinea business," became Charles
Town's leading merchant, and finally proceeded to owner-
ship and management of plantations totaling about twenty
thousand acres in the Cooper, Santee, and Ninety Six regions of South Carolina as well as along the Georgia coast.
Success eventually attended Scottish John Stuart, who,
although he failed in trade, received government appoint-
ments, acquired over fifteen thousand acres of land in
South Carolina, Georgia, and West Florida, operated
two Beaufort plantations with two hundred slaves that
yielded a thousand pounds sterling a year, rose rapidly
in the gentry, and manifested his wealth and position with
a beautiful house on Tradd Street in Charles Town. Then
there was the prosperous cabinetmaker Thomas Elfe,
whose Account Book reveals the stages by which one of
the very few fine craftsmen of the city turned the profits
of his mystery into enough land and slaves to gain him

respite from his tools and a summer at Newport. When he died in 1775 he left a small plantation on Daniel's Island, three city properties, and a personal estate of £17,176 12s. 8d.[18]

Experience apparently taught that rice and indigo were best cultivated in comparatively small units, and as a planter purchased more land and more slaves he created additional plantations. The problem of management was solved by hiring overseers—a practice strikingly much more in evidence here than in the tobacco colonies, because in the Low Country agricultural profits were great enough to warrant the expense of using them.[19] Two social consequences of the system were the release of owners who desired it from strict attention to work, and the steady development of absenteeism. Thus did the rice and indigo aristocrats enjoy not only a greater prosperity but also far more leisure than was the lot of the Chesapeake gentry.

Although wealth and leisure permitted the richest families to leave their estates whenever they wished, the unhealthy climate of the Low Country dictated the times of their departure and return, for it was generally agreed that "Carolina is in the spring a paradise, in the summer a hell, and in the autumn a hospital." Oppressive heats and fear of "the country fevers" supplemented by the attractions of Charles Town's social whirl drew them into the city by the first of May, there to remain or "escape to the Northern Colonies" until November or December, when the rice country again beckoned with its promise of good health and

[18] Carroll (ed.), *Historical Collections,* II, 478; *S.C. Gaz.,* May 22, 1742; "Quincy Journal," 453; Watson (ed.), *Men and Times,* 42; Wallace, *Henry Laurens; D.A.B.,* XI, 32–33; John R. Alden, *John Stuart and the Southern Frontier* (Ann Arbor, 1944), 162–65; *South Carolina Historical and Genealogical Magazine,* XXXV (1934), 13–16, 59, 101; Johnson, *Sea Islands,* 103, 105, 123; Fulham Palace MSS, S.C., Nos. 52, 60.

[19] *S.C. Gaz.,* Jan. 29, suppl., Feb. 26, Apr. 8, suppl., 1756.

good hunting. Residence at the plantation was thought to be imperative during the Christmas holiday week, when the slaves had their annual festival and the danger of insurrection appeared greatest. Thus the gentry led a peripatetic life that was ultimately influenced more by the urban than by the rural environment and which had the important effect of dissipating the isolation so oppressive to the Chesapeake Society.[20]

There were of course many planters who, because they lacked either the means to support a dual existence or the inclination for urban diversions, or who were situated too far away from Charles Town and Savannah, remained on their estates throughout the whole year. We may therefore properly examine the rural aspects of the Low Country life before we follow its leaders into the capital. Profits from land, rice, and indigo made possible noticeable improvements and enlargements of estates soon after 1730. Early plantation houses built "in the Old Style," simple and unadorned, had been customarily located on the "Edge of Swamps, in a damp and moist situation, which quickly kills all Europeans not season'd to the Clime. The Old Planters us'd this Method, in order to view from their Rooms, Their Negroes at Work in the Rice Fields. But this Method is now banish'd," said a resident in 1771. Larger and more imposing structures rose on higher ground, where there was a better view as well as a more healthful location. Within thirty or forty miles of Charles Town now began to appear a number of magnificent mansions—Fenwick (1730), Middleton Place (1735), Dray-

[20] Mabel L. Webber (ed.), "Extracts from the Journal of Mrs. Ann Manigault, 1754–1781," S.C. Hist. & Gen. Mag., XX–XXI (1919–20); Horace W. Smith, Life and Correspondence of the Rev. William Smith, D.D. (Philadelphia, 1880), I, 469; S.C. Gaz., Apr. 2, 1741; cf. St. J. Ravenel Childs, "Notes on Public Health in South Carolina," S.C. Hist. Assn., Proceedings (1932), 13–22; Morrison (ed.), Schoepf's Travels, II, 167, 172.

ton Hall (1738)—that challenged comparison with the most noble James and Potomac edifices in architectural qualities and elegance of formal gardens.[21]

William Middleton built Crowfield on Goose Creek in 1730, and Eliza Lucas has left us a somewhat lyric description of its splendor after a visit in 1743. Driving up a mile-long avenue she came suddenly upon the spacious lawn and a pond before the great house. The garden was perhaps the show place of Carolina, and the bowling green, "thicket" of live oaks, maze, mount, canal, and two fishponds all added to the delight of the beholder. Built of brick laid in Flemish bond, this "Capital mansion" contained twelve firerooms, had two flankers, and was surrounded with out-buildings—all in "good taste" and "superior to anything of the kind." Her excited and detailed account suggests that, familiar as she was with the Low Country, this layout, not unusual in Virginia, Maryland, and near the Northern cities, was something of a novelty.[22]

As the Carolina Society grew, an occasional great plantation was laid out in the newer regions. The mansion house, outbuildings, and gardens belonging to Joseph All-ston on Winyah Bay were "in the best order" of any that Quincy saw on his trip through Carolina. During the war Elkanah Watson visited the Savannah River estate of George A. Hall. The avenue approaching it led in two miles from the highroad through the woods to an opening "occupied by a miniature palace, elegant in its exterior and embellished by the most refined taste, in the midst of a noble plantation, and surrounded by a little village of negro

[21] Rev. Charles Woodmason, Report on the State of the Church in the Carolinas, 1771, Fulham Palace MSS, S.C., No. 51; Stoney, Plantations, 23–24, 54–57, 58–59, 119; Bernhard A. Uhlendorf (ed.), The Siege of Charleston (Ann Arbor, 1938), 327.

[22] Stoney, Plantations, 54–55, 119; Harriott H. Ravenel, Eliza Pinckney (New York, 1896), 53–54.

huts. A highly ornamented flower-garden I saw blooming on the 16th of February." [23]

South Carolina authorities believe that the ravages of fire, wind, and war destroyed most of the great colonial estates, but I suspect that there never were many great houses erected in the Low Country before 1776. This was a society in the process of growth, and its wealth was but recently acquired. The overwhelming majority of rice aristocrats lived in frame, not brick, country houses such as the modest rural dwellings of Oakland (1740) in Christ Church Parish or Tom Seabrook's on Edisto Island (1740). As one found everywhere in the thirteen colonies, there was often much architectural charm, beauty of detail, and even distinction in many of these smaller establishments, which were built and maintained for comfort. Nearly all were equipped with imported Scotch "Pavillions" of mosquito netting to hang over the beds—a prime necessity in the pestiferous Low Country. But so eager were the planters to garner profits that they neglected such amenities as the culture of gardens; for the most part only those who had been in England evinced the taste to lay out and plant elaborate ones. Indeed many a flourishing estate afforded neither flowers nor vegetables. Only the "opulent and lordly" commanded sufficient wealth to erect, furnish, and maintain establishments both on plantation and in town; and in keeping with the immediately felt needs of any new society, Carolinians got more out of showing off their mounting wealth at the capital than on swampy acres where it would not attract so much notice. The golden age of Low Country building was to come after Independence. [24]

---

[23] "Quincy Journal," 453; Watson (ed.), *Men and Times,* 42, 44, 48, 54–55; *Ga. Gaz.,* July 12, 1769.
[24] Stoney, *Plantations,* 60, 66, 164, 165, 186; *S.C. Gaz.,* June 13, 1743;

Plantation life in the Carolina Society pretty much resembled that of the Chesapeake; such differences as existed were matters of age and degree rather than of kind. Except along the Cooper and Ashley rivers, on Goose Creek, and on those Sea Islands nearest Charles Town, it developed in even greater isolation—a seclusion which the presence of much larger gangs of slaves served to accentuate. Close association with the blacks meant that the whites inevitably took on certain traits of the Negro slave. The number of personal servants required by the gentry, young and old, amazed visitors; "every child has one accompany it," exclaimed a Jerseyman, who thought that in the long run the "multitude of slaves" tended to encourage "that dronish ease and torpid inactivity which are so justly noted." In 1774 St. George Tucker noticed with surprise that Carolina gentlewomen "talk like Negroes"; and discovered "Neatness not so much in Vogue as in Virginia." Many white people, particularly of the second generation, "owe their wealth neither to art, genius, invention or industry," only to the soil, Timothy Ford reported; and their "life is whil'd away in idleness, or consumed in dissipation." [25]

Country life, enjoyed by the gentry for a few months of each year, appeared idyllic to the less fortunate. Sumptuous entertaining, accompanied by courtesy without punctiliousness, stiffness, or formality, prevailed throughout the Low Country. John Bartram noticed that each Carolina and Georgia mansion had its commodious piazza "on one or more sides," and "much conversation both sitting and walking is held in there." Steady tippling of rum punch and

Ramsay, *South Carolina*, II, 227; Morrison (ed.), Schoepf's *Travels*, II, 180.

[25] St. George Tucker, Diary, 1774, Tucker Papers (Colonial Williamsburg, Inc.); *S.C. Hist. & Gen. Mag.*, XIII (1912), 142–43; "Quincy Journal," 456; Morrison (ed.), Schoepf's *Travels*, II, 221–22.

other cooling drinks by gentlemen who had nothing else
to do in the dog days may have induced the drunkenness
which, by common consent, was the "endemic vice of Carolina"; but many agreed with David Ramsay that if the
virtues of the inferior planters "are less brilliant, . . .
their vices are fewer." Not a few Charles Town swains
were captivated by simple country girls; one summer lover
and sunshine gallant thus indiscreetly fell into halting verse
about his charmer: [26]

> So near Divinity allied,
> Is this fair Work of Nature;
> That for a Goddess might be taken
> SALLY, *the Planter's Daughter.*
>
> A form so graceful and genteel!
> (Above the middle Stature)—
> You'd swear she was the Queen of Love,
> And not *the Planter's Daughter.*
>
> But quickly you'll that Oath retract—
> Examine well each Feature,
> No wanton Venus will be found;
> It is *the Planter's Daughter.*
>
> Ye Powers (I ask no large Estate
> Or honorary Garter)
> Give me, and I am truly blest,
> SALLY, *the Planter's Daughter.*

The normal activities of a rural area did not develop
to any great degree in the rice and indigo country. To

---

[26] Morrison (ed.), Schoepf's *Travels*, II, 167; Bartram, "Diary of a
Journey through the Carolinas," 30; Ramsay, *South Carolina*, II, 391–93,
401, 410, 413; Charles Town *South Carolina Gazette and Country Journal*,
Feb. 12, 1771; *W. & M. Quart.*, 3d ser., V (1948), 398–99.

wealthy aristocrats it was of no concern that the rural Low Country had no agencies of local government, or that the only courts of justice in the entire province were located at Charles Town, as long as they could minister to their own wants and enjoy a variety of social outlets when they went to the city. In the spheres of religion and education this failure of aristocratic responsibility was striking. Although the Anglican faith enjoyed legal support in the Low Country, the number of parishes and places of worship was few for its extent, and in 1770 half of the incumbencies were reported without ministers. Carolinians and Georgians took their religion as they took other aspects of life, genteelly and with ease; they were a "sensible and Moral People." Not a single native took Episcopal orders before the Revolution. The wealthiest planters employed tutors for their children or sent them to Charles Town, with the result that their leadership and support were lacking when schools were needed in the countryside. In 1766 St. George's, St. John's Berkeley, St. Thomas, and Prince George parishes did have free schools, established by the Society for the Propagation of the Gospel, and several wealthy men willed funds for the education of poor children. But, when all allowances for the difficulty of maintaining adequate educational facilities in a rural area are made, the Carolina Society still fell considerably below the standards of the time in schooling its whites and of course did virtually nothing for the Negroes.[27]

[27] Ramsay, *South Carolina*, II, 7–8*n.*, 27, 402–408; *S.C. Gaz.*, Jan. 1, suppl., 1752; Mr. Woodmason's Account of South Carolina, North Carolina, Georgia, etc., Fulham Palace MSS, S.C., Nos. 298–300; Pub. Recs., S.C., XXXII, 367–72; *Rules of the Winyaw Indigo Society* (Charleston, 1874); *Statutes at Large of South Carolina*, III, 364–66, 378–81, 431–36; *ibid.*, IV, 23–24; Edgar W. Knight (ed.), *Documentary History of Education in the South before 1860* (Chapel Hill, 1949), I, 276–95, 314–24, 329–31, 335, 698, 712; *S.C. Gaz.*, Feb. 27, 1742; Oct. 23, 1749; Jan. 18, 1768; Frank J. Klingberg, *An Appraisal of the Negro in Colonial South Carolina* (Washington, 1941), 26, 50, 67, 72, 91, 119, 126*n.*

The social and cultural barrenness of the plantation existence is not a true index of the Carolina Society, however; its mode of life can be described and understood only in a Charles Town setting. A mobile gentry overcame the twin blights of ruralness and isolation in the city, and to it we now must turn.

"The people of Charleston live rapidly, not willingly letting go untasted any of the pleasures of life. Few of them therefore reach a great age." This shrewd insight provides an explanation for Dr. Schoepf's further observation that "luxury in Carolina has made the greatest advance, and their manner of life, dress, equipages, furniture, everything, denotes a higher degree of taste and love of show, and less frugality than in the northern provinces," as well as for Josiah Quincy's assertion that "state, magnificence, and ostentation, the natural attendants of riches, are conspicuous among this people." At Charles Town one came face to face with the Carolina paradox: the unacquisitive spending standards of an acquisitive society.[28]

This round of rapid living, facilitated by accumulating riches and abundant leisure, was most conspicuous in the homes of the great planters. Lord Adam Gordon was agreeably surprised to discover in 1765 that "almost every family of Note have a Town residence, to which they repair on publick occasions," and during the heat of the summer months. Erection of the now-celebrated single and double Charles Town houses by planters accounted for much of the city's expansion after the middle of the eighteenth century. During the five years preceding 1773, over three hundred houses, "many of them elegant," were built along the Bay, the Ashley, and in the White Point and Ansonborough sections. These, and many handsome new public

[28] Morrison (ed.), Schoepf's *Travels,* II, 168, 216–17; "Quincy Journal," 455.

edifices, such as St. Michael's Church, the State House, the Exchange, and the Theater, as well as the wide streets and several fine gardens, produced an appearance of beauty and dignity which always evoked admiration and comment from newcomers. Indeed, Elkanah Watson asserted that "perhaps no city of America exhibits, in proportion to its size, so much splendor and style." [29]

The cool and airy high-ceilinged interiors of the great town houses were elaborately decorated and elegantly furnished in the latest London modes, designed expressly to set them off to the best advantage when their owners entertained—which was almost continually. When she was not herself dining out, Madam Gabriel Manigault seems to have had guests for dinner every day, often including such colonial celebrities as the second William Byrd, Colonel Henry Bouquet, victor of Bushy Run, or Governor Henry Lyttleton. Quaker William Logan from Philadelphia was "Very Genteely and handsomely Entertained" by Joseph Wragg in 1745: "Had two Courses of Meat and after that a Desert of Preserv'd Fruit," followed by a delightful walk under the orange trees. When Josiah Quincy went to dine with Miles Brewton in 1773 he exclaimed over "the grandest hall I ever beheld, azure blue satin window curtains, rich blue paper, with gilt, mashee borders, most elegant pictures, excessive grand and costly looking glasses." Naturally, the food and drink equaled the surroundings; the Yankee gourmet admitted that the wines were better than those served at Boston, even by the

[29] Newton D. Mereness (ed.), *Travels in the American Colonies* (New York, 1916), 397; Bartram, "Diary of a Journey through South Carolina," 30; Smyth, *Tour*, II, 83; *Well's Register, Together with an Almanack* (Charles Town, 1774), 83; Uhlendorf (ed.), *Siege of Charleston*, 327–29, 333; "William Logan's Journal," *Pennsylvania Magazine of History and Biography*, XXXVI (1912), 162; Franklin B. Dexter (ed.), *Itineraries of Ezra Stiles* (New Haven, 1915), 580–81; Watson (ed.), *Men and Times*, 56.

Vassalls, Phillipses, or the great Madeira smuggler John Hancock himself. Such free and open hospitality drew unqualified praise from all and sundry. Along with Governor William Tryon of North Carolina, visitors were impressed with "the opulence and beauty of the metropolis" whose "People live in the Genteelest manner" and, as Logan added, "are Exceeding civil and kind to strangers." [30]

Like their London contemporaries, the Carolina planters, possessed by a not-unnatural urge to see and be seen, found one means in rich and costly attire of the latest English cut and style, and they maintained a steady patronage of milliners and hairdressers, who "do well here, and grow rich." The appearance of the company dazzled Josiah Quincy at his first St. Cecilia ball: he had expected the ladies to be splendid, but he also found "the gentlemen, many of them dressed with richness and elegance uncommon with us—many with swords on! We had two Macaronis, just arrived from London. This character I found real, and not fictitious. 'See the Macaroni,' was the common phrase in the hall. One may be stiled the Bag—and the other the Cue—Macaroni." [31]

Although the pursuit of pleasure took its most common form in wining and dining at city mansions, this was the era when a gentleman seemed to be almost any place except in his home. After a midafternoon dinner, numerous attractions drew him forth for the remainder of the day, and often much of the night, since the life of the town

[30] *S.C. Gaz.*, Apr. 1, 1756; Mar. 7, 1774; Alice R. H. Smith and Daniel E. H. Smith, *The Dwelling Houses of Charleston* (Philadelphia, 1917), 24-25, 35-37, chaps. ii–v, xiii; Morrison (ed.), Schoepf's *Travels,* II, 164; "Quincy Journal," 443, 444-45; "Logan's Journal," 162; Webber (ed.), "Manigault Journal," *S.C. Hist. & Gen. Mag.,* XX, 57-63, 129; William L. Saunders (ed.), *Colonial Records of North Carolina* (Raleigh, 1886–90), VIII, 210.

[31] Morrison (ed.), Schoepf's *Travels,* II, 169; "Quincy Journal," 442; Schaper, "Sectionalism in South Carolina," 274, 276.

enabled him to avoid the enforced solitude of the plantation and to emulate the gregarious gaiety of London on
the borders of the wilderness. Recreation and diversions
of all kinds were much more organized and more sophisticated than in the Chesapeake Society.

Charles Town residents formed more private societies
than any other American community; clubs existed for
almost any reason, and most gentlemen belonged to several. There was a "Whisk Club" as early as 1732, and in
succeeding years convivial gatherings with such strange
names as the Fort Jolly Volunteers, Smoaking Club, Med-
dlers, and Laughing Club were established. The aim of the
Beef-Steak Club is clear enough; since the Fancy Society
had a poet laureate, we may only guess its purpose; but
we are left in the dark about what went on when the
Brooms advertised "a special Sweep." Mrs. Manigault
was forever noting in her diary, "My son Peter went to
the Club." Young Mr. Quincy made the rounds of Charles
Town clubs in 1773. On May 12 Thomas Lynch introduced
him to the Fryday-Night Club, "consisting of the more
elderly and substantial gentlemen. About twenty or thirty
in the company, conversation on negroes, rice, and the necessity of British regular troops being in Charlestown."
Three days later, after a turtle dinner he "spent the evening
with the Monday-Night Club, . . . Cards, feasting, and
indifferent wines." But the really memorable occasion was
provided by the Sons of St. Patrick: "While at dinner six
violins, two hautboys, and bassoon with a hand-tabor beat
excellently well. After dinner six French horns in concert,
—most surpassing musick!" [32]

---

[32] Webber (ed.), "Manigault Journal," *S.C. Hist. & Gen. Mag.,* XX,
59; *S.C. Gaz.,* Feb. 12, 1732; May 25, 1747; Aug. 14, 1749; Jan. 8, 1750;
Oct. 15, 1753; Mar. 12, 1754; Sept. 28, 1765; Feb. 16, Mar. 22, 1773;
"Quincy Journal," 450-51; Morrison (ed.), Schoepf's *Travels,* II, 168-
69.

Besides social clubs there were those designed for some specific purpose or worthy cause, which, being Carolinian and eighteenth-century, always had their convivial side too. A Masonic lodge existed in 1735, and before the end of the period several more had been organized and a hall erected. The martial spirit of the planters found vent in the forming of troops of horse and in gay festivities at drills and parades. Then each of the several prominent national groups in Charles Town, usually naming themselves after the patron saint of their old country, met regularly to perpetuate the memory of the land of their birth and to assist needy members.[33]

For those interested in out-of-door diversions, fowling and hunting on the beach or in nearby woods offered great sport, as in other colonies. A genuine innovation by the Carolina Society was the establishing of the St. Andrew's Hunt in 1757 for target practice as well as the actual chase. It seems to have languished from its beginning but was revived in 1761. Inasmuch as the new hunt did not have its own pack, the *South Carolina Gazette* carried a request that "Every Member that is possessed of hounds is desired to bring them to the club" by 6 A.M. of the next scheduled hunt day. On June 20 it merged with a Charles Town club as the St. Andrew's and St. Philip's Club, at a meeting in the "hunt house, where they spent the afternoon very merry, after killing two foxes." Although it apparently did not long survive, the St. Andrew's and St. Philip's had the distinction of being one of the first fox-hunting clubs in either England or America.[34]

No true Carolinian could resist the lure of the turf. The

[33] *S.C. Gaz.*, Jan. 26, 1738; Jan. 26, 1740; Jan. 29, suppl., 1756; July 21, 1757; *S.C. & A.G. Gaz.*, Oct. 31, 1765; *S.C. Gaz. & C. Journal*, May 27, June 10, 1766.

[34] *S.C. Gaz.*, Jan. 6, 1746; Mar. 17, 1757; Mar. 7, June 20, 1761.

success of the first big horse race in 1734 encouraged the laying-out of a track named the York Course at the Quarter House, where, beginning in 1735, occasional meetings were held. Eight years later, under the management of John Hanbury, races were held nearly every month for such handsome prizes as a silver punch bowl, a gold watch, a piece of silver plate, or a purse of £150. In this year, too, there was a New Market track at Goose Creek; another New Market Course was opened on Charles Town Neck in 1754 by Thomas Nightingale from Yorkshire, who inaugurated the celebrated "Charlestown Races." The sport of kings was firmly established with the founding of the Carolina Jockey Club in 1758, which provided the running of three great features for purses as high as £1,000: the Charlestown Plate, the Colt's Plate, and the Sweepstakes.[35]

Race days were gala occasions for which the entire gentry turned out after 1743, when Mr. Hanbury erected "a Gallery for the Ladies." In fact, all classes and conditions of men were represented. Henry Laurens complained that his captains could not get their ships loaded because of "the horse races, a diversion which is carried on rather too near our town." Toward the close of the March meeting of 1756 several gentlemen had their pockets picked. When a light-fingered "Fellow was detected in the Exercise of his Art," the crowd hauled him through a nearby pond and then beat him severely "as a Reward" before they carried him to gaol.

Commencing in 1763, the *South Carolina Gazette* usually published odds before the races and always carried

[35] *S.C. Gaz.,* Jan. 25, 1734/5; Feb. 14, July 25, Aug. 15, Oct. 10, Nov. 28, 1743; Feb. 6, 1744; Apr. 10, 1755; Jan. 29, Mar. 4, 11, 1756; Feb. 1, 1768; Fairfax Harrison, *John's Island Stud* (Richmond, 1931), 101–31; John B. Irving, *History of the Turf in South Carolina* (Charleston, 1857), 33–36.

good, detailed accounts of the results, even reporting in
1769 that "William Allston: Esq.'s Chestnut Tail Horse"
won when the favorite, Mr. Lynch's Noble, "was rendered
incapable of running owing to some foul means made use
of by the Person who was his Keeper and Rider, for a
Bribe of £500 Currency." Working through the Jockey
Club the Draytons, Gadsdens, Harlestons, Hugers,
Lynches, Middletons, Ravenels, and Warings did much to
improve the breed by introducing pedigreed English stock.
All this horsiness intrigued visitors like Quincy. After an
excursion to view much of the local horseflesh in town
stables, he noted on March 16, 1773: "Am now going to
the famous Races. The races were well performed; but
Flimnap beat Little David (who had won the sixteen last
races) out and out. . . . Two thousand pounds were won
and lost at this race. . . . I saw a fine collection of very
high-priced horses, and was let a little into the 'singular
art and mystery of the turf.' " [36]

Elaborately organized cock mains never suffered neglect
from this sporting gentry. Innkeeper S. Eldridge had "a
good Pit built" in 1732, advertised seven pairs to fight all
comers at £40 per battle, and urged "all Gentlemen who
are Lovers of this Royal Diversion" to bring in their cocks
to be matched. He charged the high price of ten shillings
for each wagering spectator. Through the local newspaper
in 1735 some Charlestonians notified the gentlemen of
Port Royal that they were backing a "muffled Cock, named
Bougre de Sot," against "whoever has the Punk" to match
his spurs for £100. No odium then attached to this barbar-
ous pastime, for Gordon, Shepheard, and other respectable

[36] *S.C. Gaz.*, Sept. 12, 1743; Mar. 4, 1756; Feb. 11, 18, Mar. 24, 1764;
Wallace, *Henry Laurens*, 31; Webber (ed.), "Manigault Journal," *S.C.
Hist. & Gen. Mag.*, XXI, 12–13n.; *New York Weekly Mercury*, Apr. 18,
1768; "Quincy Journal," 451; *S.C. Gaz. & C. Journal*, Feb. 11, 1772.

and leading Bonifaces regularly promoted mains in their tavern yards.[37]

Open and daily indulgence in these and other manly amusements usually met with silence, if not approval, from the gentlewomen of Charles Town. During the agitation over the Townshend Acts, however, a "Pedee Economist" was indiscreet enough to use the columns of the *Gazette* to recommend the distaff and spinning wheel to the ladies in the cause of general frugality. He evoked the scorching reply of "Margery Distaff" that it proved little for her sisters to card and spin while their men continued to waste both time and substance "in what they call Parties of Pleasure."

"There is not one night in the week," she wrote, "in which they are not engaged with some club or other at the *tavern,* where they *injure their fortunes* by GAMING in various ways, and *impair their healths* by the intemperate use of spirituous liquors, and keeping late hours, or rather spending whole nights, sometimes, in these disgraceful and ruinous practices." Without abating her attack one jot, Margery slashed at horse racing, "by which inconceivable large sums are lost, . . . so fond are the *men* of wasting money," and she lunged home with the withering comment that foolhardy *"men* will even risk large sums on the chance strokes of *a cock's heel:* so addicted are they to extravagant dissipations, which they falsely call *Pleasure."* Although the "Pedee Economist" wisely refrained from trying to counter this not-unmerited foray, Carolina gentlemen continued to enjoy their favorite amusements, thereby inviting similar criticism from strangers. J. Hector St. John de Crèvecoeur thought that "the rays of their sun seems to

[37] *S.C. Gaz.,* Feb. 24, May 13, 1732; Nov. 29, 1735; Feb. 5, 1736; Feb. 19, 1756; Feb. 14, 1761; Mar. 28, 1768.

urge them irresistably to dissipation and pleasure." Eschewing vague philosophical reflections, Yankee Josiah Quincy was more precise in his censure: "Cards, dice, the bottle and horses engross prodigious portions of time and attention: the gentlemen (planters and merchants) are mostly men of the turf and gamesters." [38]

If the Chesapeake Society was noted for its men, the glory of the Carolina was its women. It was "acknowledged by all, but especially by strangers, that the ladies in the province considerably outshine the men." David Ramsay echoed this opinion of Hewatt when he wrote that "the name of the family always depends on the sons; but its respectability, comfort, and domestic happiness, often on the daughters." To begin with, "the personal qualities of the ladies" were greatly to their advantage; "generally of a middling stature, genteel and slender," free and unaffected in manner, they must have been lovely to look upon. Indeed, the Society for the Regulation of Manners decreed that after May 10, 1753, "no Lady do presume to walk the Streets in a Mask, unless either the Sun or Wind is in her Face; such as are very ugly or have sore Eyes always excepted." They seemed to have had but one blemish, and over this there was disagreement: some gentlemen held that they had "fair complexions, without the help of art," others maintained they were "generally of sallow complexion, and without that bloom" that distinguished their sisters elsewhere.[39]

In addition to comeliness and charm, Carolina ladies were celebrated for strength of character. They countered

[38] *Newport Mercury,* Oct. 23, 1769, quoting *S.C. Gaz.,* Oct. 5, 1769; J. Hector St. John Crèvecoeur, *Letters from an American Farmer* (Everyman's ed., London, 1912), 159; "Quincy Journal," 455; Uhlendorf (ed.), *Siege of Charleston,* 327.

[39] Carroll, *Historical Collections,* I, 504; *ibid.,* II, 478–79; Ramsay, *South Carolina,* II, 411–12; *S.C. Gaz.,* Nov. 5, 1753; Watson (ed.), *Men and Times,* 56; "Quincy Journal," 456.

"the great intemperance of the men" and their even less
gentlemanly excesses with soberness, discretion, and chas-
tity, with the result that they usually lived longer. J. F. D.
Smyth mentions that in 1775 "the Edisto or Ponpon has
been remarked by every one for the number of opulent
widows who reside on the banks of that river, and for the
perpetual round of entertainments and dissipation pursued
by the inhabitants of that gay settlement." Women faced
either prosperity or adversity with fortitude and resource-
fulness, and not a few widows managed their estates with
success. In other ways too they proved accomplished
women. According to Ramsay, they were usually of refined
manners and well educated, and several exhibited cultivated minds. The part played by Eliza Lucas Pinckney in
perfecting the indigo culture and later in raising her famous sons is an oft-told tale. Not infrequently some "females" chafed under eternal subjection to men and,
through the press, demanded a square deal, as did "E. R."
in the "Ladies Complaint":

> Then equal Laws let Custom find,
> And neither Sex oppress:
> More Freedom give to Womankind
> Or to Mankind give less.

But we understand why they lost this round of the battle
of the sexes when we read the courtly reply of "Incog":[40]

> Dear Miss, of Custom you complain:
> It seems to me you languish,
> For some dear, simple, homely Swain
> To ease you of your Anguish.

[40] Smyth, *Tour,* II, 53–54; *S.C. Gaz.,* Mar. 2, 1733/4; Aug. 15, 22, Nov.
21, 1743.

One should not conclude that no lilies grew in Low Country fields. Quite the contrary. Basing his opinion on inspection of upwards of 250 of them at a St. Cecilia concert, Josiah Quincy made one of his pungent comparisons: "In loftiness of head-dress, these ladies stoop to the daughters of the North; in richness of dress surpass them; in health and floridity of countenance, veil to them; in taciturnity during the music, greatly before our ladies; in noise and flirtation after the music is over, pretty much on a par." The most searching local critic of "the Polite Part of this Country" regretted that "Misses at Home are exercised in no Professions at all, except of Music and Dancing, which it must be confessed, make them very agreeable Companions, but will render them expensive Wives" and severely condemned many "self-conceited Girls" as witless social climbers. Yet these rice-field butterflies ultimately made excellent wives and mothers. Nearly every one of the men of culture and perspicacity who came to Charles Town to live chose a native-born wife, as much for her character and attainments as for her fortune.[41]

Enjoyment of the social life of Charles Town did not always require separation of the sexes, however. There were numerous occasions during the annual round of gaiety when ladies and gentlemen could be partners. Inasmuch as "the general topics of conversation, when cards and the bottle" did not intervene, were "of negroes, and the price of indigo and rice," discourse between the sexes, that fine art the eighteenth century so carefully cultivated, must have dragged heavily at times. Then, according to Charles Town's most acid critic, "Cards are introduced, endowed with the convenient Power of reducing all Men's understandings, as well as their Fortunes, to an Equality." A more active and less unilateral divertisement was needed,

[41] "Quincy Journal," 441; *S.C. Gaz.,* Mar. 1, 1773.

and dancing met the requirements. In 1732 the organist
of St. Philip's, a Mr. Salter, "opened an Assembly of Dancing and Cards, for the Entertainment of Gentlemen and
Ladies," and thereafter some form of subscription assembly was held annually in the planters' capital. Patronized
by Manigaults, Pringles, and other "lovely, and well-
dressed women," the Assembly eventually met twice a week
during the season, when, as one social light put it, "the
girls for fashion sake go to town." Quincy dined one evening with "Mr. Thomas Smith, Esq:, several gentlemen
and ladies. Excellent wines and no politics." Afterward
they "spent the Evening at the Assembly. Bad music, good
dancing, and elegantly disposed supper." [42]
   It is obvious that dancing was a more formalized recreation at Charles Town than in the Chesapeake Country.
This was true not only of the Assembly but also of the occasional ball. Instead of dancing in their homes, Charlestonians went out, particularly after Henry Holt, Henry
Campbell, and other masters promoted subscription balls
in the Long Room at John Gordon's, with admission by
ticket only; and there were special occasions, as in 1755
when Governor James Glen gave "a Supper and a Ball to
the Ladies at Mr. Poinsett's." Dancing and horses, it ap-
pears, often took precedence over politics. "Pray what is
your Assembly about—Dancing?" inquired Henry Laurens of an East Florida legislator in January, 1763. "Ours
break up next for that and another amusement which you
know is due in February." A handsome tribute was paid to
Terpsichore when the statesmen of South Carolina voted
to erect a "Custom House and Exchange" at public charge.
Built of brick and stucco after the Ionic order, it was

[42] S.C. Gaz., Mar. 11, 1732; Mar. 1, 1773; "Quincy Journal," 448, 456;
Carroll, Historical Collections, II, 479; Wallace, Henry Laurens, 32; S.C.
Hist. & Gen. Mag., XXVI (1925), 95; Webber (ed.), "Manigault Journal,"
S.C. Hist. & Gen. Mag., XX, 59, 61.

acknowledged to be "one of the most elegant Structures in America" when it was completed in 1773, and its preeminent feature was undeniably "the grand Assembly Room" that occupied the entire second floor.[43]

Carolinians might take their pick of the dancing teachers who made good livings instructing the rich. William Deering, newly arrived in town, opened a dancing school in January, 1750, and shortly took as his partner, William Scanlon, also from England. They inaugurated the custom of holding a master's ball for their pupils at Gordon's each November. Scanlon's "high dances" became so popular that someone paid him the dubious compliment of filching the book of cotillion figures "wrote for him by Mynheer Bockhurst of the academy at Amsterdam."

The Arthur Murray approach was first used in this country when Andrew Rutledge engaged "to make any person with a tolerable air, capable of dancing an assembly with a month's teaching," and he pressed his Gallic competitor by dancing a spirited hornpipe at his annual ball in addition to the minuet essayed by a M. Valois. Within three years he announced "Public Nights at his long room once a fortnight," baiting the ladies with free tea and coffee. Soon this prancing pedagogue employed one M. Chevalier to teach "the French dances now in vogue in Europe," and openly bragged in print that "the public is ere now, convinced of his abilities in making *genteel* dancers, and with dispatch." Under such tutelage Carolina gentlefolk, both young and old, became polite and graceful and, influenced or restrained by the greater dignity of the urban environment, were less given to jigs and country dances than Maryland-

[43] *S.C. Gaz.*, Nov. 22, 1735; Jan. 19, 1740; Nov. 7, 1743; Mar. 26, Nov. 19, 1744; Oct. 23, Dec. 13, 1751; Mar. 26, 1753; Nov. 13, 1755; Oct. 12, 1767; Jan. 17, 1771; Mar. 7, 1774; Webber (ed.), "Manigault Journal," *S.C. Hist & Gen. Mag.*, XX, 60, 209; Wallace, *Henry Laurens*, 31; *Weyman's New York Gazette*, May 11, 1767; *S.C. Statutes*, IV, 257.

ers and Virginians. Contemporaries pronounced them good dancers.[44]

Perhaps it was the sociability that accompanies concert life, even more than a love of melody, harmony, and counterpoint, that so greatly appealed to the Carolina aristocrats, but at any rate they provided steady patronage for music teachers and generous support of professional musicians. Sporadic concerts of "Vocal and Instrumental Musick" by Anglican organists were given after 1732 at the Council Chamber or at Gordon's to small and select groups. Georgians heard their first concert in Mr. Lyon's Long Room at Savannah in 1766 when John Stevens, later organist of St. Michael's, gave a benefit followed by a ball. The desire to hear regularly something a little more elaborate than chamber music led Charlestonians to found the St. Cecilia Society in 1762. According to "Rules" published a decade later this body consisted of 120 gentlemen, each of whom paid £25 a year for the privilege of attending the stated concerts and of introducing "as many Ladies as he thinks proper." For many years concerts took place at Robert Dillon's hostelry, and almost from the beginning the managers sought to bring to Charlestonians the best music obtainable. They advertised in Northern newspapers in April, 1771, for violin, hautboy, and bassoon players qualified to perform in their October series. If Josiah Quincy, whom I have so frequently quoted, found in South Carolina much to offend his ideas of fitness, he had nothing but praise for its music. When David Deas gave him a "stranger's" ticket to the St. Cecilia, he eagerly made his way to Pike's Long Room and as enthusiastically recorded his impressions: "The Concert-house is a large inelegant

[44] *S.C. Gaz.*, Nov. 27, 1749; May 21, Nov. 12, 1750; Dec. 13, 1751; Jan. 5, 1760; Feb. 14, June 27, 1761; Mar. 13, 1762; Jan. 1, 1763; Jan. 14, 1764; Oct. 13, 1766; Jan. 19, 1767.

building situated down a yard at the entrance of which I
was met by a Constable with his staff. I offered him my
ticket, which was subscribed by the name of the person
giving it, and directing admission of me by name, the officer
told me to proceed. I did, and was next met by a white
waiter, who directs me to a third, to whom I delivered my
ticket and was conducted in. The Hall is preposterously
and out of all proportion large, no orchestra for the performers, though a kind of loft for fiddlers at the Assembly.
The performers were all at one end of the hall and the company in front and on each side. The music was good. The
two bass-viols and French horns were grand. One Abercrombie, a Frenchman just arrived, played a first fiddle,
and a solo incomparably better than any I ever heard: I
have several times heard John Turner and Morgan play
a solo. Abercrombie cannot speak a word of English, and
has a salary of 500 guineas a year from the St. Cecilia Society. Hartley was here, and played as I thought badly on
the harpsichord. The capital defect of the concert was
want of an organ. Here was upwards of two hundred and
fifty ladies present, and it was called no great show." [45]

Independent concerts were not so frequent after the
formation of the St. Cecilia, but their quality vastly improved. Peter Valton, organist and composer of sonatas,
arranged a fine performance in 1765 with the Misses
Wainwright and Hallam of the American Company of
Comedians as vocalists. It was Miss Hallam's debut. The
players soon began to give musical benefits of their own—
a custom imitated in 1774 by "Signora Castella" and P.A.
Vanhagen, Jr., former "Organist and director of the City
Concert in Rotterdam"—with the permission of their em-

[45] *S.C. Gaz.*, Apr. 15, 1732; Nov. 5, 1737; Oct. 10, 1766; June 13, 1768;
Dec. 3, 1772; *S.C. Gaz. & C. Journal*, Mar. 9, 1773; *S.C. & A.G. Gaz.*,
Apr. 17, 1771; *Ga. Gaz.*, May 21, 1766; "Quincy Journal," 441–42.

ployers, the managers of the St. Cecilia Society. On a more popular level, in 1767, Messrs. Bohrer and Morgan announced that at the "New Vaux-Hall" up the Path, where they served tea, coffee, and liquors "at the Charles-Town Prices," they proposed to have "Private Concerts of Vocal and Instrumental Music" every Thursday evening at seven; in July they added a ball, for the price of one Spanish dollar. The next year a stage coach made two trips out to Vaux-Hall daily. If this enterprise succeeded, it was the nearest American approach to the celebrated London resort, since it alone offered music.[46]

A few of the gentry, of course, preferred playing or singing with friends to attending professional musicales, and they supported a number of good music teachers in the city. When St. Philip's vestry sought an organist in England after Edward Larkin's death, they estimated that he ought to earn 100–150 guineas a year by giving lessons, besides £50 from concerts and about the same from subscriptions of church members. Peter Pelham, grandson of the Boston limner and schoolmaster, taught Miss Fenwick to play the harpsichord, and won the reputation of "a very Genteel Clever young man . . . Extreamly Lik'd" by his pupils. For nearly ten years Frederick Grunzweig taught several instruments, specializing in the German flute. But the dean of local musicians was James McAlpine, who was "an eminent teacher of music" from his arrival in 1717 until his death in 1775. "His greatest Foible was Credulity, believing the most impossible Stories even of his most intimate friends." One of "the Protestant Boys, loyal and true," he so persistently feared Jesuit reprisals that he never went abroad without a pair of pocket pistols to de-

[46] *S.C. Gaz.*, Oct. 31, 1765; Jan. 19, Apr. 27, June 15, July 13, 1767; *S.C. & A.G. Gaz.*, May 29, 1767; Oct. 7, 1768; Oct. 21, Nov. 4, 1774; *S.C. Gaz. & C. Journal*, Nov. 22, 1768.

fend himself against Roman perfidy. Sometime prior to
1772 an "Orpheus Society" led by William Packrow, "first
musician," met quarterly, but we know little of its activities
other than that it was a gathering of music-lovers who
played chiefly for their own enjoyment.[47]

Any kind of theatrical entertainment always met with
enthusiastic support at Charles Town. The first of three
buildings known as the "New Theatre" was erected on
Queen Street in 1735 and opened with Otway's *Orphan,*
for which Dr. Thomas Dale supplied an effusive prologue
and epilogue. Several plays were given before May 8,
1736, when the scenery, costumes, and half an interest in
the structure were put up at auction. The religious revivals
of the forties headed by the Reverend George Whitefield
and Carolina's own Sophia Hume put a damper on the
gaiety of Anglican aristocrats, with the result that no
actors came south again until Lewis Hallam arrived in
1754 to open the second "New Theatre" on Queen Street
for a series of performances lasting from October to December. Again, in 1763, these players, now called the
American Company of Comedians, returned for a season
under the management of David Douglass. Seats may have
seemed costly (boxes 40s.; pit 30s.; gallery 20s.), but
ladies and gentlemen flocked to the plays. Madam Manigault was present when they opened on December 12 with
The Mourning Bride and when they closed on May 10 with
King Lear; in between she saw at least eight other plays
written by such favorites as Colley Cibber, Dryden, John
Lillo, Vanbrugh, and Shakespeare in the Cibber version.
One of the most sophisticated patrons of the Queen Street

[47] Vestry Minutes, St. Philip's Parish, Charleston, 220; *Letters & Papers
of John Singleton Copley and Henry Pelham,* in Mass. Hist. Soc., *Collections,* LXXI, 6–7, 15; *S.C. Gaz.,* Oct. 23, 1736; Apr. 6, 1746; Jan. 8, June
11, 1754; Apr. 22, 1756; Mar. 9, 1767; Apr. 9, 1772; Feb. 20, 1775; *S.C. &
A.G. Gaz.,* Mar. 3, 31, 1775.

Thespians was Dr. Alexander Garden, who sent to his friend Cadwalader Colden of New York a complete report of the Douglass venture: "He has met with all imaginable Success in this place since their theatre has opened, . . . since which time they have performed thrice a week and every night to a full, nay a Crowded house. Hitherto they can't possibly have made less than £110 strlg per night, for some nights they have made between 130 and 140 strlg. in one night, and I believe never under 90£ sterlg., and that for only one or two rainy Evenings. This will show you how much the people here are given to gaiety, when you compare this place in number of Inhabitants to New York. Mr. Douglass has made a valuable acquisition in Miss Cheer who arrived here from London much about the time that Mr. Douglass arrived with his company. Soon after that she agreed to go on the stage where she has since appeared in some Chief Characters with great applause, particularly Monincia in the Orphan and Juliet of Shakespear and Hermione of the Distresst Mother. Her fine person, her youth, her Voice, and Appearance, etc. conspire to make her appear with propriety—Such a one they much wanted as Mrs. Douglass was their Chief actress before and who on that account had always too many Characters to appear in." [48]

Douglass crossed to London in the summer of 1765 to engage "some very capital singers" from Drury Lane and Covent Garden to introduce "English comic opera" in the colonies. He also purchased an excellent set of scenes painted by Doll of Covent Garden for use in the third

[48] *S.C. Gaz.*, Feb. 8, 22, 1734/5; Feb. 28, 1735/6; May 8, 1736; Sept. 5, Oct. 3, 10, 17, Nov. 7, 1754; Nov. 5, 1763; *Ga. Gaz.*, Nov. 17, 1763; Sophia Hume, *Exhortation and Epistles to the People of South Carolina* (Philadelphia, 1747), 62–63; Webber (ed.), "Manigault Journal," *S.C. Hist. & Gen. Mag.*, XX, 59, 205–207; *Letters and Papers of Cadwalader Colden* in N.Y. Hist. Soc., *Collections*, VI, 281–82.

"New Theatre" on Queen Street. The dramatic season of
1765–1766 was a great success and notable for the singing
of Miss Wainwright and Messrs. Woolls and Wall in
Love in a Village and other operas. After playing for several winters in Northern cities, the American Company
gave Carolinians what was perhaps the most brilliant
season of the colonial stage in 1773–1774 when it put on
seventy-seven plays, farces, and operas—the best of the
London repertoire. The only sour notes were sounded by
the Grand Jury, whose presentment of the theater as a
public grievance because "large Sums are weekly laid out
for Amusement there, by Persons who cannot afford it,"
was quashed by a playgoing bench; and by a press attack
on the "Devil's Synagogue" by one who signed herself
"Cleopatra." With the performance of the *Tragedy of
Douglass* on May 30, the American Company closed its
career in the colonial South.[49]

In 1808, David Ramsay commented upon the fondness
of this people for British manners, and John Drayton went
so far as to assert that he found them so prejudiced in favor
of British ways that they could not conceive of imitating
or borrowing manners or culture from anywhere else. This
was true, but not the corollary so often drawn from it,
namely, that Carolinians had more contact with the mother
country than any other group of colonials and were thereby
"in their manners and customs and bearing . . . the least
provincial in America." No substantiation for this belief
has ever been adduced, nor will it be; for comparisons with
the goings and comings between England and certain other
American colonies (New York in particular) make it clear
that this is another myth we must abandon. Other streams

[49] *S.C. & A.G. Gaz.,* Oct. 31, 1765; Jan. 28, May 13, July 1, 1774; *Newport Mercury,* Jan. 13, 1766; *S.C. Gaz.,* Nov. 15, 1773; Feb. 28, May 30,
1774; *S.C. Gaz. & C. Journal,* Mar. 22, 1774.

besides the Ashley and the Cooper helped to fill the Atlantic.[50]

Nevertheless, travel played an important part in the lives of many of the Carolina Society. Natural desires to see new faces and places periodically received a real impetus from the unhealthy Low Country climate. Those who could afford it moved into town to escape the fevers, as we have seen, but a few who commanded great wealth began to summer in the Northern colonies, and just before the Revolution their numbers swelled rapidly. Valetudinarians sought cures by drinking the chalybeate waters at Bristol and Yellow Springs near Philadelphia, although they were mistaken if they fancied they would escape heat and humidity. At Manhattan some enjoyed the sea breezes and a brave couple or so tried the sea-water bathing at Gravesend beach or in enclosed privacy across the Hudson in New Jersey.[51]

Newport was the favorite summer resort of Georgians and South Carolinians. As Dr. Benjamin Waterhouse recollected, his birthplace became "the lumber room of the colonial Faculty," when more than three hundred of them made the voyage to the Island of Rhode Island during the last eighteen years of the colonial era. This enterprise required fortitude quite as much as wealth, for the journey took from seven to sixteen days and the head winds never seemed to stop blowing off Hatteras. Most people took passage with Captain Joseph Durfee in the sloop *Charlestown,* but his accommodations were not good enough for a former speaker of the Commons House of South Carolina. Late in May, 1770, Benjamin Smith, Esq.,

[50] McCrady, *South Carolina under Royal Government,* 513–14; Drayton, *View,* 217; Wallace, *Henry Laurens,* 33.

[51] Bridenbaugh, "Baths and Watering Places," 174–75; *New York Gazette or Weekly Post Boy,* June 22, 1772; Philadelphia *Pennsylvania Gazette,* June 16, 1773.

chartered a vessel to take himself, his wife, his four children, four servants, and several friends to Newport. All
went well until the ship foundered off Point Judith, but
after an exciting time of it they all arrived safely with
stories aplenty to tell throughout the summer.[52]

The annual exodus eventually reached such proportions
that it attracted widespread attention, exciting some acid
remarks from provincial patriots. The Reverend Charles
Woodmason condemned the gentry for neglecting the pure
air and mineral springs of the upcountry for Northern
climes, to the detriment of the province.[53]

Aristocratic high life at Charles Town undoubtedly encouraged the growth of religious indifference and called
forth the usual strictures. "We eat, we drink, we play, and
shall continue to till everlasting flames surprise us," cried
the Reverend Levi Durand; and a puritanical grand jury of
1743 presented as a very great grievance "the too common
Neglect of putting in Execution the Laws against Irreligion, Deism, and a licentious Ridiculing of the holy Scrip-
tures and Matters of a sacred Nature." The gentry were
just learning to play at this early date when that scourge
of diversion, George Whitefield, temporarily slowed their
pace. Five years after his first visit, he spoke of the great
change in people formerly "devoted wholly to pleasure.
One well acquainted with their manners and circumstances
told me more had been spent on polite entertainments than
the poor's rates came to; but now the jewellers and
dancing-masters begin to cry out that their craft is in danger." After 1755, however, the preachings of evangelists

[52] Carl Bridenbaugh, "Colonial Newport as a Summer Resort," Rhode
Island Historical Society, Collections, XXVI, 5, 23; S.C. & A.G. Gaz., June
8, 1770; Newport Mercury, July 25, 1768; June 18, 1770; Ga. Gaz., Oct.
25, 1769; Carl Bridenbaugh, "Charlestonians at Newport, 1767–1775," S.C.
Hist. & Gen. Mag., XLI (1940), 43–47.

[53] Fulham Palace MSS, S.C., No. 52; S.C. Gaz., May 31, 1770; Providence
Gazette, July 28, 1770.

seem to have been only one more show to such gentlefolk as Madam Gabriel Manigault, whose diary for January contains these entries: "Went to the Assembly"; "Went to the Play"; "I went to hear a Quaker Preacher [Sophia Hume]"; "Went to hear Mr. Whitefield"; "Went to a ball." [54]

But other factors than luxury, pleasure, and unbelief affected the religious life of the metropolis. From earliest times toleration of all faiths except the Roman existed, and in 1766, in addition to Churchmen, there were Presbyterians, French Calvinists, two kinds of Baptists, Quakers, Lutherans, and Jews among those who enjoyed complete freedom of worship. The ministers of St. Philip's and St. Michael's were supported at public expense instead of by tithes, a system Governor William Bull thought less onerous to dissenters than the English one. Most of the Carolina gentry preferred to worship in the Church of England, but as the Reverend Charles Woodmason sadly admitted, there were "very few Communicants in any Congregation"; the Reverend Peter Levrier, pastor of the Huguenot Church, complained in 1774 of the "great Decay and almost utter Dissolution" of his flock which, among other things, meant the extinction of the French tongue at Charles Town; and the children of prosperous Presbyterians grew to prefer fashionable Anglicanism.[55]

The tendency of Charlestonians, as indeed of nearly everybody in the mid-eighteenth century, was to regard religion as pretty much a matter of ethics and of doing good and being good, rather than of worshiping regularly or dwelling on Christian mysteries. One aspect of this

[54] David D. Wallace, *History of South Carolina* (New York, 1934), I, 414; George Howe, *History of the Presbyterian Church in South Carolina* (Columbia, 1870), I, 238; Webber (ed.), "Manigault Journal," *S.C. Hist. & Gen. Mag.*, XX, 59; *S.C. Gaz.*, Mar. 28, 1743; *Pa. Gaz.*, Apr. 23, 1747.

[55] Pub. Recs. S.C., XXXII, 367–72; Mr. Woodmason's Account, Fulham Palace MSS, S.C., Nos. 298–300; *S.C. Gaz.*, Oct. 3, 1774.

view of Christianity was the reflection in the Low Country of the new concern for the poor and unfortunate that was becoming an outstanding quality of the Enlightenment among English-speaking peoples. Lavish charity was characteristic of the newly rich gentry, satisfying in them the three desires of extending sympathy, of perpetuating one's memory, and of excelling others in public contributions. Several organizations sprang up in laudable imitation of the South Carolina Society, first and most successful of those devoted to almsgiving and good works instead of mere conviviality. Founded in 1736, it applied the generous benefactions made to it to the education and relief of the needy. "Gentlemen, especially of Distinction and Substance," joined in 1744 to support Whitefield's orphanage project in Georgia with large gifts in the hope of tying the great evangelist to Charles Town and America. Individuals vied with one another in performing charitable acts. James Crokatt distributed £1,000 among the sufferers in the fire of 1740; John Mackenzie bequeathed £7,000 sterling in 1771 to found a much-needed college in South Carolina and provided for the use of his valuable collection of books by the Charles Town Library Society until the opening of the "University." Generosity ultimately rivaled hospitality and other forms of display, leading David Ramsay to complain that "Charity is carried rather to excess in Charlestown; for the bounty of the public is so freely bestowed and so easily obtained as to weaken the incitements to industry and sometimes to furnish facilities for indulging habits of vice." [56]

One of the most deceptive of the myths about the Carolina Society is that concerning the state of culture at Charles Town. Because the term *culture* is susceptible of

[56] *S.C. Gaz.*, Apr. 9, 1741; May 30, 1771; *Pa. Gaz.*, Apr. 23, 1747; Ramsay, *South Carolina*, II, 386.

having a double meaning, at this point I must draw a sharp distinction between two kinds of culture. The word originally meant tillage, a working of the soil to produce fruitfully. From this derives the idea of culture as the development by discipline, education, and training of the intellectual, aesthetic, and moral side of human nature, the judgment of a people's attainment of truth, beauty, and virtue. In a secondary, though widely used sense, it has come to signify the purchase and collection of cultural trophies as a device of conspicuous consumption. The first meaning implies activity; the second, which I shall henceforth call *dilettante culture,* passiveness. The striking aspects of colonial Charles Town were the absence of cultural discipline and the passiveness of the city's intellectual and artistic life. The Charlestonians did have a dilettante culture, and they worked hard to cultivate Culture, as we can readily perceive from a review of their accomplishments.

"Literature is in its infancy here," Governor William Bull advised the Board of Trade in 1770. "Of Arts and Sciences we have only such branches as serve the necessities, the conveniences and the comforts of man. The more refined such as serve to adorn or minister to the luxuries of life are as yet little known here." It is folly for even the most ardent local chronicler to expect to find evidence of a highly developed cultural life in a tiny society scarcely more than five decades removed from the frontier stage. That it displayed to a marked degree what the eighteenth century called *taste,* and imported at considerable cost from the British Isles the talent to cater to it, is in itself a worthy achievement, one made possible by the existence in the Low Country of the city of Charles Town. At the metropolis planting families, which were by nature and by environment normally active and practical in their ways, came into contact with the foreigners and local men of taste who gravitated there, and thus they experienced the stimulating effects of an urban life denied the Chesapeake gentry. In a favorable atmosphere, under the lavish patronage of men of great wealth, this never-numerous gentry managed to impart to Charles Town's social life a surface brilliance and blithe insouciance that never failed to inspire strangers to superlatives. Charles Town was to Crèvecoeur the Lima of the North: "The inhabitants are the gayest in America; it is the center of our beau monde." [57]

The educational needs of the rice and indigo planters were essentially the same as those of the tobacco growers to the northward, but we have no evidence that they ever seriously concerned themselves with such matters before the last decade of the colonial era, or that anyone like the Reverend James Maury gave thought to the kind of education the region really needed. Let him who has sons and daughters see to their training according to his lights and his means was the theme of an essay in a *South Carolina Gazette* of 1732. It further emphasized that it is bad to try to educate everyone; instruction should be according to capacity, and unless he shows "genius" the craftsman's son should expect to follow in his father's footsteps. A sort of laissez-faire attitude toward education prevailed, as one might expect of a nascent aristocracy still engaged in getting and spending.[58]

Schooling of an elementary sort was available in Charles Town for those who could pay for it. Poor children went to the Provincial Free School or to schools supported by the South Carolina Society, Fellowship Society, Freemasons, and German Friendly Society, whose members annually subscribed for the instruction of a considerable number of youths. The one sustained attempt to provide facili-

[57] Pub. Recs. S.C., XXXII, 390, 392; Crèvecoeur, *Letters*, 158.
[58] *S.C. Gaz.*, Apr. 1, 22, 1732.

ties for the Negro was at the free school founded under the auspices of the Bray Associates at Charles Town in 1740 by Commissary Alexander Garden. There about sixty "Homeborn" boys and girls were taught to read the Bible and the Catechism. The curriculum had the twin objects of Christianizing and Americanizing them in the light of the cleric's belief that "this good work must not be attempted in the gross or inclusive of the whole Body of Slaves of so many various Ages, Nations and Languages, for in this view, it always has, and ever will appear insuperable." All such education for either whites or blacks bore the stigma of charity, and even the Provincial Free School was unable to offer a salary high enough to prevent its masters from accepting the easier work of a country parish. Opportunities at Savannah were even more meager and in 1768 the Grand Jury presented the want of "an established School in the town." [59]

"We have not one good Grammar School, tho' foundations for several in our neighboring parishes," Governor Bull admitted. "All our Gentlemen, who have anything of a learned education, have acquired it in England, and it is to be lamented that they are not more numerous. The expense, the distance from parents, the dangers to morals and health, are various objections against sending Children to England." As wealth accumulated in the country, some young planters were schooled in England after 1753, but the total was never as large as some recent commentators have implied. In 1765 Peter Timothy estimated that they annually took £2,000 out of the colony and had drained it of £50,000 in the past. [60]

[59] *S.C. Statutes,* VIII, 106–7; *S.C. Gaz.,* Mar. 8, 1734/5; July 19, 1760; Oct. 1, 1764; Foster, "Documentary History of Education," V, 798; *ibid.,* VIII, 9: 14ff.; Pub. Recs. S.C., XXXII, 390–91; *Ga. Gaz.,* July 6, 1768.

[60] Pub. Recs. S.C., XXXII, 390–91; "Journal of a Voyage to Charlestown in South Carolina by Peletiah Webster in 1765," Southern History Associa-

In contrast to the almost total absence of schools in the Low Country, private masters ready and able to provide at all levels almost any kind of instruction could be found at Charles Town. In 1770 Governor William Bull told English authorities that "there are teachers of Mathematics, Arithmetic, Fencing, French, Drawing, Dancing, Music, and Needlework, to fit men for the busy work and ladies for the domestic social duties of life." Most of these pedagogues conducted day schools or waited on scions of the gentry in their homes. Many, like Anne Gray, who rented "a pleasant airy house on Trott's Point," took boys and girls from distant plantations to board as well as to teach. What is today called vocational education was also in private hands. Advertisements of classes for single- and double-entry bookkeeping, mensuration, navigation, surveying, and other subjects useful to a budding planter or merchant, crowded the columns of the newspapers; notices of night classes for artisans and apprentices also appeared there. At Savannah in 1770 Peter Gandy opened an evening school "for the benefit of those that can't attend the day school, he having an assistant who will give due attendance from the hour of Six untill Nine." That hundreds of notices of private schoolmasters ran in the South Carolina and Georgia newspapers between 1733 and 1776 is some indication of the absence of any effective community sense of responsibility for providing adequate instruction for its youth.[61]

A proposal of 1723 for establishing an Anglican college in South Carolina was lost in the Assembly, and for many years thereafter aristocrats of the Low Country were in-

---

tion, *Publications*, II, 135; Wallace, *History of South Carolina*, I, 403–404; *S.C. Gaz.*, Mar. 9, 1765.

[61] Pub. Recs. S.C., XXXII, 392–93; *S.C. Gaz.*, Sept. 17, 1737; Feb. 26, 1763; July 22, 1766; *Ga. Gaz.*, Mar. 7, 1770.

different to a need for higher education. A few of them crossed to London to eat the required number of meals at Gray's Inn, Lincoln's Inn, or the Middle Temple, and several studied medicine at Edinburgh, but, as David Ramsay remarks, in the 106 years that South Carolina was a colony, less than twenty of her native sons earned a college or university degree. Efforts to promote an academy in 1750 inspired "Philanthropos" to contribute two letters on the development of a rationalized nature as the principal goal of a liberal education, but the project never matured. Sincere and concerted efforts by planters and merchants of moderate circumstances to establish a college as a patriotic and economic, as well as an educational, benefit to the province failed in the Assembly despite the large Mackenzie bequest and the support of Governor Bull, because they "had not influence enough to carry it through, and the rich did not need it." Few of the latter blushed, as did Henry Laurens at Philadelphia in 1771, at sending their sons north or to England. Having secured what they needed, the bigwigs neglected the schooling of the rest of the Carolina Society.[62]

Among a people so sociably inclined as the Carolinians and Georgians, reading was never a favorite recreation, nor was learning highly prized for its own sake. The books most frequently consulted by planters were those supplying useful information or the sermons and devotional tracts so popular everywhere at this time. Although several residents of the city assembled small libraries, the book-buying public was never large. One of the principal collections was that of John Mackenzie, who left over eight hundred vol-

[62] Knight, *Documentary History of Education,* I, 369; Ramsay, *South Carolina,* II, 383; *S.C. Gaz.,* Aug. 6, 13, 1750; Nov. 30, 1769; Mar. 8, 1770; May 30, 1771; E. Alfred Jones, *American Members of the Inns of Court* (London, 1924); J. H. Easterby, *History of the College of Charleston* (Charleston, 1935), 9–15.

umes at his death, although the one or two hundred books listed in the inventories of such prominent men as Thomas Gadsden and Joseph Wragg are far more typical. Yet the city did not lack good bookshops. In 1754 Robert Wells opened one in connection with his printing business and soon had a large selection. After 1768 Nicholas Langford on the Bay threatened him with competition when he began issuing printed catalogues of his many titles. These and other booksellers made regular importations of the most recent English publications and sold subscriptions to the several London magazines and newspapers, thereby facilitating the development of a taste for reading among such of the gentry as desired it.[63]

A far more effective stimulus, however, came with the establishment of the Charles Town Library Society in 1748 by seventeen citizens. That this group numbered nine merchants, two lawyers, a schoolmaster, a peruke-maker, a printer, a physician, and only two planters eloquently underscores the vital contribution of the city to the literary culture of the Low Country. Although the Library Society never attained the scientific and educational objectives of its founders, within two years it had 130 subscribers and in 1770 a collection of nearly 2,000 books. And they were being read, or at least taken out, for the librarian had to advertise in 1756 for the return of 48 overdue volumes. Savannah followed the lead in 1763 with the opening of the Georgia Library Society, whose books were purchased in 1775 by the new Savannah Library Society.

Back at Charles Town an enterprising bookseller, George Wood, announced in 1763 a circulating library for those who desired lighter reading than that afforded by

[63] Frederick T. Bowes, *The Culture of Early Charleston* (Chapel Hill, 1942), 54–61; *S.C. Gaz.*, Apr. 15, 1732; Sept. 17, 1737; May 21, 1754; Apr. 15, 1756; Aug. 28, 1768; Nov. 2, 1769; *S.C. & A.G. Gaz.*, Jan. 30, 1767; Feb. 5, 1771; *South Carolina and Georgia Almanack* (Charles Town, 1770).

the classics and treatises in the Library Society. His catalogues listed "a collection of curious books, consisting of
histories, voyages, travels, lives, memoirs, novels, plays,
etc." The public did not give him much encouragement,
however, and after four years he advertised "upwards of
one thousand volumes" for sale. Samuel Gifford came over
in 1772 to open a "Circulating Library, on the same Terms
as in London," but that is the last we hear of him.[64]

The presses of Charles Town and Savannah played a
most significant part in dispensing useful knowledge to the
Low Country. In 1732 Lewis Timothy began publication
of the *South Carolina Gazette,* which was continued after
his death by his wife and his son Peter. Robert Wells, a
Scot of superior intelligence and education, founded the
South Carolina Weekly Gazette in 1754, which was succeeded ten years later by the *South Carolina and American
General Gazette.* With the appearance of James Johnston's *Georgia Gazette* in 1763 at Savannah and Charles
Crouch's *South Carolina Gazette and Country Journal* in
1765, the Low Country had four newspapers serving it.
Both Timothy and Wells turned out unusually good sheets,
which attained as high a standard as any in the colonies.[65]

Charles Town's printers published very few books as
compared with Northern craftsmen. This was in part because of the small sale they could expect, and also because
almost no literature was produced in the region. Demon-
stration of taste is one thing; creation of works of taste
is another. Yet there were two books written in the coun-

---

[64] Anne K. Gregorie, "The First Decade of the Charleston Library So-
ciety," S.C. Hist. Assn., *Proceedings* (1935), 5–6; *S.C. Gaz.,* Apr. 26, 1750;
Jan. 22, 1756; Mar. 5, Aug. 13, 1763; July 20, 1767; Nov. 12, 1772; *S.C. &
A.G. Gaz.,* July 3, 1767; *S.C. Gaz. & C. Journal,* Apr. 6, 1773; "Quincy
Journal," 447; McCrady, *South Carolina under Royal Government,* 512;
Ga. Gaz., Sept. 8, 1763; Apr. 6, 1768; May 17, 1775.

[65] Brigham, *History and Bibliography of American Newspapers,* I, 125;
II, 1036–42.

try which command our attention on account of both their high quality and their local themes, even if the authors were not natives. Dr. Lionel Chalmers came from Scotland with an Edinburgh degree and spent what time he could spare from a busy practice studying the Low Country climate and its effect on the human constitution. When he published his conclusions at London in 1776 under the title *Essays on the Weather and Diseases of South Carolina,* it received an enthusiastic notice in the *Monthly Review.* It was, in fact, the most important American contribution to general medicine made during the colonial period. The Reverend Alexander Hewatt also was a Scot and educated at Edinburgh. He served as pastor of the Presbyterian Church at Charles Town from 1763 to 1775, when he returned to England because of Tory sympathies. There, in 1779, he brought out in two volumes *An Historical Account of the Rise and Progress of the Colonies of South Carolina and Georgia.* He undertook the study because the only general history of the colonies, William Douglass' *Summary,* was too thin on the Southern colonies. Writing at first solely for his own amusement, he grew serious and resorted to such original materials as he could procure through his friend Governor Bull. He was honest, admitted his bias, and acknowledged frequent confusion in dealing with a "new field." His history of political events has long been superseded, but, in keeping with the historical theory of the Enlightenment, the pages he devoted to a description of the people are priceless to the chronicler of today.[66]

The universal curiosity of the eighteenth century about natural philosophy was shared to a certain extent by the

[66] Carl and Jessica Bridenbaugh, *Rebels and Gentlemen* (New York, 1942), 297, 336; *W. & M. Quart.,* 3d ser., VI (1949), 660; Alexander Hewatt's *History* is reprinted in Carroll, *Historical Collections,* I; see especially lxxii–lxxiii, 501–16.

planting gentry, but they were not inspired to give their time to the study of the new science. Both gentlemen and ladies attended courses of public lectures on "amusing and pretty, as well as useful experiments" in natural history or electricity, offered occasionally by Hugh Anderson, Lewis Evans, William Johnson, and others. From permanent residents of Charles Town—principally Scottish physicians, joined by a few merchants and a craftsman or two— came the meager Carolina scientific contributions of these years. Dr. John Lining reported the first colonial studies of "non-infectious diseases," based on fluctuations of perspiration, kept meteorological observations from 1740 on, and corresponded with Benjamin Franklin about the new electrical fire. In addition to his careful work on fevers, Dr. Lionel Chalmers made studies of tetanus and meteorology. But the foremost figure was Dr. Alexander Garden, whose botanical work brought him into correspondence with Baker, Collinson, Ellis, Hales, Huxham, Linnaeus, and Shipley in Europe and all of the prominent colonial scientists between 1752 and 1775; it also won him membership in the Royal Society of Arts and Sciences at Upsala, the Edinburgh Society, the American Philosophical Society, and the Royal Society of London. He was tireless in collecting specimens of new plants and sending them or drawings made by Postmaster George Roupel to London, and in encouraging the expeditions of the Bartrams; but his efforts to awaken interest among his neighbors proved unavailing. In 1760 he told George Ellis that "ever since I have been in Carolina I have never been able to set my eye upon one who had barely a regard for Botany." [67]

[67] *S.C. Gaz.*, May 19, July 19, 1739; May 18, 1745; Oct. 31, 1748; Mar. 2–Apr. 30, 1752; Apr. 13, May 4, 1765; *Ga. Gaz.*, May 16, 1765; *S.C. & A.G. Gaz.*, Mar. 25, 1768; *Providence Gazette*, Jan. 28, 1769; *The Philosophical Transactions of the Royal Society of London, . . . 1665, to the Year 1800* (London, 1809), VIII, 683; *ibid.*, IX, 478; *Gentleman's Maga-*

Every attempt of Garden and William Bull, himself an Edinburgh graduate, to organize scientific activities in the Low Country was warmly seconded by the Timothys, who always gave ample space to philosophical news in their *Gazette*. Still their ardor went for nought. A proposal by some members of the Royal Society for a provincial botanical garden to conduct useful agricultural experiments met with a cold refusal from the planting interest in the Assembly on several occasions between 1757 and 1769. Bad weather unfortunately prevented local members of the American Philosophical Society from observing the Transit of Venus on June 3, 1769. Four years later, urged by Governor Bull, the Charles Town Library Society appointed a committee to collect and prepare materials for "a full and accurate Natural History" of the region and "fitted up a Museum" in which an orrery ordered from David Rittenhouse of Philadelphia was to be given a prominent place. To this promising undertaking, however, the onset of revolution put an end.[68]

If literature and science were denied the encouragement and support of rich planters, this was not the case with the polite arts. In truth, no other American community gave them more wholehearted patronage. We have seen that Charles Town residents generously subscribed for Douglass' theaters and regularly attended the performances of the players. Large audiences and ample funds to hire the best musicians were never lacking for the St. Cecilia Society. Similarly, the *South Carolina Gazette* boasted in

zine (1753), 431; Lionel Chalmers, *An Account of the Weather and Diseases of South Carolina* (London, 1776), I, 47; *ibid.*, II, frontispiece; Sir James E. Smith (ed.), *A Selection of the Correspondence of Linnaeus and other Naturalists* (London, 1821), I, 414, 419, 431–32, 446, 461, 476–77.

[68] *S.C. Gaz.*, May 28, 1750; June 17, 1751; Apr. 1, 1757; Nov. 24, 1759; Oct. 1, 1763; Aug. 31, 1765; Mar. 2, 1769; Mar. 22, 1773; *S.C. & A.G. Gaz.*, May 13, 1768; June 12, 1769; *S.C. Gaz. & C. Journal*, June 8, 1773; *Charleston Museum Quarterly*, I (1923–25), 3–11.

1774 that "many Gentlemen of Taste and Fortune are giving the utmost encouragement to Architecture." A series of destructive fires culminating in the great conflagration of 1740 cleared out many of the crude old structures of an earlier day and, like the fire of London, made possible the erection of new and more beautiful structures, which a prosperous gentry could then afford. Co-operating in the one activity where gentlemen, master craftsmen, and professionals could associate with social approval, Carolinians worked out from English and West Indian elements a distinctive urban architecture in the unique single and double houses, with side piazzas and detached kitchens, that rose from the ashes of 1740 and soon spread to the newer districts of Ansonborough, Laurens Square, and the Gadsden Lands. The double house reached its highest development in what is certainly the handsomest surviving urban dwelling of the colonies, that which Miles Brewton built at a cost of £8,000. There were "besides, in other parts of the Town many Houses that cost a thousand and twelve hundred pounds sterling." For parish churches in a small city, St. Philip's and St. Michael's were adapted with unusual appropriateness of elegance and size from more monumental models. These and many other buildings, like the State House, Guard House, and Exchange, combined with "many grand palaces, every one of which has porticoes with Ionic and Doric pillars" to make the Charles Town of 1776 a sightly seaport.[69]

Although the Carolina Society never produced a native

[69] *S.C. Gaz.*, May 6, 1751; Apr. 11, 1761; Sept. 14, 1767; Mar. 8, 1770; Jan. 31, Mar. 7, 1774; *S.C. & A.G. Gaz.*, Sept. 23, 1768; Aug. 23, 1769; Beatrice St. Julien Ravenel, *The Architects of Charleston* (Charleston, 1945), 18–54; Smiths, *Dwelling Houses of Charleston;* Bridenbaugh, *Cities in the Wilderness*, 372; Mr. Woodmason's Account, Fulham Palace MSS, S.C., Nos. 298–300; Pub. Recs. S.C., XXIV, 307–9; Carroll, *Historical Collections*, II, 486; *Charleston Year Book, 1887* (Charleston, 1888), frontispiece; Stoney, *Plantations*, 43–45; Uhlendorf, *Siege of Charleston*, 329.

painter, its members spent large sums on artists. Arriving
in 1739, Jeremiah Theus, a capable Swiss who could produce a stylish and convincing portrait, became painter-in-
ordinary to the gentry, enjoying almost a monopoly from
the departure of Alexander Gordon in 1754 to the end of
the last French War, when the "celebrated limner" John
Wollaston made several visits to Charles Town and won
commissions from the Manigaults. About the same time,
also, such rice nabobs as the Pinckneys, Elliotts, Middletons, and Smiths began to employ the best English face
painters during prolonged trips to London. Fashionable
Ralph Izard, or his wife, the former Elizabeth de Lancey
of New York, sat for West, Zoffani, and Gainsborough
and was Copley's first patron in Europe. Some idea of the
current artistic taste of gentility is gained from a London
letter of 1751 from young Peter Manigault to his mother
about his portrait by Allan Ramsay: "Tis done by one of
the best Hands in England and is accounted by all Judges
here, not only an Exceedingly good Likeness, but a very
good Piece of Painting: The Drapery is all taken from
my own Clothes, and the very Flowers in the Lace, upon
the Hat, are taken from a Hat of my own; I desire Mr.
Theus may see it." Peter did not go to William Keeble as
Thomas Smith had recommended, because although his
"Likenesses (which are the easiest Part in doing a Picture,) were some of them very good," he could not match
Ramsay's ruffles, which "are charmingly, and exactly like
the Ruffles I had on when I was drawn." [70]

In the decade before the Revolution, Lewis Turtaz,
Letitia Sage Benbridge, and the brothers Stevenson popu-

[70] *S.C. Gaz.*, Sept. 6, 1740; Oct. 22, 1744; June 1, 1767; *S.C. & A.G. Gaz.*,
Sept. 9, 1774; Anna W. Rutledge, "A Cosmopolitan in Carolina," *W. & M.
Quart.*, 3d ser., VI (1949), 637–43; Ravenel, *Eliza Pinckney*, 231; Webber
(ed.), "Manigault Journal," *S.C. Hist. & Gen. Mag.*, XX, 128–29, 209, 257;
Anna W. Rutledge, *Artists in the Life of Charleston* (Philadelphia, 1949),
116.

larized miniature-painting at Charles Town, while Abraham Delanoy, Thomas Laidler, the Stevensons, Turtaz, and the senior Warwell competed as portraitists. When Theus was reaching the end of his long career in 1772, Henry Benbridge arrived from Philadelphia to capitalize on the charm of his wife Letitia and the international renown of his portrait of Pasquale Paoli; he virtually became the arbiter of taste in the Low Country. Savannah had an anonymous painter in 1767 who advertised "Altar-Pieces, Landscapes, Sea Pieces, neatly finished."

At this time at least eight drawing schools drew their support from the wish of Charles Town's young ladies to learn the rudiments of a fashionable art. A beginning at collecting art was made by Hector Béranger de Beaufain and by Judge Egerton Leigh, the latter possessing paintings, or copies of paintings, by Paul Veronese, Giordano, Correggio, and Guido Reni. "Landskips" and all manner of "genteel Prints" adorned the walls of many a Low Country mansion.[71]

Little did these Southern aristocrats suspect that during this same period one of the greatest achievements of colonial art was taking place in Georgia and Florida, one destined to receive rare and merited praise from English connoisseurs. The ink and water-color drawings of the country's marvelous flora and fauna by the youthful William Bartram had romantic and dramatic qualities which marked him as the originator of the genre later made famous by John James Audubon.[72]

Considering the comparative youth of the Carolina So-

[71] *S.C. Gaz.,* Nov. 10, 1766; Apr. 27, 1767; Nov. 14, 1768; Mar. 8, 1770; Mar. 26, May 14, 1772; Apr. 5, 1773; June 6, 1774; Jan. 2, 1775; *S.C. & A.G. Gaz.,* Mar. 13, 1767; Nov. 11, 1774; *S.C. Gaz. & C. Journal,* May 15, Oct. 3, 1770; Oct. 15, 1771; Sept. 21, 1773; Bridenbaughs, *Rebels and Gentlemen,* 166, 168, 171, 173, 194; *Ga. Gaz.,* Feb. 18, 1767.

[72] Bartram, "Diary of a Journey through the Carolinas," 19; William Bartram's drawings are in the British Museum (Natural History), London.

ciety, its members were most successful in bringing music, the theater, capable painters, and prevailing modes of architecture to their capital, whence they might eventually penetrate inland as the society matured. Among a people who failed to produce a substantial and numerous middle class, practitioners in the arts never appeared, but they were imported from across the seas. Still if no native Carolinian or Georgian scaled Parnassus, there were those who made votive offerings to the Muses, and Peter Timothy could with propriety claim that "great Attention is . . . paid to the fine Arts." [73]

Following the praiseworthy custom of eighteenth-century historians of assessing the "temper and character" of a people, I will now sum up the traits of the Carolina Society. May I remind you that I am dealing here with the two thousand or so dominant whites—the aristocracy with "plenty of the Good Things of Life"—who gave the society its peculiar tone. The planting and mercantile gentry of the Low Country were intelligent, and their quickness in grasping the essentials of everyday matters enabled them to manage their affairs with ease. Men of mild temper, they were "not without a quick sensibility of any designed affront," according to Dr. Chalmers, but their passions soon subsided. Agriculture, rather than trade or the professions, attracted them because it seemed to offer the most lucrative rewards and guarantee the greatest social approval. Moreover, successful planting in a lush new country required neither a deep knowledge of farming nor much steadiness of application. Hence, as young men married early and took to planting, domestic and business cares soon absorbed all of their interests and energies. Gay, lively, affable, and fond of dress, their taste ran to extravagance, which contemporaries discovered "was beginning

[73] *S.C. Gaz.,* Mar. 7, 1774; Ramsay, *South Carolina,* II, 269.

to creep into Carolina." Few men lived to the age of sixty; old age set in with many at thirty. The Reverend Alexander Hewatt, who knew what he was talking about, pointed out in 1775 that "in the progress of society, they have not advanced beyond that period in which men are distinguished more by their external than internal accomplishments. Hence it happens, that beauty, figure, agility and strength form the principal distinctions among them, especially in the country. . . . They are chiefly known by the number of their slaves, the value of their annual produce, or extent of their landed estate." This is the familiar story of the plutocratic stage of any rising people.[74]

Not only did the Carolina gentry lay waste their powers in the accumulation of fortunes, but society and environment combined to form their character. It was universally admitted that because of the climate and the comparative ease of existence under slave labor in a fruitful country, most men lacked the questing curiosity, energy, and perseverance essential to outstanding achievement in the arts and sciences or in statecraft. The few who went to school in the British Isles usually distinguished themselves by their knowledge; but the large majority educated at home, Hewatt found, had their "ideas confined to a narrower sphere" and "made little figure as men of genius or learning." "Nothing that I now saw raised my conception of the mental abilities of this people," said Quincy, and Dr. Garden reached the same conclusion about "the gentlemen planters, who are absolutely above every occupation but eating, drinking, lolling, smoking, and sleeping, which five modes constitute the essence of their life and existence." [75]

[74] Pub. Recs. S.C., XXIV, 318–19; Carroll, *Historical Collections,* I, 504–8; Chalmers, *Weather and Diseases,* I, 38; *S.C. Gaz.,* Mar. 1, 1773.
[75] Carroll, *Historical Collections,* I, 504; "Quincy Journal," 442; Smith, *Correspondence of Linnaeus,* I, 519–20; Fulham Palace MSS, No. 60 (1771).

Between 1730 and 1776, these men and women, the
gentlemen and ladies of South Carolina and Georgia, were
busily engaged in fashioning a way of life for the Low
Country. Here was an aristocracy in the making. At the
same time that from town and country they were building
up their fortunes by engrossing the land and dominating
the rice and indigo economy, they were further consolidat-
ing their privileged position by controlling both houses of
the provincial assemblies and hedging the prerogatives of
royal governors. Living at the extreme southern limits of
the continental colonies, on the edge of a wilderness, this
little group of whites surrounded by a vast, terrifying
population of servile blacks built its future under unique
conditions. After 1750 a stream of settlers from the Northern colonies flowed over the upcountry, but between them
and the Low Country lay the Pine Barrens which effectively
kept them apart until the close of the period—and with
almost fatal consequences for the two distinct societies.
Expansion took place within the Low Country's ample
boundaries, and unlike the situation in Virginia and Maryland few cadets of established families sought their fortunes in the back settlements. A glaring example of the
selfish preoccupation of this nascent gentry with its own
concerns is the failure of the South Carolina Assembly to
provide local government for either town or country; no
matter where a man lived, if he wanted justice he had to
seek it in Charles Town. "But this Province from the beginning has always been in a few Hands. It was settled long
before Pennsylvania, and see the difference, between a
Land of Freedom, and a land of Oppression," cried a clerical champion of the upcountry. "Nor has one real disinterested public spirited Person, devoid of Party and Self Interest, ever yet appear'd in this country, which greatly

wants such a Phenix to give a new Turn to Things." [76]

Prosperity and success attended the efforts of planters and merchants until the outbreak of the War for Independence brought to the Low Country economic stagnation, devastation by fire and sword, and the tragedy of civil war. They escaped the insufferable provincialism that ordinarily accompanies such a narrow self-centered pursuit of the interest of a single class, because through Charles Town, and to a lesser degree Savannah, they were forced into contact not only with imperial commerce as was the Chesapeake Society, but to an even greater extent possible only in urban centers with the civilizing influences of the age of the English Enlightenment. Charles Town generated the meliorating currents the Carolina Society so greatly needed. It nurtured a society of genuine elegance. At times, nevertheless, its quickening influence seemed to observers close upon the scene to produce incongruous effects on aspiring gentlemen: "Their whole Lives are one continued Race: in which everyone is endeavoring to distance all behind him; and to overtake or pass by, all before him; everyone is flying from his inferiors in Pursuit of his Superiors, who fly from him, with equal Alacrity. . . . Every Tradesman is a Merchant, every Merchant is a Gentleman, and every Gentleman one of the Noblesse. We are a Country of Gentry, *Populous generosorum:* We have no such Thing as a common People among us: Between Vanity and Fashion, the Species is utterly destroyed. . . . The better Sort of Gentry, who can aim no higher, plunge themselves into Debt and Dependance, to preserve their Rank." Here was a people in flux, with attainment of

[76] Schaper, "Sectionalism in South Carolina," 324–38; "Quincy Journal," 454–55; Burnett (ed.), *Letters of the Members of the Continental Congress,* I, 517–18; Fulham Palace MSS, Nos. 52, 56, 60.

wealth and status the prime objective of all and sundry, who not infrequently mistook glittering tinsel for pure gold, sophistication for true worth.[77]

During the prerevolutionary decades the Carolina Society was taking form with inordinate rapidity. Newness and wealth were its outstanding characteristics. In forty years or less, a planting plutocracy arose on the basis of fortunes amassed in rice and indigo or in trade and sought to transform itself into an aristocracy after the Old World pattern. Unlike the illusory wealth of the Chesapeake gentry, that of the Carolinians was real; for its time, it was the big money. Upon favored possessors it conferred a precious endowment of abundant leisure and the coveted privilege of living in the city, at the same time that it sucked dry the rural Low Country. Absenteeism signalized a lack of gratitude to their acres for the wealth produced and bred a callous social irresponsibility that more than counterbalanced the growing gentility of the rich planters. Their residence at Charles Town or abroad throughout most of the year deprived the area of the leadership of gentlemen, resulted in a feeble church and feebler schools, and, above all, fastened inadequate justice on those remaining behind, many of whom could still remember the vast amount of unpaid service performed by the resident squirearchy of Old England. Nobility did not seem to obligate these Carolina planters, at least not as far as the countryside was concerned.

Charles Town, the great center for the beneficiaries of the Carolina Society, was like Humphrey Clinker's London, "the great wen" that drained the vigor from the rural areas. At the same time, however, it also provided the delightful vision of the elegant life, elevated above the common sphere, "glittering like the morning-star, full of

[77] *S.C. Gaz.*, Mar. 1, 1773.

splendour, vitality, gaiety." There the rice and indigo gentry displayed and consumed their wealth (once they got it) in the most lavish way possible. Theirs was not the grasping materialism, vulgarity, and grossness we associate with the Gilded Age of nineteenth-century America; it was circumscribed by a still powerful aristocratic tradition with a clean-cut standard of taste, a clean-cut standard of honorable occupations, and a clean-cut standard of prestige, specifying approved ways of spending money. The very fact of status, accepted as a yardstick, regulated their behavior and gave it tone. At Charles Town the butterfly charm of the women also attached to the men. Here was the only leisure-class Society of colonial America; here, the only people among whom "the unbought graces of life"— enjoyment, charm, refinement—became the *summum bonum*.

Granted that the Carolina Society was devoted almost exclusively to the rapid amassing and just as rapid consuming of property; granted that as yet it had put down no cultural roots, that it had produced no native scientist, painter, musician, or scholar; granted that transplanted Englishmen, Scots, or colonials from the North filled the ranks of its clergy, teachers, and physicians; granted that its native sons knew little Latin, less Greek, and seldom read books; granted, too, that its leading men lacked the precious political experience the Virginians acquired by participation in a flourishing parish and county government, and the comprehension of men and measures revealed by Adamses, Franklins, and Lees in the Continental Congress; granted that it had no ambitious middle class to serve as tradesmen and artisans from whose ranks could come recruits for the arts and sciences; granted that the prime causes of these deficiencies were the climate and the unvoiced but determining presence of the Negro; granted all these, we must I think, still conclude that much had been accomplished in these years toward the founding of a distinctive manner of life—one that adumbrated also many future possibilities. Its outlines were just appearing as the alarm sounded at Lexington. The matured, fully fashioned Carolina Society still lay far in the future along with the new republic.

III

The Back Settlements

IN THE year 1791 William Bartram published at
Philadelphia one of the first seminal literary works to
come from the pen of an American. His *Travels through
North and South Carolina, Georgia, East and West
Florida, the Cherokee Country, the Extensive Territo-
ries of the Muscolgulges, or Creek Confederacy, and the
Country of the Choctaws* became almost immediately a
veritable source book for such writers of the romantic
school as Chateaubriand, Coleridge, and Wordsworth. In
this fascinating volume the Good Quaker gave classic form
to the concept of the American Indian as a Noble Savage.
William Bartram's contacts with the Southern tribes,
whom he regarded as unspoiled children of nature, came
principally during journeys from 1773 to 1778. Over
twenty years earlier his equally Good Quaker father, John
Bartram, concluded realistically, after different forest
experiences, that "unless we bang the Indians stoutly, and
make them fear us, they will never love us, nor keep the
peace long with us." [1]

The startlingly opposed views of father and son in-
cisively symbolize the radical changes in the interior of

[1] William Darlington, *Memorials of John Bartram and Humphry Marshall* (Philadelphia, 1849), 256; John L. Lowes, *The Road to Xanadu* (Boston, 1927), 9, 365, 453, 455, 506; N. B. Fagin, *William Bartram and the
American Landscape* (Baltimore, 1933).

the South between 1730 and 1776. During this period the
aboriginal denizens of the upcountry wilderness witnessed
its gradual transformation into a land of farms and tiny
villages and into an organized rural society, which inexorably expelled Ignoble Savages like themselves. The emo-
tions poetic men recollected in tranquillity might trick them
into believing that in the misty past Atala and René actually did dwell on the banks of the Holston, Yadkin, Congaree, or Altamaha, but I am not here concerned with romantic myths. Instead I am seeking historical reality, and
it will be useful to reconsider many fixed ideas about this
newly settled land and to probe the real nature of the society that began to emerge; for this is a tale of beginnings
in a region eastern contemporaries casually referred to as
the "Back Country," "Back Parts," or the "Back Settlements"—labels that I find more accurate than those commonly used. Only at the outbreak of the Revolution can we
begin to discern the contours of a new society.

The Back Parts consisted of an irregularly shaped area
running southwest from Mason and Dixon's line for more
than 600 miles to just beyond the southern banks of the
Savannah River and varying from 20 to 160 miles in width.
Beginning west of the Monocacy River with Frederick
County, Maryland, it included the Great Valley and that
portion of the Virginia Piedmont west of a line from Charlottesville due south to the North Carolina boundary, as
well as the North and South Carolina Piedmont between
the fall line and the Great Smokies. In extent this was a
larger territory than the Chesapeake and Carolina countries combined.

The Back Country differed markedly from Tidewater
and Low Country. It was an upland region of many hills,
of fertile limestone or stiff clay soils, of many varieties of
trees and towering forests, and of vastly superior climate.
Although the Blue Ridge separated the Valley of Virginia

from the Piedmont, several gaps afforded connections. In North Carolina the sparsely settled western half of the coastal plain tended to set the Piedmont off from the country of the Albemarle, Pamlico, and Cape Fear, while in South Carolina a strip of sand hills, often called the "Pine Barrens," interposed a virtual no man's land between the Low Country and the Back Parts. In Virginia and Maryland ready access to the Valley was possible via the Potomac and James, but the rivers of North Carolina flowed southeastward through South Carolina to the ocean, cutting off any easy approach to the Piedmont from Edenton, New Bern, or Cape Fear.

Only an occasional white hunter or fur trader was to be found in this whole vast area in 1730. Indian, deer, and beaver dwelt there in forest majesty, unmolested. Less than four decades later over 250,000 people of European, American, or African birth occupied the country from which the trees, the Indian, the deer, and the beaver were rapidly vanishing.[2] The population of the Southern Back

[2]   ESTIMATES OF BACK COUNTRY POPULATION, 1776

		Per Cent of Colony's Population
Western Maryland	40,000	20.0
Great Valley of Virginia	53,000	11.8
Southwest Piedmont of Virginia	8,000	13.0
North Carolina Piedmont	61,695	40.0
South Carolina Piedmont	82,942	49.0 *
Georgia Back Country	4,682	14.5
TOTAL	250,319	

* 79 per cent of South Carolina's white population.

Sutherland, *Population Distribution*, 195, 201, 226–27, 240, 259–60, 266, 268; Freeman H. Hart, *The Valley of Virginia in the American Revolution* (Chapel Hill, 1942), 6–8; Evarts B. Greene and Virginia G. Harrington, *American Population before the Federal Census of 1790* (New York, 1932), 125, 152–53; *Colonial Records of North Carolina*, V, 320, 471–72, 565, 575; *ibid.*, VI, 1027, 1039–40; *ibid.*, VII, 539, 540–41; *ibid.*, VIII, xlv; Fulham Palace MSS, S.C., No. 11; State of South Carolina, 1770, Chalmers Papers, S.C,

Country did not compose a uniform society. One of the most striking features about it was that in different parts various groups of its people lived in several stages of development at the same time. Why this was so becomes immediately evident as the process of settlement is traced.

Into a land of promise spied out by a handful of Indian traders and hunters came thousands of people. At its inception this was not the usual westward movement of American-born population from Tidewater and Low Country, but rather a southward thrust from Pennsylvania of immigrant Germans from the Palatinate and of Scotch-Irish from Ulster, lured hither by seaboard speculating gentry with cheap lands to sell. In time, however, eastern colonials of English extraction moved westward to join the migration. We will mistake the true nature of the first great internal folk movement of American history if we see in it either the hand of God or the working out of a logical process. Some men and their families knew precisely what they wanted. National cultural traits, unwillingness or inability to pay the high prices asked for land in Penn's Woods, and the persuasive come-south-where-it's-cheap blandishments of the Dulanys, Hites, and Beverleys, the agents of Lord Granville, and the Assembly of South Carolina not only started the people on the way south but ensured a continuation of the march. That most of them just went was confirmed by the shrewd remark of Frederick William Marschall, the Moravian leader, as he watched the wagons roll through Wachovia: "The migrations of men are like the movements of a flock of sheep, where one goes the flock follows, without knowing why." [3]

[3] Herbert L. Osgood, *The American Colonies in the Eighteenth Century* (New York, 1924), II, 483; *Archives of Maryland*, XXVI, 25–26; Charles E. Kemper, "Early Westward Movement in Virginia," *Va. Mag.*, XIII (1905), 113, 118–19; Ellis M. Coulter, *The Granville District*, in *James Sprunt Studies in History and Political Science*, XIII (Chapel Hill, 1913),

The southwestward trek of immigrants from Pennsylvania had its official beginning in the summer of 1730 when a group of Germans, led by Adam Miller, located at Massanutten on the South Branch of the Shenandoah River, near the present Luray, in Virginia. Four years later a party of native Quakers from Pennsylvania established a meeting at Hopewell on the Opequon, and by 1736 permanent Scotch-Irish settlements had appeared on William Beverley's manor halfway up the Great Valley. As the people passed through Maryland on their way to "Chenando," many of them, especially Palatines, took up choice lands along the Monocacy River, and by 1743 each nationality had more or less staked out a claim to the lands of Maryland and Virginia in which its future expansion would take place. Methodically the superior German husbandmen selected only limestone soils and pre-empted the best lands of Calvert's county of Frederick (1748) and the northern half of the Shenandoah Valley from Harrisonburg to the Potomac. Under the leadership of James Patton and others, the Scotch-Irish occupied the south Valley, moving to the southwest until, in 1775, they had settled communities on the banks of the Holston and the Clinch and stood at the threshold of Cumberland Gap. So completely did this contentious folk dominate Augusta County that two Moravian missionaries traveling from Georgia to Bethlehem in 1749 wrote of their great relief when "we passed confidently and safely through the Irish settlements." [4]

39–40, 47–48; *Va. Gaz.*, Sept. 7, 1739; Robert L. Meriwether, *The Expansion of South Carolina, 1729–1765* (Kingsport, 1940), 17–30; Fries (ed.), *Records of the Moravians*, I, 294.

[4] Kemper, "Early Westward Movement," 113–33, 287, 295–97, 351, 360–61; Joint Committee of Hopewell Friends (comps.), *Hopewell Friends History, 1734–1934, Frederick County, Virginia* (Strasburg, 1936), 7, 14–15; John W. Wayland, *The German Element in the Shenandoah Valley of Virginia* (Charlottesville, 1907), 39–40, 92; Stephen B. Weeks, *Southern Quak-*

At the same time that the Germans and Scotch-Irish
were peopling the Valley, Virginians of English descent
were working their way westward into the Piedmont lands
lying between the James River and the North Carolina
line and forming the county of Brunswick, out of which by
1767 eight new counties were fashioned. This region was
occupied much more slowly than the Tidewater extension
north of the James, because the Staunton, the Dan, and
their tributaries all drained into North Carolina by way
of the Roanoke instead of into the Old Dominion. In this
region, however, westward-moving Virginians met and
mingled with the immigrants from the North who de-
bouched from the Valley onto the Piedmont plateau by
following the Staunton River through Wood's Gap, Mag-
goty's Creek Gap, or later, Fancy Gap.[5]

The occupation of Virginia's new settlements went on
for nearly two decades before the southward-flowing tide
reached the borders of North Carolina. Some venturesome
Scotch-Irish squatted on Lord Granville's lands and on the
banks of the Hico, the Eno, and the Haw about 1740, but
no great influx occurred until a decade later. From then
until the outbreak of the last French War, Scotch-Irish,
Germans, and Englishmen swarmed southward to take up
the rich bottom lands of the Yadkin and Catawba valleys.
The three western counties of Orange, Rowan, and Anson
had scarcely one hundred fighting men in 1746; yet only
nine years later the number was "at least three thousand,
for the most part Irish Protestants and Germans, and day-
ley increasing." When the United Brethren purchased
their great Wachovia tract in 1752, Bishop Spangenberg

ers and Slavery (Baltimore, 1896), 71; Cunz, Maryland Germans, 57–64,
114; Lewis P. Summers, History of Southwest Virginia (Richmond, 1903),
43; Va. Mag., XI (1903), 126, 225–33, 374.

[5] Robinson, "Virginia Counties," 131–35; Kemper, "Early Westward
Movement," Va. Mag., XII, 342–43; ibid., XIII, 4.

referred to it as "probably the best left" in the province.[6]

Although Governor Arthur Dobbs of North Carolina reported that the Indians, stirred up by the French after 1754, put a "total stop" to immigration from Pennsylvania and New Jersey and drove many settlers away from their lands on the Yadkin and Catawba, migration continued, albeit of a different nature. The descent of the French and Indians on the Valley of Virginia in 1754 to burn and murder set the exodus in motion at about the same time that it shut off the coming of new immigrants from the North. Population from the back parts of the colony shifted to unseated lands in another. From the comfort and safety of his palace in Williamsburg in 1755, Governor Robert Dinwiddie advertised to the inhabitants of Augusta County, who "have most shamefully deserted their Plantations, for Fear of an Enemy, . . . leaving every Thing that they have, and seek[ing] for Settlements in some other Country," that Colonel Washington's ranger companies could now guarantee them "the utmost Security." Honeyed words could not arrest this flight of fear, however, and soon the Reverend James Maury was warning Councilor Philip Ludwell that Piedmont Virginians were moving southward in "such numbers" as to "appear almost incredible." In one week of October, 1756, three hundred persons went by Bedford Court House on their way to Carolina, and "five thousand more had crossed James River, only at one ferry, that at Goochland Court House." Others were following, continued the vicar; ". . . many of these are not the idler and the vagrant pests of society

[6] *Col. Recs., N.C.,* V, 24–25; *ibid.,* IX, 49; Sutherland, *Population Distribution,* 229–31; Fries (ed.), *Records of the Moravians,* I, 59; Samuel J. Erwin, *Colonial History of Rowan County,* in *James Sprunt Studies in History and Political Science* (Chapel Hill, 1917), XVI, 10–14; William K. Boyd (ed.), *Some Eighteenth Century Tracts Concerning North Carolina* (Raleigh, 1927), 440, 443.

. . . , but the honest and industrious, men of worth and property, whom it is an evil to a community to lose." Besides fear of Indian attack other weighty reasons impelled many Virginians to give up cleared and fertile lands; among the dissenters in particular, release from paying taxes to support the Anglican Church made a mighty appeal. Several years after the elimination of the red and Gallic menaces the Wachovia Moravians learned of "some thousands more who wish to leave Virginia" and Maryland and start life anew.[7]

North Carolina was not without its Indian troubles too, but they never created the hysteria aroused in the Old Dominion. The freer and safer air and the fertile soil of the Granville District satisfied many Virginia malcontents, and as the great trek accelerated after the war, good farming land became scarce. In 1765 a Moravian diarist laconically recorded that "more travelers passed than in any previous year." Governor Dobbs was more informing: "I am of opinion this province is settling faster than any on the continent, last autumn and winter, upwards of one thousand wagons passed thro' Salisbury with families from the northward, to settle in this province chiefly; some few went to Georgia and [East] Florida, but liked it so indifferently, that some of them have since returned." And still they came. Not until the War for Independence brought bloody civil strife to the Carolina Piedmont did immigration slacken.[8]

Just as the populating of North Carolina was delayed two decades until choice Virginia lands were pre-empted,

[7] *Col. Recs. N.C.*, V, liv; *ibid.*, VI, 613–14; Cunz, *Maryland Germans*, 80–81; *Md. Gaz.*, Mar. 11, 1756; July 19, 1763; *Archives of Maryland*, VI, 484; *Va. Gaz.*, Oct. 10, 1755; *W. & M. Quart.*, XIV (1906), 95–96; Anne Maury, *Memoirs of a Huguenot Family* (New York, 1872), 431, 463; Fries (ed.), *Records of the Moravians*, I, 304–305.

[8] *Col. Recs. N.C.*, VII, 248; *ibid.*, IX, 821–22; Fries (ed.), *Records of the Moravians*, I, 294, 297, 360, 392, 413.

so the penetration of the back parts of South Carolina by the Scotch-Irish and Germans waited upon the settlement of its northern neighbor. In fact, the presence there of the Cherokees forestalled white occupation until after 1760. In the meantime, however, Welsh, Scots, and Palatines arriving at Charles Town between 1735 and 1750, were speeded up into the Middle Country by provincial authorities to develop the new "townships" laid out by the Assembly at Amelia and Orangeburg on the headwaters of the Edisto, at the Welsh tract on the Pedee, and at Saxe Gotha and the Congarees. Others ascended the Savannah to New Windsor, opposite Augusta. From the outposts of the Low Country the newcomers fanned out after the end of the Cherokee War, coincident with the arrival of the vanguard of the great southward migration in the still debatable land on the borders of the two Carolinas. But the northern immigrants soon took over the upcountry, making it the southern limit of what we may with propriety call *Greater Pennsylvania*.[9]

As the Ulster Scots came down the Valley of the Catawba, which in the southern province becomes the Wateree, they located first along the Waxhaw Creek. This region became one of the most heavily populated of the Back Parts. In the newly settled Rocky Mount district in 1767, a missionary found people already crowded together, "thick as in England." John Stuart wrote from Charles Town in 1769 that "the Country near the line is very full of Inhabitants, mostly Emigrants from the Northern colonies; it is remarkable that in going hence to the Frontiers I rode at Times 30 and 40 miles without seeing any house or hut yet near the Boundary, that Country is full of Inhabitants, which in my memory was con-

[9] Meriwether, *Expansion of South Carolina*, 45, 65, 79, 91, 113, 118–23, 133–35, 136, 154, 160.

sidered by the Indians as their best hunting Ground, such
is their rage for settling far back." Indian paths now became routes of migration as pioneer families pushed along
them to take up lands on the small streams forming the
Broad, the Saluda, and the Savannah. Little colonies of
Virginians, North Carolinians, English, Swiss, and Huguenots, as well as many single families or even lone individuals, continued to arrive from the North and from
the Low Country, where gentlemen were acquiring a new
interest in filling up the interior of their province. In 1772
Alexander Chesney landed with his family from Ireland
and immediately proceeded from Charles Town to Winnsboro by wagon. The next year he moved far inland to the
Pacholet, a branch of the Broad in Ninety Six District,
where he raised a cabin on his own four hundred acres.

South Carolina's population living above the fall line
doubled by 1765, when it reached 10,000, while at the same
time that of the larger though more sparsely settled Middle Country rose to 12,000, most of it English leavened
by a few Welsh and Germans. In 1763 between March
and July, upwards of 300 families crossed Ninety Six on
their way to settle near the Savannah River. But the aston-
ishing accretion came in the succeeding decade, when the
population soared from 22,000 to nearly 83,000, 50 per
cent of the population of the whole colony and 79 per cent
of its white inhabitants. Indeed, it should be noted that
the last part of the colonial interior to be settled contained
in 1775 slightly more than half of all its people.[10]

[10] *Col. Recs. N.C.*, VIII, 1; Rev. Charles Woodmason, Journal, 1767–1769
(New York Historical Society), 19; G. D. Bernheim, *History of the German
Settlements and of the Lutheran Church in North and South Carolina* (Phil-
adelphia, 1872), 161, 168, 177; *Ga. Gaz.*, July 7, 1763; Meriwether, *Expan-
sion of South Carolina*, 260; E. Alfred Jones (ed.), "The Journal of Alexan-
der Chesney, a South Carolina Loyalist in the Revolution and After," Ohio
State University, *Bulletin*, XXVI (1921), 3–4; John H. Logan, *History of
Upper South Carolina* (Charleston, 1859), I; Alexander Gregg, *History*

The question naturally arises, how did these pioneers with their families and household goods reach their destinations in the Back Settlements? We are all familiar with the Lancaster Pike, the National Road, the Santa Fe, Oregon, and California trails, but only an occasional student can tell you of the route by which the expansion of Pennsylvania took place. It has as much color and romance as the others and should be better known. There isn't even a highway marker for it. On the Fry and Jefferson *Map of the Most settled Parts of Virginia* is shown "The Great Wagon Road from the Yadkin River through Virginia to Philadelphia distant 435 Miles." Beginning at the Schuylkill River Ferry opposite the colonial metropolis, the Great Philadelphia Wagon Road ran west through Lancaster to Harris' Ferry on the Susquehanna River; thence through York to Williams' Ferry across the Potomac, where it entered the Shenandoah Valley, passing through Winchester, Stephensburg, Strasburg, and Staunton, crossing the James at Looney's Ferry (Buchanan), and swinging almost due south to the site of Roanoke. There it turned eastward through the Staunton River Gap of the Blue Ridge, then veered southward again close to the Blue Ridge, crossing the Blackwater, Pigg, Irvine, and Dan to its original terminus at Wachovia on a branch of the Yadkin. After 1760 it was extended down the North Carolina Piedmont through Salisbury, and then on through the Catawba Valley to Pine Tree (Camden) in South Carolina where the road from Charles Town joined it as it bent westward then south, forking beyond the Congaree for Ninety Six and Augusta.[11]

of the Old Cheraws (New York, 1867) ; Mouzon, *Map of North and South Carolina.*

[11] Joshua Fry and Peter Jefferson, *Map of Virginia;* Mouzon, *Map of North and South Carolina.*

Like most of our historic highways, the Great Philadelphia Wagon Road followed the meanderings of old Indian trails; in fact it was only made possible by the willingness of the Iroquois at the Treaty of Lancaster in 1744 to permit the use of their Great Warrior's Path through the Shenandoah Valley, and in North Carolina it took the course of the Cherokee Trading Path for many miles beyond Salisbury. Prior to 1760, "the bad road began" south of Augusta Court House in the Valley of Virginia, but thereafter it was passable over its entire length of over 735 miles for the sturdy wagons devised by the Pennsylvania-German craftsmen of the Conestoga Valley. Year after year, along this narrow-rutted intercolonial thoroughfare coursed a procession of horsemen, footmen, and pioneer families "with horse and wagon and cattle." In the last sixteen years of the colonial era, southbound traffic along the Great Philadelphia Wagon Road was numbered in tens of thousands; it was the most heavily traveled road in all America and must have had more vehicles jolting along its rough and tortuous way than all other main roads put together.[12]

This was primarily a movement of humble folk, of families hopefully seeking a cheaper, better, and freer life than they had hitherto known. Among them existed a marked disparity of wealth. Poverty was the common badge of the majority of Ulsterites, although here and there a man of property could be found. Their nearest rivals were the Highland Scots, who came late in the period. I am inclined to think that despite the fact that most of the Palatines

[12] Thomas P. Abernethy, *Three Virginia Frontiers* (University, La., 1941), 33, 53; *Va. Mag.*, XII, 56–61, 150–53, 271; Fries (ed.), *Records of the Moravians*, I, 41, 75–77, 143n.; *Col. Recs. N.C.*, VII, 248; Dexter (ed.), *Stiles Itineraries*, 64–65; Robert G. Albion and Leonidas Dodson (eds.), *Philip Vickers Fithian: Journal, 1775–1776* (Princeton, 1932), 13, 21; *Va. Gaz.* (Rind), July 7, 1774.

and Swiss were also poor, there was a larger number who possessed at least a little property than among the other groups. At any rate it is clear that by their cautiousness in selection of land and care in their husbandry, by their willingness to work hard, and by sharing tools and effects with one another, they seemed from the very first to make a better life of it than the Scotch-Irish. Among the westward-moving colonials the widest range existed, from abject poverty to considerable wealth in land and slaves. A pair of horses or yoke of oxen, a small wagonload of household and farm effects, plus some cattle, hogs, and poultry made up all the capital of the average family.[13]

A contemporary referred to these migrants as "a mixd Medley from all Countries, and the off Scouring of America," and with much truth, for their characters differed mightily according to imported national attitudes, and according to how and when they settled during the forty-five years over which their coming was spread. Certainly the most pronounced social trait of each of the European nationalities was clannishness. If the families of one did not migrate southward together, they did take up neighboring tracts of land and develop their own distinctive community. Above all this meant the preservation of native tongues, the prevalence of many varieties of English dialects, of Highland and Lowland brogues, and of Rhenish and Swiss variants of *Hochdeutsch*. Scattered among the great expanses of the inland South, multilingual enclaves persisted for years, sustained by a national exclusiveness that could never have survived in the seaboard cities of America, where intermingling forced by daily intercourse bred a genuine cosmopolitanism. Refreshed each year by the arrival of more kinsmen and friends from the Old

---

[13] Schaper, "Sectionalism in South Carolina," 317; Woodmason, Journal, 3–4; Cunz, *Maryland Germans,* 114; *Col. Recs. N.C.,* IX, 259, 1159, 1167.

World and all but ignored by their eastern colonial neighbors, each little group clung tenaciously to its cultural
heritage and resisted with all its strength what has been
called the Americanizing process. Young men were strong
to wive, but marriage within the national, and therefore
religious, fold was the rule, not the exception. In a broad
sense these wanderers often proved more attached to their
native lands and Old World ways than the men of the
coastal societies. In the choice of farm land, agricultural
methods, and craft techniques, in diet, religion, and language, this truth is patent.[14]

Of all the national groups the Scotch-Irish were the most
numerous, and it is not surprising that in the long run they
came to dominate, nor that Charles Lee sardonically referred to their society as a "Macocracy." The first of them
entered the Valley of Virginia in groups, but throughout
the Back Parts thereafter they tended to migrate in single
families. They also seem to have had a psychological repugnance to making permanent homes until they had
moved several times. Many of them, after a brief stay on
less desirable acres in the northern sections, pushed along
the Catawba Valley to South Carolina after peace with the
Cherokees had thrown open choice tracts. Andrew and
John Pickens served as justices of the peace at the first
court of Augusta County, Virginia, in 1745; six years later
they had located at the Waxhaws below the South Carolina
boundary; and in 1762 John and Andrew, Jr., received
warrants to parcels of land in the Savannah Valley. Likewise four Augusta County Calhouns (among them Patrick,
the father of the "Cast-iron-man") moved to Long Cane

[14] Woodmason, Journal, 3; Cunz, *Maryland Germans,* 114; Hugh Williamson, *History of North Carolina* (Philadelphia, 1812), II, 68, 79–80;
Col. Recs. N.C., V, xl; Bernheim, *German Settlements,* 99–102, 152, 179–
80; Fulham Palace MSS, No. 91.

Creek north of Augusta, Georgia, where they quickly assumed leadership of the Scotch-Irish in that growing district. Thomas Sumter and Moses Thompson are two others who had the same origin and destination.

Devoid of organization at first, the individual traits of these Ulsterites rose quickly to the surface. Undisciplined, emotional, courageous, aggressive, pugnacious, fiercely intolerant, and hard-drinking, with a tendency to indolence, they nevertheless produced ambitious leaders with the virtues of the warrior and politician. As viewed by others, these were hard and unlovely qualities, effective in a new country withal.[15]

By contrast, the Palatine Germans, the next largest element of the population, once having selected new lands, usually stayed put, and their group activities stood out prominently, attaining the greatest development among the Moravians in North Carolina. Also they were pacific, law-abiding, stolid, deeply pious, temperate, and devoted to the social ideal of a well-ordered society. At the same time they were shrewd and calculating and determined to achieve worldly prosperity as well as spiritual joys to a degree that led those who knew them not to accuse them of materialism.[16]

The Welsh, Swiss, and English Quakers each banded together, while those of colonial birth, already familiar with wilderness conditions, showed the most individual enterprise of all. Greater wealth, superior social status,

[15] Wayland F. Dunaway, *The Scotch-Irish of Colonial Pennsylvania* (Chapel Hill, 1944), 102–18, 181–83; Meriwether, *Expansion of South Carolina,* 50, 133–35, 138–40; Summers, *History of Southwest Virginia,* 53, 57; *Lee Papers* in New York Hist. Soc., *Collections,* VI, 457–58.

[16] Richard H. Shryock, "British Versus German Traditions in Colonial Agriculture," *Mississippi Valley Historical Review,* XXVI (1939), 46–48; Cunz, *Maryland Germans,* 114; Bernheim, *German Settlements,* 167, 185; Meriwether, *Expansion of South Carolina,* 65, 252.

and a voice in Tidewater and Low Country councils were the portion of the English colonials, whose influence with the Scotch-Irish was to become very important.

As we estimate the effect of the American environment upon these newcomers, it is well to bear in mind constantly that they were newcomers, and that down to 1776 reinforcements from the Old World arrived annually. Although eventually Tidewater social and political institutions were to gain ascendancy, for the period under consideration mutual suspicion was stronger than the forces of common humanity, especially in religious matters— which then meant nearly all matters. At times all along the western fringe of settlement, Indian threats had the effect of bringing all nationalities together, as at the Moravian villages, where kindness shown by the United Brethren to more than 120 terrified refugees, regardless of nationality or sect, provided one kind of counterpoise to social divisors. And during the passage of from twenty-five to forty years, the native colonials, the Scotch-Irish, the Scots, and the Welsh could in some measure find a common ground for the preparation of a new ethnic amalgam, but the formula for it was not perfected in these years. We surely err, however, if we apply the concept of the *melting pot* to the Back Settlements, which, to choose a Biblical metaphor all its inhabitants would have readily understood, much more accurately resembled the Tower of Babel.[17] Fate designated the Back Settlements as the scene of cultural conflict for many decades.

The Back Country never witnessed the complete return to nature or social disintegration often implied by historians and sociologists. Those who migrated from one developing section to another, still wilderness, were inclined to accept far lower standards for civil society than immi-

[17] Fries (ed.), *Records of the Moravians,* I, 135, 180, 195–96, 210, 234.

grants fresh from the ordered communities of Europe. And, although this was a free population when compared with its eastern neighbors, every one of its members accepted the strong eighteenth-century consciousness of class and heartily respected both status and wealth, which, as the country developed, were further emphasized by the introduction of white servitude and Negro slavery.

None of these peoples had any training suitable for pioneering, and at no time in the period did anywhere near half arrive possessed of the skills they would need. Only the native-born and those who had already tried it once and then moved on knew how to use an ax or hoe properly. As a consequence most newcomers had to clear their acres and get out their first crops the hard way. I can find no evidence to support the customary assertion that their Ulster experience made the Lowland Scots better settlers after the initial stage, if, indeed, at all. They were content to live on a lower level of comfort and economy, which declined progressively from Virginia to Georgia, and the second generation knew far less of European ways than the first. The truth is that the German habits of co-operative labor produced the most immediate and best results and strikingly accentuated the shiftlessness of the Scotch-Irish and the inferior husbandry of the English.

The fundamental social unit, the family, was preserved intact throughout what was in reality a transplanting and reshuffling of European folkways. The conquest of the Back Parts was achieved by families, and, as the Reverend Charles Woodmason discovered at the Waxhaws, the people like the country were fruitful, for nearly every cabin contained from eight to twelve children. Besides performing prodigies of work and bearing numerous children, the women served as the conservators of tradition and civilization, ensuring the preservation of much that was rich and vital for guiding the new society upon which their men were expending so much physical and political vigor.[18]

The figure of a stream, now rapid now sluggish, has naturally come to writers describing the great migration; but they have overlooked the further analogy that running water carries materials in suspension which settle to the bottom as the flow slows down or ceases. And this was certainly true of the flow of people throughout Greater Pennsylvania. It was overwhelmingly a stream of simple folk, but along with it swept a "mixt Multitude" consisting among others of country gentlemen, soldiers, lawyers, land speculators, merchants, Indian traders, embryo entrepreneurs, men of culture, parsons, travelers, artisans, rogues, criminals, and ne'er-do-wells of every kind. The grand total of such opportunists was never large, but in a new country the extent of their influence was profound if incalculable. They supplied an initial overlay of culture to a nascent, bucolic society of peasant farmers. From their ranks emerged most of the interior's leaders, good and bad. Glibly vocal, usually literate, they counted ambition, ready wit, and a smattering of rudimentary education as more productive capital than their small grubstake of money. Coming as individuals unhampered by wives and children, these men were definitely on the make. If some lacked valuable eastern connections to smooth the path to affluence and power, experience guided them in their dealings with innocent husbandmen. One imagines them journeying along the Great Philadelphia Wagon Road brimming with projects and alertly scanning the Back Country for the best opportunity to exert their talents.

Just as the settlement of the interior of each colony took place at different times, so also within each province, and indeed within districts, social development varied with age

[18] Woodmason, Journal, 10; Erwin, *Rowan County,* 52.

as well as with nationality. Roughly speaking, as one went southward from Maryland and the Valley of Virginia (parts of which had been occupied for forty-five years and already gave an impression of permanence), to South Carolina and Georgia, whose oldest inhabitants had arrived scarcely seventeen years since, fewer signs of a rural order were evident. In any part of the Back Settlements too the easternmost areas were generally more populous. The degree of what we call civilization in any locality depended principally upon the number of people living there, but the maturing and enriching effect of time was also essential. We will shortly learn how true this was even of the Waterees, which, in 1766, the Reverend Mr. Woodmason found "most surprisingly thick settled beyond any Spot in England of its Extent." [19]

The first men to seek a living in the Back Country were the Indian traders, but their traffic was transient, since the influx of farming families drove out the game and the Indians. A few traders, like Robert Goudey of the Congarees and Ninety Six, remained to deal with the settlers; but most of them moved on to the west. Hunters experienced the same pressure, although some continued to hover near the settlements, supplying them with fresh meat. Poor "Lifelet Larby," a Blue Ridge Nimrod, after many an escape from the redman, fell a victim to the Teague in 1730 when he went "down among the Inhabitants to buy powder and bullets" and was murdered by three runaway Irish servants lest he inform against them. North Carolina hunters brought thousands of deerskins and many beaver pelts to the Moravians at Salem to exchange for store goods. [20]

Prevalence of large natural meadows and canebrakes, formerly fired by the Indians, encouraged cattle raising on

---

[19] Woodmason, Journal, 10.
[20] Meriwether, *Expansion of South Carolina,* 15, 113, 123; Schaper, "Sectionalism in South Carolina," 294–95; *Va. Gaz.,* June 10, 1737.

a large scale where deer, elk, and bison once had fed. Before settlement grew too dense and the "unbounded range" was fenced in, cattle were allowed to run free and forage for themselves until roundup time came and they were herded "in ganges under the auspices of cowpen keepers." Thus neglected, the stock was stunted and inferior to the cattle of Pennsylvania and New Jersey. "It is not an uncommon thing to see one man the master of from 300 to 1,200, and even to 2,000 cows, bulls, oxen, and young cattle," reported a traveler in North Carolina. Gradual transformation of the several areas into farm lands brought about the decline of great herds, but since the majority of farmers themselves kept cattle, the total number of heads steadily increased. Some were butchered for their hides, tallow, and meat, which was salted down and barreled. Distance from markets, however, made it necessary for drovers to push herds long distances on the hoof up the Great Road to Philadelphia, or later, to Cape Fear, Petersburg, and Charles Town. On October 20, 1774, a Moravian diarist at Salem noted: "During this month and last more than 1,000 head of cattle have been driven by here on the way to Pennsylvania." [21]

The attraction of inexpensive, fertile lands had started the southward movement of population. In Pennsylvania the average farm was 128 acres, and the price was high. In 1732 Maryland made a bid for the foreigners by offering 200 acres to heads of families and 100 to single men, free and unburdened by quitrents for three years. But in Western Maryland and the Valley of Virginia, most of the Scotch-Irish and Germans purchased from speculators,

[21] Logan, *History of Upper South Carolina*, I, 1–22, 122–49; Cresswell, *Journal*, 269; Carman (ed.), *American Husbandry*, 240–42; *Charleston Year Book, 1883*, p. 395, 410; Gregg, *Old Cheraws*, 68n., 76, 109–10; Schaper, "Sectionalism in South Carolina," 295; Boyd (ed.), *Some Eighteenth Century Tracts*, 444–45; Fries (ed.), *Records of the Moravians*, I, 39, 111; *ibid.*, II, 835.

who had made haste to acquire large grants which they sold off in small parcels at low but profitable prices. In the Valley the average settler took up from 300 to 400 acres, and by 1775 real estate had so risen in value that ordinary land in Frederick and Berkeley counties brought 30 shillings an acre and choice lots went for as high as 50 shillings.[22]

Such conditions speeded many of the poorer settlers further southward. In the Granville District, which covered the upper half of North Carolina, the regular grant was 640 acres; in the lower part of the province it was usually less, and in South Carolina, holdings ranged all the way from 50 to 500 acres, with most of them around 175. Thus it fell out that the medium or small farm rather than the great estate predominated here in contrast with the seaboard. Had contemporaries been able to fly over the region they would have been struck by the manner in which the green expanse of timberlands was being dotted with clearings of reddish-brown soil. Many places were more thickly populated than the plantation lands of the Tidewater or Low Country.[23]

The primary tasks facing the farmer and his family on their new tract were providing some sort of shelter and clearing the ground for planting. The log cabin has become the symbol of the pioneer, but romantic haze has shrouded the fact that this birthplace of great Americans was seldom as snug an abode as we imagine or as we reproduce today. Many of the Scotch-Irish contented themselves with "open Logg Cabbins," consisting of a roofed log structure closed on the sides and back but open on the front to the elements.

[22] Hart, *Valley of Virginia*, 11–13; *Va. Gaz.*, Jan. 20, 1737/8; Apr. 18, 1745; Sutherland, *Population Distribution*, 194–96; *Archives of Maryland*, XXVI, 25–26; Cresswell, *Journal*, 50.

[23] Coulter, *Granville District;* Court of Pleas and Quarter Sessions, Rowan County, N.C., (MS Minutes, Film, N.C. Dept. Archives & Hist., Raleigh), 157, 158; *Col. Recs. N.C.*, V, 149; Schaper, "Sectionalism in South Carolina," 277–78, 317–18.

In such primitive shelters during the bitter February cold of 1767 the Reverend Mr. Woodmason found many Presbyterian inhabitants of Lynch's Creek, "with hardly a Blanket to cover them." More widespread among other groups, and the second stage for these Ulsterites, was the house made of green logs, notched on the ends and rolled into place, after which the interstices were plugged with a mixture of clay and grass or moss; it was roofed with clapboards and bark. German settlers often hewed the logs square and fitted them securely and neatly together with greater care, thereby making a more weather-tight and permanent dwelling. They also tended to place the chimney in the center rather than at the end of the roof, with an eye to installing stoves at a later date. Logrollings were community enterprises, accompanied by much merriment. Twenty people, among them some Moravians, helped Hans Wagner raise his cabin on the Yadkin in 1754, though one of the industrious Brethren moralized that "things never go well at such a gathering for more time is spent in drinking brandy than in working." [24]

Clearing land was backbreaking toil for which few settlers were prepared either in technique or physique. "Their method upon entering their Lands," wrote Governor Arthur Dobbs, "is to cut down where they build their Loghouses, all the Trees fit for logs near their Houses, lest they fall upon them, as many are blown up by the rocks every season, and as many as will make rails to fence their corn field." Clearing space for the cabin and an acre or two for a small corn crop was all that could be undertaken the first year. This was done by girdling the trees between

[24] Woodmason, Journal, 3, 13, 31; Meriwether, *Expansion of South Carolina*, 165; Fries (ed.), *Records of the Moravians*, I, 96, 106; Schaper, "Sectionalism in South Carolina," 277–78; Gregg, *Old Cheraws*, 57–58; Joseph Doddridge, "Notes on the Settlement and Indian Wars of the Western Parts of Virginia and Pennsylvania," in Samuel Kercheval, *History of the Valley of Virginia* (4th ed., Strasburg, Va., 1925), 264–65.

two and three feet from the ground and allowing them to bleed to death. In time they would blow down, fall down, or be felled, and each year by this procedure more acres were gradually cleared for cultivation. The Scotch-Irish and the English did not bother to dig up the stumps, merely planting crops among them. The Germans, on the other hand, because they came with the intention of being permanent farmers and reckoned the resulting well-cleared field worth the toil expended on it, ordinarily did not girdle the trees; they cut them down, burned off the branches, and pulled out the stumps by the roots.[25]

The system of agriculture practiced in the Back Settlements was the same from Maryland to Georgia. Each farmer sowed his newly cleared lands, where the rich soil was two feet deep, with Indian corn for several years until the yield noticeably declined. At first he got about eighty bushels per acre, then commonly sixty or seventy. If it went below that he often tried black-eyed peas or beans, which produced thirty or forty bushels to an acre, for two or three years. Or, as markets opened, he increasingly put in wheat after several crops of maize had taken out some of the soil's richness. Experts denounced the "bad husbandry" of the back inhabitants, who mined the soil and were content with "an insufficient hand-hoeing or two," and neglectful of both weeding and manuring. All agreed, however, that the Germans were superior farmers, as their deeply plowed fields in the lower Shenandoah Valley, Wachovia, and along the Congarees with their variety of crops and ever-present vegetable gardens showed.[26]

[25] *Col. Recs. N.C.,* V, 362–63; Theodore E. Schmauk (ed.), Benjamin Rush, *An Account of the Manners of the German Inhabitants of Pennsylvania* (Lancaster, 1910), 58; Shryock, "British vs German Traditions in Colonial Agriculture," 47; Lyman H. Butterfield (ed.), *Letters of Benjamin Rush* (Princeton, 1951), I, 333, 400–402, 406.
[26] Carman (ed.), *American Husbandry,* 242–43, 248–59, 273–74, 316, 318; Schmauk (ed.), Rush, *Manners of the German Inhabitants,* 56–57, 65;

Regional additions to these basic products resulted in a mixed agriculture that not only guaranteed a certain self-sufficiency but still further differed from the system of the Chesapeake and Carolina countries. Maryland and the upper or Scotch-Irish part of the Valley of Virginia south of Augusta Court House (Staunton) produced large quantities of hemp and flax. As early as October, 1751, sixty wagonloads of flaxseed arrived in Baltimore from Frederick County in two days. Parliamentary and provincial bounties encouraged twenty-three Ulsterites of Botetourt County to register nearly fifty thousand pounds of hemp at the court in the summer of 1771. Settlers around Winchester and in southern Virginia, as well as transplanted Virginians in the Carolina Piedmont, grew considerable quantities of tobacco. The rich soil of the Old Cheraws produced more pounds per acre than the best lands of the Old Dominion. Potatoes were grown in both of the Carolinas, and in the Middle Country of the southern province, indigo became a lucrative staple. German farmers everywhere planted barley from which their brewing malt was made, and the Scotch-Irish cultivated rye and barley to use in their whisky, for bourbon, or corn, had not yet been developed.

Other well-known phases of farm life rounded out back-country husbandry. Apple and peach orchards provided the juices for the two most widely consumed beverages, cider and brandy; in addition orchard windfalls provided succulent forage for the ever-increasing quantities of hogs raised on every tract for meat and market. Cattle were kept for their hides, tallow, meat, and small milk supply, and sheep for the wool that went into linsey-woolsey homespun cloth.[27]

Shryock, "British vs German Traditions in Colonial Agriculture," 51–53; Woodmason, Journal, 19.
[27] Md. Gaz., Oct. 30, 1751; "Court Records, Botetourt County," in Lewis

Agriculture thus existed in every stage of development, from the newest clearing with its girdled trees on the South Carolina border to the advanced German farms around Winchester or the unique Moravian "Oeconomy" at Wachovia. By the opening of the seventies the small farm had become the means by which at least 95 per cent of the people of the Back Settlements made a living. Where once there had been nothing but forest, new farms kept appearing as the countryside was transformed from the rank wilderness into a rural society.

The back inhabitants lived by a mere subsistence farming up to about 1750 in Maryland and in the north part of the Great Valley, and somewhat later in the Carolinas. This necessitated the fabrication in the home by the members of the family of all items needed except salt and iron —wooden furniture and utensils, homespun cloth, soap, and candles. Just about the time the few precious manufactured articles brought along in the wagon from Pennsylvania gave out, however, some localities commenced producing a small surplus of corn, wheat, hemp, hogs, or cattle for sale, which made possible the first division of labor. Among the Scotch-Irish and Germans were many artisans who preferred working at their crafts to laboring in the fields, and they were ready to perform their mysteries in exchange for food and other necessities as a supplement to the work of wives and children on the farm. In this they were but following the time-honored European custom of rural artisans. Doubtless the most prominent and useful of the country specialists was the miller who ground corn and wheat for local custom. When two Moravian missionaries traveled through Virginia in 1749, they met, among

P. Summers, *Annals of Southwest Virginia, 1769–1800* (Abingdon, Va., 1929), 70–71; Nelson, Letter Book, 36; *Col. Recs. N.C.*, V, 316–18; Carman (ed.), *American Husbandry*, 184–85, 243, 316–17; Pub. Recs. S.C., XXXII, 393–400; Cresswell, *Journal*, 49, 195–96; *Va. Gaz.*, Jan. 20, 1737/8; Apr. 18, 1745.

others, "an awakened shoemaker" named Philips, Casper, a weaver, and Hackmeyer the blacksmith.[28]

Production of a surplus not only stimulated the rise of crafts through local exchanges of goods and services, but also necessitated a search for markets and for a supply of much-needed manufactured goods. In the earliest days commerce with distant Lancaster, Bethlehem, and Philadelphia was carried on by means of the Great Wagon Road, and it never entirely ceased. By 1775 a "Lower Road" ran across Virginia east of the Blue Ridge, giving a more direct route to Wachovia, although most vehicles continued to go by the Valley road. The Moravians regularly sent letters and orders for articles to Pennsylvania by their own wagons or entrusted them to friends traveling that way. As late as 1773 they procured Philadelphia leather fire buckets at a dollar each.[29]

Enterprising leaders of the Back Country and eastern merchants avid for the profits of the interior trade combined in seeking ways and means to divert the northbound traffic eastward or southward. At Piney River in Albemarle County in 1749, the Reverend Robert Rose devised what became the standard means of carrying "down . . . upland streams eight or nine hogsheads of tobacco" by lashing two canoes together and stowing the barrels athwart the gunwales. Virginia authorities were quick to sponsor roads from the Tidewater to the Valley—the 1755 edition of Fry and Jefferson's *Map* shows three routes us-

---

[28] Julia C. Spruill, *Women's Life and Work in the Southern Colonies* (Chapel Hill, 1938), 81; Colonial Office 5: 1331, pp. 237–38; Rev. Robert Rose, Diary (Typescript, Institute of Early Amer. Hist. & Culture), 127; *Va. Mag.*, VII (1900), 404; *ibid.*, XI (1903), 116, 231; *ibid.*, XXXI (1923), 249; Bridenbaugh, *Colonial Craftsman*, 22–24, 29–30; Ct. of Pleas & Quart. Sess., Mecklenburg County, N.C., Minutes, Oct. 4, 1774; Meriwether, *Expansion of South Carolina*, 62, 172–74.

[29] Osgood, *American Colonies in the Eighteenth Century*, IV, 109; Fries (ed.), *Records of the Moravians*, I, 143n.; *ibid.*, II, 765, 777.

ing Vestal's, Williams', and Ashby's gaps to connect Winchester with deepwater ports on the Potomac and Rappahannock. Many acts of the Assembly also permitted and encouraged the opening of roads and bridges or the erection of ferries to improve communication and travel between the valley of the James and the new transmontane country in the southwest. Similarly the Virginians went out after the trade of the North Carolina Piedmont by tapping it at Bolling's Point, where the "Lower Road" crossed the James and shipping produce down river to the rising towns of Richmond and Manchester.[30]

An outlet to the seacoast became a vital problem to the people of Rowan, Anson, and Mecklenburg counties in North Carolina, who found themselves about three hundred miles equidistant from Bolling's Point and Charles Town, and nearly as far from Wilmington on the Cape Fear River. The businesslike Moravians tried every route as roads were cut from Bethabara eastward through Guilford to Edenton, to Springhill and Cross Creek (Fayetteville) on the Cape Fear, and south along the Waxhaw, or by way of Charlotte to Pine Tree Hill (Camden) on the Wateree, where the road from Charles Town terminated. As population mounted, an important development of side roads increased to link new settlements with the main highways. Bethabara, and later Salem, the Moravians found, became "more and more a house of passage" as countless poor but passable ways were cut through the woods. Brother Gottfried Reuter, as roadmaster of Dobbs Parish in 1774, had signs posted at all nearby crossroads giving

[30] *Va. Gaz.* (Rind), May 4, 1763; July 21, 1768; William W. Hening (ed.), *The Statutes at Large . . . of Virginia* (Philadelphia, 1813–23), VIII, 16–17, 152, 546–47, 548; *ibid.,* IX, 247–48; Albion and Dodson (eds.), *Fithian Journal, 1775–1776,* 162–63; Cresswell, *Journal,* 267; Rose, Diary, 103, 104; Maury, *Memoirs of a Huguenot Family,* 388–89; Fries (ed.), *Records of the Moravians,* I, 44, 209, 234; *Col. Recs. N.C.,* VI, 969; "Botetourt Recs.," 236.

direction and the distance to the nearest settlements "to the great satisfaction of travelers."[31]

Eventually Low Country merchants like Henry Laurens and the Kershaws succeeded in inaugurating a wagon trade from North Carolina to Charles Town. There higher prices for produce and a greater variety of inexpensive European goods could be had than at Cross Creek or Wilmington, which greatly appealed to back country farmers and artisans. When the colonial postmaster general ordered a fortnightly post between Wilmington and Cross Creek in 1774, the interior may be said to have achieved reasonably satisfactory communications with the Atlantic seaboard.[32]

Henry Mouzon's *Map* of 1775 clearly indicates that Upper South Carolina was amply provided with highways connecting it with its seaport market. The roads from Augusta, Orangeburg, and the Congarees had formerly been pack-horse trails to the Indian country and were later widened to thirty-five feet to accommodate wagons. Freights were very high, as the Reverend Mr. Woodmason learned in 1766 when he had to pay seven guineas to the wagoner for carrying his books and other effects from Charles Town to Pine Tree Hill. It cost the Chesneys one penny per pound to ship their goods to Winnsboro in 1772, but Alexander got it back when he later went into the freight business for himself. The amazing production of grains and meats in the Back Parts rendered the province

[31] Fries (ed.), *Records of the Moravians,* I, 27, 44, 105, 209, 214, 229, 234, 237, 241, 267, 284, 285, 290, 301, 339, 356, 380; *ibid.,* II, 762, 763, 810–11, 835; *Col. Recs. N.C.,* VI, 968; Christopher C. Crittenden, *The Trade of North Carolina* (Chapel Hill, 1936), 23, 30–32, 75, 76, 88; Mecklenburg Co., Minutes, 1774–85, *passim;* Walter Clarke (ed.), *State Records of North Carolina* (Goldsboro, N.C., 1904), XXIII, 753, 851, 908, 918.

[32] Crittenden, *Trade of North Carolina,* 91, 92; Fries (ed.), *Records of the Moravians,* I, 235, 277, 358; *ibid.,* II, 868; Wilmington (N.C.) *Cape Fear Mercury,* May 11, 1774.

self-sufficient, and some commodities yielded a surplus for export by 1760, whereas in former times South Carolina had been a good customer of Pennsylvania and New York. According to Governor William Bull, "as many as three thousand wagons per year come in from the Back Country" and several Charles Town merchants built large yards behind their stores to care for them, while others opened branch offices beyond the city's gates. On December 5, 1771, a citizen counted 131 wagons on their way in to town, the previous high being 30.[33]

Although these crude thoroughfares were not all that one would have desired, abundant evidence demonstrates that a network of highways spread over the Back Country within a relatively short time after settlement. The popular cry was for more and better communication, not a wail over no roads at all, as we have often been led to think. The authorities, moreover, seem to have responded promptly and, on the whole, generously to demands for bridges and ferries.

A highly significant, though usually little-noticed phenomenon of growth in the Back Parts was the rise of more than twenty little inland villages and towns between 1738 and 1776. Fifteen of them—Frederick, Hagerstown, Shepherdstown, Martinsburg, Winchester, Stephensburg, Strasburg, Woodstock, Staunton, Fincastle, Salem (Bethabara), Salisbury, Charlotte, Camden, and Augusta—were located along the seven-hundred-mile route of the Great Philadelphia Wagon Road. Others, such as Bath, Hills-

[33] Council Journal, S.C. (MS, Columbia), XV, 32; Weston (ed.), *Documents connected with South Carolina,* 178; *Boston Chronicle,* Dec. 12, 1768; Pub. Recs. S.C., XXIII, 357; *ibid.,* XXXII, 282, 295–96; *S.C. Gaz.,* Dec. 5, 1771; Smyth, *Tour,* I, 205; Mereness (ed.), *Travels,* 399; Mouzon, *Map of North and South Carolina;* Woodmason, Journal, 12; Jones (ed.), "Journal of Alexander Chesney," 3, 8; McCrady, *South Carolina under Royal Government,* 389.

boro, Springhill, Cross Creek, Cheraw Hill, and Ninety
Six Court House, appeared at the head of navigation or
on important east-west roads.

These towns grew up in answer to certain deeply felt
needs of the inhabitants, and, properly located, have continued to thrive for the most part because they meet the
economic demands of today. They started at a crossroad,
on the banks of a river at a ferry, near a gristmill, or at a
county courthouse, and always in the midst of a well-
populated district. Obviously, they served as stages along
the Great Road, supplying entertainment and shelter for
travelers at their taverns. Soon too they became neighborhood centers, attracting artisans and serving as market
towns as well as providing for the needs of government.

Frederick Town on the Monocacy was laid out in 1745
and almost entirely settled by Palatines of the Lutheran
and Reformed faiths. It flourished from the beginning as
a focus for the surrounding farmers, who gave employ-
ment to many artisans and enabled it to pursue a large grain
trade with Baltimore. Its people also profited from the
southward flow of immigrants through Frederick. Well
known for the manufacture of stockings and guns, the two
thousand inhabitants dwelt in well-built houses of brick or
field stone. Lieutenant Thomas Anburey thought the town
made "a very noble appearance" and praised the gentility
of some of the principal burghers.[34]

Another important community inhabited by Germans
was Winchester on Opequon Creek, the gateway to the
Valley of Virginia, and the largest inland town south of
Lancaster. Established in 1745, it was regularly laid out
in squares on which an Anglican and a "dutch" church, be-

[34] Eddis, *Letters*, 101–102; *Va. Gaz.* (Rind), Nov. 11, 1773; Cresswell,
Journal, 133; Anburey, *Travels*, II, 181–82. For Hagerstown, see Eddis,
Letters, 133–34; Albion and Dodson (eds.), *Fithian Journal, 1775–1776*,
9–10; *Md. Gaz.*, May 20, 1773.

sides many houses of brick and stone, were erected, and nearby rose a Quaker meeting. It had acquired a market house, a gaol, several merchants' stores, and many crafts-men's shops, as well as taverns like Philip Bush's Golden Buck, by 1770. At this seat of Frederick County, lawyers had much local legal business, and one could even be inoculated against the smallpox by one of the village medicos at this time. Southbound settlers brought in much trade, but Winchester's great prosperity derived from the fact that it was the starting place of a considerable traffic in wheat, tobacco, and iron carried by many wagoners, among whom was Daniel Morgan, through the Blue Ridge gaps to Alexandria, Falmouth, and Fredericksburg.[35]

The seat of Rowan County, Salisbury, was located near the Yadkin in central North Carolina in 1753. Three years later it contained only seven or eight houses, the gaol, and the courthouse. Its growth continued to be slow, but as the number of taxables in Rowan increased from 2,800 in 1765 to 3,957 in 1770, Salisbury gained in importance because people found it "a healthy, pleasant Situation, well watered and convenient for Inland Trade." Already a borough town with a seat in the Assembly, its nascent urban development was signalized by special legislation in 1770. "An Act for regulating the Town of Salisbury" provided for eleven town commissioners, appointed for life, to supervise streets, building laws, markets, and fire protection, and to enforce the requirement that lot owners on Corbin and Innes streets clear and fence their lots within a year. Within three years—or four if they lived on the parallel lanes—they had to erect on each lot a building

---

[35] *Va. Gaz.*, Apr. 24, Oct. 10, 1752; *Va. Gaz.* (Rind), Apr. 28, 1768; Mar. 22, July 26, 1770; Sept. 26, 1771; *Va. Gaz.* (Purdie & Dixon), July 2, 1772; Cresswell, *Journal,* 49; Anburey, *Travels,* II, 272–73; Miles Malone, "Falmouth and the Shenandoah Trade Before the Revolution," *Amer. Hist. Rev.,* XL (1935), 693–703.

twenty-five by sixteen feet "in the Clear, of Brick, Stone, or Frame, or Hewed Logs," having a brick or stone chimney. The inhabitants were overwhelmingly Scotch-Irish and mostly artisans, who filled the needs of the surrounding countryside by operating tanneries, cooperages, smithies, and mills, or by fabricating hats, leather breeches, shoes, saddles, and guns. The fact that three silversmiths could earn a decent living by 1774 testifies to the incipient wealth of Salisbury and Rowan County. Eight or more taverns and ordinaries catered to travelers and those attending court sittings by selling whisky at six shillings a gallon and whisky punch at one shilling, and by daringly offering "Lodging with clean Sheets." [36]

About 1750 a colony of Irish Quakers, headed by Samuel Wyly and Robert Milhouse, erected saw- and gristmills at Pine Tree Hill in South Carolina where the Catawba becomes the Wateree. Eight years later Ancrum, Lance, and Loocock of Charles Town sent Joseph Kershaw, a rising young Yorkshireman, up to the Waterees to establish a branch of their mercantile house. He bought out Wyly's Mills, built a store and additional mills, laid off lots, and made numerous other improvements at Pine Tree Hill. Specializing in upcountry produce, Joseph Kershaw's company, which included as partners his brother Eli and John Chestnut, proved an immediate success and soon branched out with stores at Cheraw Hill on the Pedee and at Granby, just below the forks of the Congaree. Under the aegis of Kershaw, who encouraged wheat culture throughout the region, Pine Tree Hill was renamed Camden in 1768 and became a principal entrepôt for the North and South Carolina back parts, and a starting and outfitting

[36] *Col. Recs. N.C.*, V, 355; Rowan Co., Minutes, I, 48, 61, 110, 259, 283, 331, 495, 628, 661; *ibid.*, II, 253, 284, 310, 390; *ibid.*, III, 55; George B. Cutten, *Silversmiths of North Carolina* (Raleigh, 1948); Clarke (ed.), *State Recs. N.C.*, XXIII, 810–13; Erwin, *Rowan County*, 20–23.

point for settlers "going to the Mississippi to take up land." Many of the Scotch-Irish who came to the Waterees resided in Camden, where they soon greatly outnumbered all other residents, built a Presbyterian meetinghouse, and set the tone for the neighboring area. The situation was very healthy, artisans were active, trade was brisk, and soon Camden was on its way to "becoming the most considerable inland town in this part of America." [37]

Unique among the western settlements was the "Oeconomy" established by the United Brethren in 1753 at the Wachovia tract in Rowan County, North Carolina. Carefully planned in advance at the church center in Bethlehem, this undertaking embraced all human activities—religious, economic, and industrial—and was, without doubt, the best integrated and most successful community in the Southern colonies. The first Moravians founded a little farming village, called Bethabara, where they lived together in the European manner and went out daily to the fields. Shortly they opened a tavern and a store and introduced certain necessary handicrafts that they found lacking in other Piedmont localities. So well did the Moravians serve the country that in 1763 they proudly claimed that "Bethabara has been so far the pantry for all the settlers in this neighborhood." But this village and adjacent Bethania were intended to be farming villages exclusively, and in 1766 work began on Salem, a town "not designed for farmers but for those with trades." [38]

Every interior town I have mentioned was laid out with some degree of regularity prior to settlement and in this respect contrasted markedly with the more or less casual

[37] Ramsay, *South Carolina*, II, 216, 596–97; Fries (ed.), *Records of the Moravians*, I, 270, 277, 307, 333; *S.C. Gaz.*, July 12, 1760; Sept. 17, Nov. 5, 1763; Dec. 29, 1766; *Va. Gaz.* (Pinkney), Oct. 6, 1774.
[38] Fries (ed.), *Records of the Moravians*, I, 59, 73, 124, 138, 149, 251, 267; Bridenbaugh, *Colonial Craftsman*, 26–27, 185.

arrangement of most coastal communities. But at Salem the work of Frederick William Marschall and Gottfried Reuter, a skilled draftsman, represents genuine town planning based upon the twin concepts of meeting the needs of a "Congregation Town" and the contemporary taste for order and beauty. Brother Marschall drew heavily for inspiration upon such German towns as Niesky and Gnadenberg, studiously avoiding the straggling appearance of familiar unplanned Pennsylvania towns. The result was and still is both satisfactory and satisfying.[39]

Salem was in full operation by 1772. There workers in iron, wood, and leather did not restrict themselves to the cruder and simpler branches of their mysteries, for one could find gunsmiths, sickle- and sieve-makers, wood turners, millwrights, and pipe organ-makers, as well as mere blacksmiths and carpenters. Gottfried Aust's pottery not only turned out common articles but produced a good quality of queen's ware. A distillery, merchant mill, brewery, brickyard, and tannery processed materials more for outside custom than for the Moravians. Their store and tavern were the busiest places in Salem, and the prudent Palatines finally decided to cut out credit at both when six hundred persons owed over £1,800, much of which consisted of bad debts. In 1773 "for the convenience of strangers coming to town," signs were placed over the doors to all artisans' shops. Although the population of Salem never exceeded three hundred, by its example and achievement in successful community living and production it stood preeminent in the Back Country. Only the language barrier prevented the United Brethren from making an even greater contribution toward the creation of an orderly, prosperous, and cultured society.[40]

[39] Fries (ed.), *Records of the Moravians*, I, 313–15, 323–24, 325, 327, 374, 404.

[40] *Ibid.*, I, 335, 387, 413, 435; *ibid.*, II, 657, 697–98, 700, 705, 724, 767, 771, 827, 857, 858, 867, 895, 899.

Many of the new clearings were so remote from the towns that for necessities settlers had to rely upon country stores that sprang up here and there. Robert Lanier kept one near Shallow Ford on the Yadkin, and John Moore on the Catawba sold pottery from Bethabara to folk whose only utensils were of wood. Probably the largest country store above the fall line in South Carolina was that of Robert Goudey who supplied Cherokee traders as early as 1747 at the Congarees and later maintained a branch at Ninety Six. When he died about 1775, more than four hundred persons in the Saluda Valley owed him money. At these and similar emporiums, farmers paid in corn, wheat, barley, pork, or beef for salt, a little iron, rum or whisky, and the few notions they did not procure from the many peddlers who penetrated to the most remote of the Back Settlements.[41]

Notwithstanding the newness of the upcountry, certain industrial enterprises operated successfully. Wherever sufficient water power was found in grain-growing districts, gristmills appeared, and as soon as a surplus of corn or wheat was available, merchant mills flourished. Iron ore, found near limestone deposits, particularly in Maryland and the north part of the Shenandoah Valley, as well as the presence of ample firewood for charcoal, attracted ironmasters from Pennsylvania and other eastern provinces. Hermon Husband of later Regulator fame managed the Fountain Copper Works of Frederick Town, Maryland, in 1760. The Carolinas had at least four iron furnaces and one silver mine operating in 1775.[42]

[41] *Va. Gaz.*, Apr. 17, 1746; Apr. 24, 1752; *Va. Gaz.* (Purdie & Dixon), Mar. 21, Sept. 5, 1771; *Va. Gaz.* (Dixon), Nov. 24, 1775; Fries (ed.), *Records of the Moravians*, I, 162, 251, 252; ibid., II, 792; *Col. Recs. N.C.*, XXIII, 371; Meriwether, *Expansion of South Carolina*, 63, 132, 169, 170, 174, 176.

[42] Rose, Diary, 183; Rowan Co., Minutes, I, passim.; ibid., II, 78; Fries (ed.), *Records of the Moravians*, I, 46, 190; *Md. Gaz.*, Dec. 11, 1760; Aug. 9, 1766; June 11, 1767, suppl.; *Va. Gaz.* (Rind), Jan. 11, Oct. 4, 1770;

In the days when a pioneer's food supply and often his life depended upon his firearms, lead was an indispensable commodity, hard to obtain from the seaboard because of its scarcity and weight. In 1756 Colonel John Chiswell discovered lead deposits on the upper reaches of the New River in the Valley, not far from the present Wytheville. With his son-in-law Speaker John Robinson and Colonel William Byrd III, he purchased the property and commenced mining. Nearly two years later, Byrd constructed Fort Chiswell nearby to protect the diggings and the recently arrived settlers from Indian attack. From the start, men of the western country patronized the undertaking by traveling long distances for its product. Moravian George Loesch made regular trips to New River to buy three hundred pounds of lead at a time. As if in return for the custom, Colonel Chiswell purchased bread and meal for his workers and the garrison at the fort from the Bethabara mill. In November, 1763, wagons departed from Wachovia on the eighty-two-mile journey by way of Fancy Gap with two thousand pounds of corn meal, leaving an even larger portion of the order for the next trip. When the fight for freedom broke out, Chiswell's mines proved of incalculable value to the new Commonwealth of Virginia.[43]

Fulling mills were needed to process the homespun cloth woven in nearly every cabin of the Back Parts. The Scotch-Irish were famous weavers. By the time Tidewater and

Oct. 22, 1772; *Va. Gaz.* (Purdie & Dixon), Jan. 3, Sept. 26, Oct. 17, 1771; Feb. 4, July 8, 1773; June 16, 1774; Kathleen Bruce, *Virginia Iron Manufacture in the Slave Era* (New York, 1931), 21–22; *Col. Recs. N.C.,* VIII, 496; Jones (ed.), "Journal of Alexander Chesney," 10; Bridenbaugh, *Colonial Craftsman,* 25–26.

[43] Thomas P. Abernethy, *Western Lands and the American Revolution* (New York, 1937), 79–80; Fries (ed.), *Records of the Moravians,* I, 249, 276, 288, 312; *Va. Gaz.* (Purdie & Dixon), Aug. 13, 1767; Dec. 21, 1769; Apr. 5, 1770.

Low Country leaders started opposing British restrictions
with nonimportation measures, the interior was clothing
itself with its own fabrics, and the prospects of eventually
finding an outlet for a surplus made great appeal. In the
southern Virginia Piedmont, Lieutenant Anburey was astonished in 1777 to discover that "inhabitants of the lower
sort" cultivated cotton, which they "cleaned by means of
a machine called a gen," carded, spun, and wove it into
cloth "little inferior to that made at Manchester" and
worn by nearly all the people in the summer months. "Spinning wheel and flax-breaks at every house," exclaimed
Nicholas Cresswell during a visit to Frederick and Berkeley counties in the Valley. "They will make more coarse
linen in these two Counties than will be used in their families. Some few people make very fine linen, thirteen or fourteen hundred warp, but don't bleach it very well." In 1770
the "Maryland Factory in Frederick Town" offered an
all-around service, including dressing of flax and hemp,
weaving of all sorts, and constructing of looms. Industrial
development, like everything else in the Back Parts, was
uneven, varying from the crudest to the most advanced
forms and demonstrating that the remarkable efflorescence
of household industries and skilled crafts that we customarily think of as coming only with the peace of 1783 had
already begun in 1775.[44]

In the peopling of the Back Country, colonial governments played a dual role: their action in making land grants
and, in certain cases, their extension of provincial authority
to the interior encouraged both rapid settlement and eco-

[44] *Va. Gaz.* (Rind), June 15, 1769; *Va. Gaz.* (Purdie), May 10, 1776; *Va.
Mag.*, XXXI (1923), 249; *Col. Recs. N.C.*, VII, 249; *ibid.*, VIII, 154; Meck-
lenburg Co., Minutes, Oct. 4, 1774; Meriwether, *Expansion of South Caro-
lina*, 83, 173; Anburey, *Travels*, II, 423–25; *Boston Chronicle*, Dec. 12, 1768;
Bridenbaugh, *Colonial Craftsman*, 23–24; Cresswell, *Journal*, 192; *Md.
Gaz.*, Sept. 9, 1746; Sept. 20, 1770.

nomic exploitation; conversely, the burgeoning west created situations often calling for control by local government long before the eastern gentry saw fit to provide it. If geographic, demographic, and economic conditions were much the same throughout the interior, giving strong support to the social concept of a uniform Greater Pennsylvania, the expansion policies of the five Southern colonies acted variously either as unifying forces or as political divisors.

Virginia and Maryland authorities were quick to set up county and parish institutions in freshly opened areas. The westward movement of the Chesapeake Society began in the late seventeenth century as venturesome people passed beyond the fall line onto the Piedmont plateau, year by year clearing lands for tobacco culture, merging the new with the old, and organizing local governments authorized by the assemblies. Between 1732 and the outbreak of the Revolution, Virginia established twenty-one new counties east of the Blue Ridge, of which fifteen, together with five new Valley counties, comprised the Old Dominion's portion of the Back Country. Almost as soon as a region acquired enough inhabitants to warrant it, local self-government through parish and county was arranged. In 1743 and 1745 the Valley was divided into the counties of Frederick and Augusta, and in 1770 and 1772 further cut up to form Botetourt and Berkeley, Dunmore and Fincastle. Similarly, the Maryland Assembly erected the western portions of the Calverts' domains into the county of Frederick in 1748. Officials of both provinces continued to show concern for the new settlements by passing numerous acts to create towns.[45]

These prompt grants of home rule to back regions at-

[45] Robinson, "Virginia Counties," 128–40; Owen, "Virginia Vestry," 136–38, 142; Hening (ed.), *Statutes*, V, 179–80; Sutherland, *Population Distribution*, 194.

test the existence of marked political wisdom in the Chesapeake Society. The fact that the Back Parts were adjacent
to older districts; that a substantial proportion of the
settlers came from the east with its ideals and attitudes;
that above all political leaders of both colonies were not
only deeply interested in western lands but also fully cog-
nizant of the needs of the interior and saw to it that their
fellows in the Assembly were kept informed about them;
and that many themselves had moved or intended to move
there—all made the extension of Tidewater institutions
both prompt and easy. It is true, of course, that the newer
counties were very large and that the seaboard retained a
preponderance of members in the lower houses; yet it is
also true that in free elections the western voters frequently chose Tidewater aristocrats like George Washington and George Johnston to represent them and that a
Valley aristocrat like George William Fairfax sat on the
Council of State. I have searched fruitlessly for evidence
that before 1776 political sectionalism—western resentment of eastern overrepresentation and rule—was an issue,
either open or covert, in Maryland or Virginia. Nor were
there any undercurrents of economic or social unrest. The
rise of Patrick Henry so frequently ascribed to a cham-
pioning of the cause of the interior has no foundation
in fact; rather was it the signal for a redistribution of
power among the Virginia gentry. Actually, Maryland
and Virginia succeeded to a remarkable degree in solv-
ing their own little imperial problems by ensuring their
western settlements law and order, guaranteeing security
of life and land titles, and providing representation at
Williamsburg and Annapolis.[46]

Neither of the provincial governments of the Carolinas
could point to a like achievement. A belt of unoccupied

[46] Barker, *Maryland*, 24; Bridenbaugh, *Seat of Empire*, 48–71.

country long separated the North Carolina Piedmont from the Albemarle, Pamlico, and Cape Fear regions, permitting the two to grow independently for many years. Furthermore, North Carolina had no well-knit society of its own whose ideals and institutions could be carried westward. Nor was this condition ameliorated, as in Virginia, by a substantial westward movement of native colonials. Despite such unpropitious circumstances, the creation of Bladen County in 1731 marked the beginning of a real effort by the eastern authorities to supply effective local government to the interior as the need for it became apparent. During the administration of Gabriel Johnston, seven counties were set up, including the important ones of Granville, Anson, Orange, Rowan, and Mecklenburg, between 1741 and 1752; while during William Tryon's term of five years, 1765–1770, four more were created. At the close of the era North Carolina had sixteen county governments in operation between the fall line and the Great Smokies. At the same time parish vestries came into being with each county, since the Church of England was established by law.[47]

As we leaf through the pages of the court records of such counties as Rowan and Mecklenburg or read the fascinating Moravian diaries, it is evident that very early in the course of settlement justices of the quorum earnestly sought to give the new areas something more than a veneer of local government. They acted favorably on petitions for the opening of new roads; indeed, not infrequently they assumed the initiative in such matters. Action taken on all manner of "internal improvements"—roads, bridges, ferries, appointment of supervisory committees, payment of wolf and wildcat bounties, and designation of public

[47] Williamson, *History of North Carolina*, II, 246; Fries (ed.), *Records of the Moravians*, I, 37, 54, 154, 433.

DATE DUE

JUL 18 '88			
2-18-93			
MAY 1 7 1996			

mills—compares favorably with similar work of contemporary boards of selectmen in the interior towns of New England. Rowan justices also handled a large volume of business connected with registering wills, probating estates, and in particular, recording deeds and determining land titles. Sitting as an orphan's court, one of their primary duties was to bind out orphan and bastard boys and girls to trades to relieve the community of charge for them; and their concern for the welfare and decent treatment of apprentices, indentured servants, and slaves is often reflected by the records. Licensing of taverns, setting of liquor prices and ferry rates, registering of brands and earmarks, care of the poor, and the appointment and supervision of minor officials—these are some more of the manifold responsibilities which the transplanted system of English local government required gentlemen justices to discharge without remuneration and which in these counties they discharged on the whole very well.[48]

In spite of this prompt and very real contribution of county and parish institutions to the stabilizing of civil society in the interior, so bitter became the unrelieved resentment of the Scotch-Irish and others against these county officials in the sixties that it exploded between 1766 and 1770 into the mob violence, open rebellion, and bloodshed popularly known as the Regulation. It can scarcely be termed a democratic revolution in the sense that a change of institutions was sought. It is "not our Form or Mode of Government," a Granville petition insisted, "nor yet the Body of our Laws that we are quarreling with, but with the Malpractices of the Officers of our County Courts, and Abuses that we suffer by those that are impowered to manage our publick Affairs." There can be no doubt that

[48] Rowan Co., Minutes, 1752–76, especially I, 42, 46, 61, 110, 331, 350, 510, 561, 667; *ibid.*, II, 79, 93; Mecklenburg Co., Minutes, Oct. 4, 1774; Jan., 1775.

the primary incitements to insurrection were the insolence and venality of certain public officials—judges, sheriffs, "mercenary tricking Attornies, Clerks, and other little Officers," who were almost exclusively native-born adventurers of English descent, and who had sniffed from afar opportunities for wealth and power in a new country.[49]

The objectives of the Regulators were never very clear. They charged that taxes bore unfairly on Piedmont counties, and that inhabitants struggling to get a foothold in the land were least able to bear the incidence. Although responsible groups like the plain-spoken Moravians had no complaints against the officials whom the Regulators charged with rapaciousness, the payment of quitrents, mismanagement of the currency, hatred of the Established Church with its tithes, and anger at the abuse of land laws that allowed those with "influence" to engross the choicest parcels were surely legitimate grievances. Their rage focused on the county sheriffs, whose office and powers lent themselves to embezzlement of funds, unreasonable distraining of the property of tax delinquents and debtors, and collusion in peculation with other officials of the courthouse rings quite as much as to disinterested service for the common weal.

My sympathies instinctively go out to these simple and greatly abused farmers, but sentimentality has no place in historical judgments. Nowhere in the thirteen colonies was so complete a measure of individual liberty enjoyed by the common people as in Piedmont North Carolina, and when an Anson County petition to the Assembly in 1768 recited that "we have too long yielded ourselves slaves to remorseless oppression," we ought, perhaps, to attribute such hy-

[49] Julian P. Boyd, "The Sheriff in Colonial North Carolina," *N.C. Hist. Review*, V (1928), 150–80; *Col. Recs. N.C.*, IX, 314, 329–30; Hermon Husband, "An Impartial Relation," in Boyd (ed.), *Some Eighteenth Century Tracts*, 254–55.

perbole to Scotch-Irish individualism and question the extent to which it was actually true. Their expressed grievances were good reasons for direct action; that left unexpressed was what I conceive to have been the real or basic reason: a general reluctance to accept any bridling of their hitherto unrestricted freedom in the interest of what seems reasonable to any proponent of a well-ordered society. To exchange the state of nature for the civil compact pleased them not, especially when the officials were not of their own nation and faith, and an actual payment of taxes was involved.[50]

This was a situation charged with emotion, an emotion that has ever since obscured certain relevant matters. Governor Tryon had made an unpopular but courageous and honest attempt to place the colony's disordered finances on a sound basis, but it was his misfortune that most of the sheriffs were rascals and that some judges were corrupt, as the Regulators claimed. Dishonest and incompetent sheriffs, however, were common to the entire province; they were not exclusively a scourge to the Back Country but rather a concomitant of a bad system. Much has been said about taxation, but very little about paying taxes. As of October, 1768, only 1,017 of 3,059 Rowan taxables had paid their 1766 levies; a year later 1,833 "refractory Regulators" still remained in arrears.[51]

The leaders of the Regulators were, for the most part, colonials of English background, like Hermon Husband and Rednap Howell; but the rank and file were chiefly Scotch-Irish with a few Germans. Highly emotional harangues from an eloquent and sincere, though equally un-

[50] John S. Bassett, "The Regulators of North Carolina," in Amer. Hist. Assn., *Annual Report* (1894), 142–94; Boyd (ed.), *Some Eighteenth Century Tracts,* 201–46, 253–74. *Cf.* Butterfield (ed.), *Letters of Benjamin Rush,* I, 401–402.

[51] Boyd, "Sheriff in Colonial North Carolina," 167–68; Rowan Co., Minutes, I, 661; *ibid.,* II, 60, 147, 217.

stable, man like Husband roused his followers to a disas-
trous violence which the fiery Quaker had never contem-
plated. Fear and coercion forced many reluctant farmers
into Regulation ranks, and not a few men used the movement as a cloak for lawlessness and unscrupulous designs
on other people's property, leading the Moravians to in-
quire pertinently whether the remedy did not exceed the
abuse.

In its stage of dignified protest through petitions, the
Regulation had won the sympathy and support of most
responsible people in the interior counties, but after the
manhandling of Colonel Edmund Fanning and the damage
done to property at Salisbury they fell away. Six leading Presbyterian ministers publicly denounced mob action, as did at least one German; and the Reverend
Alexander Meiklejohn, who had earlier sought to medi-
ate between the Regulators and the government, now
turned against them and preached an influential sermon to Tryon's troops from Rom. 13:1–2. Governor
Tryon's policy of maintaining law and order in the back
country at almost any cost is more comprehensible when
one reads his correspondence and realizes that he knew
he had a large following in the rebellious districts, not the
least of which came from the Presbyterian clergy.[52]

The inexperience of the leaders was fatal, as the complete collapse of the cause after the Alamance defeat
proved. As propagandists, however, they excelled. By
pamphlet, ballad, and stump speech they made Colonel
Fanning the symbol of misgovernment and extortion, although his crime seems to have been only that he was
Tryon's friend. Hermon Husband shrewdly published *A
Fan for Fanning* at Boston in 1771 where Governor

[52] Boyd (ed.), *Some Eighteenth Century Tracts,* 395, 399–412; Fries,
(ed.), *Records of the Moravians,* 367–96, 446–70; *Col. Recs. N.C.,* VII, 111;
ibid., VIII, 218.

Thomas Hutchinson had become anathema to patriots, thereby successfully gaining Yankee sympathy and giving substance to the rising intercolonial suspicion that the only good royal governor was a dead one. Rednap Howell's broadside, *When Fanning first to Orange Came,* has probably blackened a name forever. The Regulators may have lost the war, but they certainly won the history.[53]

South Carolina also had its Regulators, although they were not so celebrated in song and story; and, be it observed, their course was not taken in opposition to government, as in the northern colony, but because they had no government at all. As the Scotch-Irish, followed by many Virginians and some Palatines, moved into upcountry South Carolina after 1750, no effort was made at Charles Town to provide them with any local government. The vacuum thus created immediately sucked in most of the lawless and disorderly characters of the entire South. That law-abiding people of the Cheraws, Waterees, and Congarees suffered acutely from predatory bands of ruffians has always been known, but the exact nature and extent of their trials is revealed in dramatic fashion in the papers of the Reverend Charles Woodmason, formerly a Charles Town merchant and official, who went to the Waterees in 1766 as the only Anglican clergyman in the western parts of the colony.[54] His report to the Bishop of London is so vivid that I cannot improve on it: [55]

[53] Arthur P. Hudson, "Songs of the North Carolina Regulators," *W. & M. Quart.,* 3d ser., IV (1947), 477.

[54] Woodmason, Journal, 6, 7, 20; Schaper, "Sectionalism in South Carolina," 334-35; Gregg, *Old Cheraws,* 130-31.

[55] Charles Woodmason, to Bishop of London, 1771, Fulham Palace MSS, S.C., No. 55; *S.C. Gaz.,* July 27, 1767; Oct. 4, 1773; Meriwether, *Expansion of South Carolina,* 95; *Va. Gaz.* (Purdie & Dixon), Oct. 24, 1766. For crime in the back parts of Virginia, see *Va. Gaz.,* Oct. 21, Nov. 25, 1737; Oct. 11, 1751; *Va. Gaz.* (Rind), Mar. 4, Apr. 22, 1773; Hart, *Valley of Virginia,* 11-12; for North Carolina, see Fries (ed.), *Records of the Moravians,* I, 40, 41, 48, 151, 157, 164, 243, 247, 249, 303, 329, 333, 336, 360, 377, 379, 432, 460; *ibid.,* II, 734, 773, 798, 815, 818, 824.

"Here Vile and Impudent fellows, would come to a Planters House, and Tye him, Lye with his Wife before his Face, Ravish Virgins, before Eyes of their Parents, a dozen fellows in succession. . . . They carried off about twenty of the finest Girls in the Country into the Woods with them, and kept them for many Months, as their Concubines in common . . . , and [they] never could be brought back to a Life of Virtue when regain'd by their Friends. They would put Irons in the Fire and burn the Flesh of Persons to make them confess where they conceal'd their Money. All the Merchant Stores were broke up. No Peddlars with Goods could travel. No Woman venture abroad. And Numbers abandon'd their Habitations. . . . They penetrated, at length, to the Lower Settlements and stole many Negroes. Even from one of the Council. And had they not so done, it was a Doubt whether they would not have reign'd much Longer, but when their own House was on Fire, They then thot on their Neigh[bors]. Yet the Good natur'd Country People, pursu'd these fellows over the mountains, hoping that this Instance of Regard would operate in their favor. But it signified very little.

"The Villains had their Confederates in ev'ry Colony. What Negroes, Horses, and Goods was stollen Southwardly, was carried Northerly, and the Now'd Southward. The Southward shipp'd off at New York and Rhode Island for the French and Dutch Islands, the Now'd carried to Georgia and Florida, where smuggling Sloops would barter with the Rogues and buy great Bargains.

"Our Senators treated all Representations of these Things as Idle Tales, Nay, there were those who wd assert there were not a thous'd people in the Back Country. Ev'ry Complaint was adjudged Chimerical. Instead of attend'g to the Internal Concerns of their Country, and Welfare,

Security, and Prosperity, and Trade of the Inhabitants, They spent seven Years in wrangling and disputing about Politics and Privileges, and the Concerns of Gt. Br. and other foreign matters."

Thoroughly desperate, the back inhabitants, at length wearying of the depredations of the robbers and neglect by Charles Town, "rose in Arms, pursu'd the Rogues, broke up their Gangs, burnt the dwellings of all their Har- bourers and Abettors, Whipped and drove the Idle, Vi- cious, and profligate out of the Province, Men and Women without distinction, and would have proceeded to Charles- town in a Regular Corps of 3000 men, and hung up the Rogues before the State House in presence of Govr. and Council," had not the Reverend Mr. Woodmason "by great Pains" prevailed with the "multitude . . . to lay aside desperate Resolutions" and to seek redress in a con- stitutional way. After he corresponded with the authorities and was promised that upcountry grievances would be carefully considered, he drew up a "Remonstrance." [56]

The Remonstrance of 1767 presented to the Commons House of Assembly by the Reverend Mr. Woodmason's parishioners prayed among other things that justice not be confined exclusively to Charles Town, and that circuit courts and courts of general sessions with appropriate officers be constituted throughout the province. When the document, signed by 4,000 in the name of 50,000, was read to the House, an uproar followed, and "the Lawyers died very hard." Those who brought it in felt that the Back Country was completely ignored and that every artifice was used to defeat their proposals, so that they decided never to supplicate colonial authority again; or as Mr. Woodmason put it, "Finding that they were only amus'd and trifled with, all Confidence of the Poor in the Great

[56] Woodmason, Journal, 24–25, 26, 55, 58–59.

is destroy'd and I believe will never exist again." Mr. Woodmason sought in vain to explain the reasons for *The Groans of the Back Country* in Charles Town newspapers, but he met with refusal from the printers, "who dar'd not" take his pieces, and he had to issue his pamphlet in Virginia. Disgusted with the obtuse and unenlightened conservatism of the "humane gentlemen" of the Low Country, he sardonically denounced them in a letter to Henry Laurens: "Have Patience, have Patience! has for many Years been the preoccupation of our Political Quacks, to the Country People. Their Patients have apply'd this Anondyne, till they are become Paralytic and require more sovereign Remedies." [57]

At long last in 1769 the Assembly tossed a crust to the stricken upcountry by replacing the old counties with six new districts and assigning a circuit court to each. The interior districts were Cheraws, Camden, Orangeburg, and Ninety Six. Two years later in a blistering letter to John Rutledge, Charles Woodmason eloquently exclaims that if much has been granted, "then much remains undone." It is still necessary for us to travel two or three hundred miles to the city to sue for £3 or take out a marriage license; officers can still come among us bearing a "Letter de Cachet" and jail us for debt unless we can raise bail within ten days; as yet we have no workhouses, hospitals, or bridewells; and I continue to live in "Dred of Villains robbing my House, steal'g my Horses and Cattel, ravishing my Wife and Daughrs," because you give me no lawful protection. In all he lists twenty-four grievances unredressed by those many taskmasters, those Low Country "Sons of Liberty," whose insolent treatment of the upcountry far

[57] Woodmason, Journal, 25, 55; *S.C. Gaz.,* June 15, 1765; Fulham Palace MSS, S.C., Nos. 51, 52, 57, 62, 91.

exceeds anything they can charge against the King or Parliament.

Consider how, he continues, just "to humour a few Noisy Bell weathers and swaggerers, who bellow for Liberty," the Assembly has in recent years spent not less than £20,000 on the ballroom it calls the Exchange, a statue of William Pitt, the Wilkes fund, and the trips of Christopher Gadsden and others to the New York Stamp Act Congress, while it denies schools and churches, roads and bridges to the upcountry! [58]

I have treated this affair in detail to bring out the fact that the Back Country was not at all satisfied with what has been called "the generous concession" of the planters in 1769. It was a case of too little too late. Even a moderate like the Reverend Mr. Woodmason, who frequently deplored the "Great Insolencies, . . . Wickedness and Impudence" of "those fellows that call themselves Regulators," in 1771 openly expressed his belief that the men who stood up to Scoville on the banks of the Saluda in 1769 could not for long be prevented from making their delayed march on Charles Town. If, once they discovered the pressing nature and right reason of the demand by the upcountry for civil government, the gentry had endeavored to fill the void in the true spirit of the eighteenth-century liberalism they loudly professed, the fierce and costly internecine strife of the Revolutionary War could have been avoided, with much saving of lives and property, and the Back Parts won as a unit to the cause of liberty.[59]

* * * * *

[58] Fulham Palace MSS, S.C., Nos. 60, 62; Schaper, "Sectionalism in South Carolina," 337–38.

[59] Woodmason, Journal, 55–56, 59; William Bull to Lord Dartmouth, May 5, 1773, Chalmers Papers, S.C., I, 185; R. W. Gibbes (ed.), *Documentary History of the American Revolution* (New York, 1855), 128, 225–38.

The presence of so many substantial Tidewater people among the population of small farmers in the Valley of Virginia created a good market for bound servants, which merchants like William Allison of Falmouth quickly exploited by selling "meere Irish" or occasionally English, Scots, or Germans for £15 to £24 each. The bulk of the servants were convicts rather than freewillers, which doubtless explains the frequency of theft and other delinquencies among them. Harsh treatment and the relative ease of escape impelled many servants to run away into the wilderness. From Augusta County in March, 1772, John Jefferson, weaver, William Johnson, "a tolerable good scholar," and John Guin, plasterer, lit out on two horses; while in October Scotta Marshall and Anne Banks ran away from Botetourt, "on the headwaters of Holston's River." Fewer servants were found in the Carolinas, but the problems were the same. When Joseph Ellis of Rowan was returned after eloping from his master in 1754, the court ordered him to pay for the time and work lost by serving sixteen months beyond his original term, and after another attempt at escape the following year it added an additional four months to his indenture. In every colony women servants giving birth to bastards, and there were many, usually had to work an extra year to compensate their masters for time lost.[60]

Slave labor, though costly, found as much favor in the interior as on the seaboard among those who could afford it. By 1775 Western Maryland and the Valley contained 12,758 slaves, and districts in upcountry South Carolina acquired many blacks after 1760. Moses Kirkland, the notorious Tory, used 60 at his indigo plantation. A preva-

[60] Hart, *Valley of Virginia*, 16–18; Summers, "Botetourt Records," 151, 173, 186, 204, 232; *Va. Gaz.* (Rind), Mar. 12, Oct. 22, 1772; Rowan Co., Minutes, 47, 83, 145, 237.

lent attitude of the day was expressed by two Virginians who visited the Moravians at Bethabara in 1772 : "Among other questions they asked how many negroes we had? Answer, two. They were the more surprised to find that white people had done so much work." Many slaves were skilled artisans. The only blacksmith near Staunton in 1753 was a free Negro who had come with a Scottish wife from Lancaster and who understood and read German very well. We are reminded that the white man's ways often produced curious effects on the Negro when we read that Jack, a literate runaway Negro farrier, "speaks in the Scotch-Irish dialect, and in conversation frequently uses the words *moreover* and *likewise*." [61] If the proportion of the total population that was black never reached 10 per cent during this period, its presence was both a symptom and a portent of the ultimate composition of this society.

Much confusion exists about the nature of class arrangements in the Back Settlements. The region had its gentry, which sought to give it an aristocratic cast: the gentry owned and controlled large tracts of choice lands, servants, and slaves, which made this goal attainable, and they exercised social and political influence as well. The accepted social theory that divisions of people into better, middling, and inferior sorts accorded with the law of Nature never encountered a serious challenge; it had existed since the beginning of time. The body of peasant farmers wanted and asked for the leadership of gentlemen. The assumption that family did not count in the Back Parts is without foundation in fact, albeit the aristocracy was never as tightly constituted as in the lowlands.

[61] Sutherland, *Population Distribution,* 201; Meriwether, *Expansion of South Carolina,* 160, 173; Gibbes (ed.), *Documentary History,* 197; Fries (ed.), *Records of the Moravians,* II, 780; *Va. Mag.,* XII (1904), 147-48; *Va. Gaz.* (Purdie & Dixon), Oct. 20, 1775; Mar. 22, 1776; *Va. Gaz.* (Rind), Oct. 22, 1772.

The founders of the interior gentry were men from the east, good or bad, but generally able. They came west with an already assured status achieved through family, wealth, or education. Dr. Thomas Walker of Castle Hill, physician, land speculator, explorer, vestryman, and legislator, was as active as any gentleman in the opening of the western parts of the Old Dominion. Thomas, sixth Lord Fairfax, built Greenway Court near Winchester in 1752, becoming the only resident peer in America, and participated freely in local affairs. Judge Richard Henderson and William Johnston of North Carolina, and South Carolina's Reverend Charles Woodmason and John Stuart, Indian agent for the Southern colonies, are other colorful examples of this inland gentry.[62]

Newcomers from the Northern colonies or immigrants direct from Europe promptly stepped forward to join these men in leadership of the back inhabitants. In their case too wealth, family, education, and native talents paved the way to place. Among those who came from other provinces was Edmund Fanning of Long Island, Berkeley scholar and graduate of Yale College, lawyer, public official, and promoter of higher education, who achieved the unmerited reputation of being the most hated man in all the Back Parts. Samuel Wyly, Quaker merchant from Pennsylvania, who founded Pine Tree Hill; the Reverend Peter Muhlenberg, Lutheran leader and Revolutionary commander; and the Reverend David Caldwell, graduate of Princeton and foremost Presbyterian in North Carolina, were outstanding clerical aristocrats. From their ranks, both the Scotch-Irish and Palatines produced laymen

[62] Thomas Walker, *Journal of an Exploration in the Spring of the Year 1750* (Boston, 1888) ; Natalie J. Disbrow, "Thomas Walker of Albemarle," Albemarle County Historical Society, *Papers*, I, 5–10; *D.A.B.*, VI, 256; *ibid.*, VIII, 530–31; Abernethy, *Western Lands*, 124, 134–35; *Col. Recs. N.C.*, VII, xv; Alden, *John Stuart;* Woodmason, *Journal.*

of substance and cultivation, who rose rapidly in the new country to the status of local gentry. In the records of Augusta and Botetourt counties, the names of Campbell, Preston, and Lewis are always accompanied by the title "Gentleman." Frederick William Marschall of the Moravians showed himself not only a master of languages and town planning but also a diplomat in dealing with other nationalities and the great leader of the most successful community experiment in the South.[63]

Men such as these belie the second William Byrd's overdrawn account of "Lubberland," which, be it noted, he made back in the twenties. By 1776 they and their families had forsaken the log cabin for framed houses furnished with many comforts, and some, like Isaac Zane, one of the lords of the Valley, lived amid a luxury and splendor rivaling Tidewater planters. The gentry gave the tone to and set the pace of existence which others envied and hoped eventually to imitate. Conspicuous display had its place even then. In 1775 a rich Dan River planter named Fearnly, recently come to Virginia from Antigua with one hundred slaves, called at the Moravian settlements in his coach accompanied by his wife, a Mr. Galloway, and servants. Nor did the vaunted leveling spirit of the Back Country prevent the growth of aristocratic arrogance and exclusiveness. When "an impertinent Constable" attempted to serve Colonel John Chiswell with a warrant at his quarter near Rockfish Gap in 1750, the irate gentleman ordered him off the plantation for "Rude behaviour and provoking him." From Winchester on May 24, 1775, the Reverend Philip Fithian walked out with some friends to "a lovely Farm of Mr. Whitehead's; an old Englishman of York-

[63] *D.A.B.*, III, 465; *ibid.*, VI, 265; *ibid.*, XI, 206; Summers, "Botetourt Records," 198, 212, 230; Abernethy, *Western Lands*, 80; Meriwether, *Expansion of South Carolina*, 50, 161–62, 164.

shire by birth. Left home early. Has been through America
with a Sett of Pictures and Magic Lanthorn, by which he
has made a Fortune. Is acquainted with many of the highest
Rank in Jersey, Pennsylvania, and Virginia. An intimate
acquaintance of Lord Fairfax in this County. Talks much
of Lords and Ladies." [64]

Important political positions went first to gentlemen
everywhere in the interior. Their interest ordinarily
weighed on the side of conservatism and counted heavily
in seaboard councils, particularly in the matter of land
grants. In Virginia and North Carolina, Scotch-Irish and
German leaders sat on the vestries of the Established
Church, ordered local government pretty much to their lik-
ing, and made no effort to change the institutions of the
parish. The great Virginia assault on parish vestries, culminating in their abolition during the War for Independence, received far more impetus from Tidewater liberalism
and anticlericalism and the rise of Newside Presbyterian-
ism in the Chesapeake Society than from any quickening
of so-called backwoods democracy. Actually, democratic
control of the parish failed to materialize in the Back
Country.[65]

Women of all classes and conditions lived in the Back
Parts, although they numbered perhaps only one third of
the men. Such a disparity and the genuine need for their
labor and company gave them an importance European
women never enjoyed. Physical strength and endurance
were as highly prized in women as in men. From all indica-
tions a large proportion must have been bad housewives
and worse cooks. At Cheraws in 1766, the Reverend Mr.

[64] Bridenbaugh, *Colonial Craftsman,* 24–26, 157; Fries (ed.), *Records
of the Moravians,* II, 876; Rose, Diary, 63; Albion and Dodson (eds.),
Fithian Journal, 1775–1776, 15.
[65] Owen, "Virginia Vestry," 3, 136, 142, 167, 170; Fries (ed.), *Records
of the Moravians,* I, 305, 319; Woodmason, Journal, 39.

Woodmason condemned "all the Cooking of these People, being exceeding filthy and most execrable," and consisting only of clabber, butter, "fat musty Bacon," and corn bread. In neatness and culinary arts the German *Hausfrauen* noticeably surpassed their English and Scotch-Irish sisters.[66]

Visitors universally acclaimed the shapeliness and beauty so frequently encountered among the young girls of the Back Settlements, particularly the Scotch-Irish and English. Even more did they exclaim over gentility discovered on the edge of the forest. Visiting Berkeley County, Virginia, Cresswell thought a Miss Grimes "A blooming Irish Girl," but favored almost to the point of marriage Miss Kitty Nourse, "one of the most sencible, agreeable, and well-bred girls, that I have seen since I left England." When Governor Henry Hamilton was being taken to Williamsburg after his surrender to George Rogers Clarke, his captors stopped overnight with Colonel William Inglis on New River. "A beautyfull Girl, his daughter, sat at the table," reported Hamilton, "and did the honours with such an easy and gracefull simplicity as quite charmed us." [67]

The freedom from convention enjoyed by the women of the west and the absence in many places of opportunities to legalize marriages encouraged a disregard of accepted moral standards. This was of course most noticeable among servant girls, who gave birth to numerous bastards, not infrequently mulattoes, and proved a perennial problem to county courts. Much more significant, however, were "the abandon'd Morals and profligate Principles"

[66] Woodmason, Journal, 9, 32, 34, 48; Spruill, *Women's Life and Work,* 81–83, 242.
[67] Woodmason, Journal, 29, 60; Cresswell, *Journal,* 97–100, 177; Henry Hamilton, Journal (Houghton Library, Harvard University), May 5–6, 1779; Weeks, *Southern Quakers,* 128.

the Reverend Mr. Woodmason discovered in the South Carolina upcountry. There, as in the interior of other provinces, many men and women lived together without ever marrying, because no clergyman was available. Others of the second generation to live in the most remote and wild portions of the Back Parts had never received any instruction in morality, but might be swayed by missionaries. What really shocked the sensible clergyman was the fact that "thro' the licentiousness of the People, many hund[reds] do live in Concubinage, swapping their Wives as Cattel, and living in a State of Nature, more irregularly and unchastely than the Indians." On August 16, 1768, he preached at Flatt Creek to a curious gathering who had never before heard a minister or the Lord's Prayer. "After the Service," the dismayed parson wrote, "they went out to Revellg, Drinking, Singing, Dancing and Whoring, and most of the Company were drunk before I quitted the Spott." Many experiences at divine services led him to conclude on what seems a modern note: ". . . their yg. Women have a most uncommon practice, wch I cannot break them of. They draw up their Shift as high as possible to the Body, and pin it close, to shew the roundness of their Breasts and slender Waists (for they are generally finely shaped) and draw their petticoat close to the Hips, to shew the fineness of their Limbs, so that they might as well be Puris Naturalibus. Indeed Nakedness is not censurable or indecent here, and they expose themselves often quite Naked, with Ceremony, Rubbing themselves and their Hair with Bears oil, and tying it up behind in a Bunch like the Indians, being hardly one degree removed from them." [68]

Lest this picture of the poorer South Carolina females

[68] Summers, "Botetourt Records," 135, 138, 140, 148, 151, 159, 163, 169, 173, 186, 204, 210, 219, 235, 240–41; Rowan Co., Minutes, II, 85; Woodmason, Journal, 3, 4, 11–12, 52, 54–55, 56, 57, 60–61.

seem overdrawn, we find the Botetourt County Court in the Valley of Virginia concerned with the many cases of immorality among the Scotch-Irish. Down the Valley at Winchester, Isaac Zane, a disowned Quaker, openly kept a mistress; and Nicholas Cresswell, who was certainly no prude, recorded of West Augusta, "nothing but whores and rogues in this country," and mentioned with disgust that a certain major, his two brothers, and his son enjoyed a mistress in common, "tho' these are the first people in this country." Possibly because they settled in groups where a stricter morality could be inculcated, the Quakers and the German sects seem to have been more circumspect in their behavior. This seamy side of life is naturally seldom mentioned, but it was a potent moral factor in the molding of Back Country society.[69]

The wilderness environment exerted a profound influence upon the manners and psychological attitudes of the back inhabitants that persisted when regions grew into settled rural communities. The struggle against Nature demanded unremitting labor, labor which not infrequently went unrewarded. Clearing land and developing a good farm called for more effort than many were willing to put forth when with a little corn patch and some hunting one could get by. Droughts and crop failures often brought some localities close to starvation, and with the passage of time, of course, the deer and other game disappeared. In October, 1766, Joseph Kershaw opened his store without charge to the Scotch-Irish farmers about Camden, whose families were in want of food.[70]

The loneliness and fear engendered in people fresh from the quiet, populous, agricultural villages of the Old

[69] Cresswell, *Journal,* 99–100, 105; Weeks, *Southern Quakers,* 128; Summers, "Botetourt Records," 162, 181–82, 225.

[70] Fries (ed.), *Records of the Moravians,* I, 103, 104; *Col. Recs. N.C.,* IX, 323; Woodmason, Journal, 4, 13, 32, 34, 38, 47, 48, 51.

World were depressing. "The wolves here give us music every morning, from six corners at once, such music as I never heard," Bishop Spangenberg sardonically reported. So numerous were wolves and panthers that authorities offered good-sized bounties for their "scelps." Then too, in many parts the Indian menace was never absent in colonial days. Although the Back Country was generally a healthy region, many settlers suffered from the ague, the popular label for malaria and rheumatic disorders. The Reverend Mr. Woodmason attributed the poor health of his parishioners to living in "Cold Cabins, unfloored and almost open to the sky" in a land of heavy dews and rains. At Granny Quarter in January, men and women attended services barefooted—the women clad only in a shift and petticoat, the men in shirt and trousers. Contributing to bad health was the monotonous and inadequate diet of pork, corn bread, "Butter, Milk, Clabber, and what in England is given to the Hogs and Dogs." The Germans seem to have been the only farmers to raise vegetables and other grain than corn, rye, and wheat.[71]

Medical attention to the needs of the settlers was at first wholly lacking, but as the country became thickly populated more physicians were available than is usually thought. By 1770 some able doctors practiced in the Valley of Virginia: Adam Stephen had studied at Edinburgh, as had William Fleming, while William Dunlap of the Cowpasture turned out to be one of America's early ovariotomists. East of the Blue Ridge in Albemarle, Doctors Thomas Walker and William Cabell cared for a large population. The typical eighteenth-century quack even made his way to the forks of the Broad and Saluda, where, according to the

[71] Fries (ed.), *Records of the Moravians*, I, 51–52; *Col. Recs. N.C.*, VII, 111; *ibid.*, IX, 313; Woodmason, Journal, 9, 29, 31, 32, 38, 56; Gibbes (ed.), *Documentary History*, 283.

South Carolina Gazette, Dr. Abraham Anderson advertised to cure "Consumption, Cancker or inward Imposthumes." No sooner did the Moravians erect their buildings at Bethabara than patients flocked from all over the Piedmont to Brother Kalberlehn. "The people are very thankful that he is willing to serve them," remarked the diarist. Dr. Kalberlehn died of typhus in 1759, but Dr. August Shubert carried on the good work, winning many friends and convincing many suspicious sectarians that the Moravian faith was certainly no league with the Devil.[72]

Despite the good beginning made before 1776, it must be evident that what are known today as psychic factors deriving from these unfamiliar and unanticipated conditions had much to do with determining social attitudes and habits in the Back Settlements. The prevalence, in a fertile country that merely awaited the slightest tillage to reward the husbandman abundantly with all kinds of foodstuffs, of a shiftlessness that amazed all observers is partially explained by this natural and psychic background. Whether pellagra and hookworm disease prevailed at this date is not known. That Scotch-Irish folk would sit "hovering over a few embers" in bitter February weather rather than stir about to cut firewood is beyond our comprehension. "They are very Poor owing to their Indolence," we are told. "They delight in their present low, lazy, sluttish, heathenish, hellish life, and seem not desirous of changing it. Both Men and Women will do any thing to come at Liquor, Cloaths, Furniture, etc, etc, rather than work for it." [73]

In Back Country lore the infallible panacea for hard

[72] Blanton, *Medicine in Virginia,* 19, 81, 238–43, 363–65; Summers, "Botetourt Records," 97; Disbrow, "Thomas Walker," 7–9; Fries (ed.), *Records of the Moravians,* I, 94, 95, 171, 216–22, 238, 268, 273; *S.C. Gaz.,* June 19, 1762; Woodmason, Journal, 36, 37, 53.
[73] Woodmason, Journal, 14, 31, 52; *Col. Recs. N.C.,* IX, 329.

work, bad diet, and discouragement was liquor in generous and frequent doses. Intemperance was an endemic vice in all ranks. Hard cider and peach or apple brandy were the commonest beverages, rum was consumed in large quantities, but in these prebourbon days, rye whisky was the grand elixir. On returning from a trip across the mountains to Augusta Court House in 1750, the Reverend Robert Rose admitted, "I have drunk more whiskey than ever I did before, and find when a Man is heartily fatigued any thing will do instead of Claret." Less gentle and prosperous people never faced the need to make the distinction. Temperate Germans preferred their beer, but English, Scots, and Ulsterites insisted upon whisky, which they consumed in quantities that strain modern credulity—witness the accounts of William Calhoun's purchases. One found "People continually drunk" in the west. Before an Episcopal service at Pine Tree Hill in 1767, ornery Presbyterians felt it necessary to give out "2 Bbls of Whisky to the populace to make drunk and for to disturb the Service." At the climax of the harvest in August, Mr. Woodmason wrote apprehensively: "Now will come on their Season of Festivity and Drunkenness. The Stills will be soon at Work to make Whisky and Peach Brandy. In this Article both Presbns and Episcopals very charitably agree (vizt) That of getting Drunk." Under such a dispensation it is scarcely remarkable that the backwoods tavern became one of the two principal institutions, rivaled only by the church.[74]

The manners one noted among these people were as varied as anything else in the interior parts. Some inhabitants were "as wild as the very deer," others crude, many quiet, sober, and diligent, a few genteel and cultivated.

[74] Rose, Diary, 200; "Journal of William Calhoun," Southern History Assn., *Publications,* VII, 180, 185–87; Woodmason, Journal, 4, 7, 27, 28, 38, 53; *Va. Gaz.* (Rind), July 18, 1766; Apr. 28, 1768; Fries (ed.), *Records of the Moravians,* I, 105, 109, 110, 121, 157, 241.

Yet the basic stock was stanch, and many a traveler told of rude kindnesses that men went out of their way to perform for total strangers. Quaker Samuel Wyly introduced the Reverend Mr. Woodmason to the inhabitants of Pine Tree Hill, Presbyterian Captain Dougherty took care of him when he fell violently ill, and once a rough backwoodsman carried him across a swollen stream on his shoulders. The plain, warmhearted character of all and sundry went with a country where people knew their own faults and limitations better than outsiders did. "Lord, grant that I may always be right," prayed a stiff-necked Scotch-Irishman, "for thou knowest that I am hard to turn." [75]

Simple sports and frolics of the conventional Anglo-Saxon kind constituted the diversions of the Back Country. Religious worship was the primary recreation, but it had to compete for attention with others on the Sabbath. In South Carolina "Amg the low Class, it is abus'd by Hunting, fishing, frivolity and Racing. By the Women in frolicing and Wantoness. By others in drinking Bouts and Card playing." These, with logrollings, harvest frolics, country dances, weddings, and an occasional horse race, completed the recreations of the West.[76]

Presence of many excellent mineral springs encouraged the development of a curious backwoods phase of the current European rage for taking the waters. Matthew Bramble had his American counterparts in the Great Valley of Virginia. At the "Health Springs" in Berkeley, Virginia, "many sick people" were already in attendance when two Moravians visited them in 1747; but the great vogue for the waters came after 1756 when Lord Fairfax made a present of the springs and surrounding land to the prov-

[75] Woodmason, Journal, 3, 15–16, 36; Dunaway, Scotch-Irish, 182; Rowan Co., Minutes, III, 7.
[76] Woodmason, Journal, 45; Cresswell, Journal, 97; Gibbes (ed.), Documentary History, 231; Spruill, Women's Life and Work, 110–11.

ince "for the welfare of suffering humanity." George Washington found about two hundred back inhabitants at the springs in August, 1761, and in the seventies the town of Bath grew up to provide needed shelter and supplies for the annual influx of visitors, who included such eastern gentry as the Dulanys of Maryland, James Madison, and the Nortons of York Town. In 1776 Philip Fithian was astonished to find at the springs over four hundred people, representing a true cross section of the frontier, from the buckskin reeking of bear's grease to the perfumed dandy of Williamsburg and Annapolis. The springs of the Valley enjoyed the greatest popularity, but North Carolina spas at New River and near the Roanoke also attracted many invalids and summer visitors. Although South Carolina developed no watering place, the salubrity of the upcountry climate and the cost of going to Newport drew attention to the High Hills of Santee. "They are therefore now thinking of their own poor despised Back Country, and are now flocking up where I am, to build Summer Seats and Hunting Boxes," writes the Reverend Mr. Woodmason in 1771, adding that land not worth a shilling an acre three years since now brings a guinea.[77]

A powerful competitor with all other forms of recreation, and stronger than government as a force for discipline, organized Protestantism emerged as the most influential institution of the Back Country. Churches sometimes appeared in a region before the authorities extended law and order to it, as in the case of the Hopewell Friends Meeting, which preceded by nine years the first county court in the Valley of Virginia; or in South Carolina, where

[77] *Va. Gaz.* (Purdie & Dixon), June 7, Aug. 30, Sept. 20, 1770; Brant, *Madison,* 108; Hening (ed.), *Statutes,* IX, 247, 248; *New York Weekly Post Boy,* Apr. 20, Aug. 20, 1744; *Col. Recs. N.C.,* VII, 100–101; Fulham Palace MSS, Nos. 51–52; Foster, "Documentary History," V, 809–10; Bridenbaugh, "Baths and Watering Places," 160–64.

Quaker, Baptist, and Presbyterian meetings flourished in
the absence of any civil authority for many years. Representing "the dissidence of dissent," as Burke said, a large
majority of the people were Calvinists and thus might have
been expected to contribute measurably to the social and
cultural unity of growing settlements, as indeed they did;
but the compelling religious feature of the entire interior
was the existence in its most virulent form of a fierce sec-
tarianism.[78]

Such a condition stemmed directly from the presence of
many sects and nationalities. To a man, the Scotch-Irish
worshiped according to the Westminster Confession, as
did the Scots and some of the English. The Presbyterians
outnumbered all other denominations combined. Save for
a few Moravians and Dunkers, the Palatines belonged
to the German Reformed (Calvinist) or Lutheran com-
munions, which probably had as many members as the
Church of England. In the South the Society of Friends
underwent a rebirth, when new meetings sprang up all the
way from Hopewell to Guilford and on through Pine Tree
Hill to Cane Creek and Georgia, but the Quakers never
attained the size of other sects. From most humble beginnings the Baptists, "who called themselves Newlights (not
of the flesh of Mr. Whitefield) but Superior Lights from
New England," made signal gains late in the period, serving notice on both Presbyterians and Anglicans that in
missionary work, among the poor and those of no faith
especially, they faced a real rival. Just as the separation
from the mother country occurred, Methodism rooted itself around Leesburg in the Virginia Piedmont.[79]

[78] *Hopewell Friends History*, 7.
[79] E. W. Caruthers, *A Sketch of the Life and Character of the Rev. David
Caldwell, D.D.* (Greensboro, 1842), 26, 27, 30, 80; *Va. Gaz.* (Purdie &
Dixon), Mar. 28, 1766; Cunz, *Maryland Germans*, 61, 68, 77; Wayland,
German Element in the Shenandoah Valley, 92, 104, 122; Rowan Co., Min-

In the remote Back Parts, among native-born settlers, were many nothingarians, to whom any form of religious observance was a great novelty. The Reverend Charles Woodmason also discovered large numbers of such folk in the most populous areas of his huge parish of St. Marks, near the North Carolina boundary. At Granny Quarter the people had not "the least Rudiments of Religious Manners or Knowledge (save of Vice) among them. Such a Pack, I never met with, neither English, Scots, Irish or Carolinian by Birth." They belonged to no denomination, had never seen a minister or heard a sermon, scripture reading, or prayer "in their Days." As a consequence they had no understanding of the commonest principles of morality; men and women never married, and their children went unbaptized. Christian teachings could win over many of the ignorant, and in two years the Anglican clergyman covered three thousand miles as an itinerant, raising about thirty congregations, marrying almost three hundred couples, and baptizing twelve hundred children. Others, "Idle People without either Religion or Goodness," and "the lowest vilest Scum of Mankind," seemed beyond the reach of the Gospel.[80]

Sectarian animosities flared up time and again in a most unchristian manner. Brother Marschall reported in 1772 to the Bethlehem authorities that at Salem "the situation is as usual, that is to say many of our neighbors are bitter against us, partly because we are a godly people, partly because of our outward prosperity." Two years later Bap-

---

utes, II, 207, 251; Woodmason, Journal, 3, 10; Bernheim, *History of the German Settlements,* 99–102, 148–54, 179–80; *Col. Recs. N.C.,* V, 1170, 1175, 1177; *ibid.,* VII, 284–88; *ibid.,* VIII, 229, 655, 732, 734–35; *ibid.,* IX, 1003; Weeks, *Southern Quakers,* 70–71, 89, 95, 96, 104, 119; *Minutes of the Kehukee Baptist Association,* in *James Sprunt Historical Monographs,* V (1904), 3, 9–10, 15–22; Cresswell, *Journal,* 138, 141, 143.

[80] Woodmason, Journal, 3, 20, 28, 40, 47, 48, 57, 60, 63; Fries (ed.), *Records of the Moravians,* I, 251, 752–53, 755, 761, 788–804.

tists on the Yadkin warned Brother Utley against preaching in their settlements. Where members of Lutheran and Reformed churches were few in numbers, they frequently joined for worship but customarily separated as soon as each felt they could support a separate congregation. Because Newlight Baptists proselyted so successfully with an unlearned ministry, they incurred the resentment of other denominations, for, remarked a Moravian in 1766, they were "the only ones in the country who go far and wide preaching and caring for souls." On Swift Creek in South Carolina there was a "gang" of ignorant Baptist and Methodist preachers, according to an Anglican, "yet the lower Class chuse to resort to them rather than to hear a Well connected Discourse." At times the nothingarians cried a plague on them all. "They complained of being eaten up by Teachers and preachers, Imported from New England and Pennsylvania, Baptists, New Lights, Presbyterians, Independants, and an hundr. other Sects. So that at one Day you might hear this System of Doctrine, the next Day another, next Day another, retrograde to both. Thus by a variety of Taylors whoud pretend to know the best fashion in wch Xt's Coat is to be worn, none will put it on." [81]

Surpassing all other Protestants in bigotry and fierce denominationalism were the Scotch-Irish Presbyterians, and the lengths to which they went are almost unbelievable. That Charles Woodmason was an Episcopal partisan is admitted, but that he possessed a full measure of Christian compassion for the suffering back inhabitants regardless of creed is also true. He was buoyed up by his faith, by the patience of Job, by great personal integrity and bravery,

[81] Fries (ed.), *Records of the Moravians,* I, 84; *ibid.,* II, 678, 816, 824, 867, 889; *Col. Recs. N.C.,* VII, 252–53, 285–86; Woodmason, Journal, 5, 9, 10, 17, 45–46, 53; Fulham Palace MSS, Nos. 51–62.

and by his sense of humor. If he posted announcements that he would preach on a certain day, the Presbyterians would change the date on the notice; they gave out quantities of whisky two hours before his service to get the listeners thoroughly drunk. They branded him a Jesuit for conducting church on the fifth of November. Crafty bigots gave the itinerant false directions so that he lost his way in the woods. They stole the keys to the meetinghouse at Camden, and after two years they expelled him from his parish. Once they started fifty-seven dogs fighting outside the church, forcing the clergyman to dismiss his congregation; but he caught one bitch, took it to a deacon's house, and slyly intimated that it was one of the fifty-seven Presbyterians he had just converted. They condoned robbery of his lodgings, opened his mail, and framed him disreputably on a moral charge. Because all upcountry magistrates were Presbyterians he could expect no defense from the "Envy, Malice, and Temper of the presbyterians," whom he not unnaturally regarded as "certainly the worst Vermin on Earth." Despite such treatment, however, he ministered to them faithfully, delivered some of their babies in remote cabins, taught their children, interceded for them at Charles Town, and drew up their "Remonstrance" against Low Country neglect. Perhaps Mr. Woodmason took some comfort from the realization that the Presbyterians hated the Baptists more than the Episcopalians, "and so the Rest," and that all sectaries regarded the Church of England as second best.[82]

Throughout the Back Settlements mutual dislike and mutual suspicion more often than not triumphed over brotherhood and charity to a degree unknown in the urban communities of colonial America, and definitely served to accentuate national differences and to prolong group ex-

[82] Woodmason, Journal, 27, 28, 32, 33, 41–42, 44, 49, 51.

clusiveness. To this, ignorance and rural isolation heavily contributed. One thing was certain: everywhere the sectaries outnumbered the Established Church and steadfastly opposed its pretensions. In North and South Carolina tithes were seldom collected, while laws validating only Anglican marriages were openly and resentfully nullified. Religious heterogeneity was a fact in the interior, whatever the theory of the law; separation of church and state would have to come eventually. Nevertheless we shall do well to remember that the toleration born of the Enlightenment and voiced by some liberal Tidewater Anglican gentlemen had no interior echoes before 1775; such Christian fellowship as obtained in the West derived from two brute facts: the religious ignorance or indifference of the native-born and the inability of any one sect to impose its creed upon the rest.[83]

Each immigrant group and many religious bodies ardently desired to assure children a common-school education and, even though accomplishments never equaled aspirations, made commendable efforts to that end. The Ulsterites had behind them the ancient repugnance of the Lowland Scots for illiteracy, the tradition of a highly trained ministry, and the vigorous support of the Presbyterian Synod at Philadelphia and the College of New Jersey at Princeton. Schoolmasters made their way to the Valley of Virginia and the Piedmont. In far-off Botetourt in 1771 complaint was made to the court against Jacob Jackson "for not educating his children in a christianlike manner." Prior to 1763 the Valley acquired a classical school when the Reverend John Brown opened "Augusta Academy," and in 1775 the Hanover Presbytery assumed responsibility for this flourishing school with a new master, since Brown was then teaching near Fincastle and prepar-

[83] *Col. Recs. N.C.*, I, xxv; *ibid.*, VIII, 15; *ibid.*, IX, 7, 251, 623–24.

ing to establish a "seminary" at Round Oak. Even more success attended Presbyterian efforts at education in North Carolina, where capable Princeton-bred ministers founded a succession of schools after 1755. Joseph Alexander, Ephraim Brevard, Waightstill Avery, and Henry Paltillo led in the work. Crowfield Academy, a classical school at Bel Mont in Mecklenburg County, and David Caldwell's "Log College" near Newmarket enjoyed the greatest reputation of any of these little clerical schools, the latter attracting students from as far north as the Potomac. Because it was a newer region, South Carolina lagged in education. It had not a single school in 1766, but within two years at Camden an "Old Presbyterian fellow" opened a pay school for his sect, and in 1768 the residents of Ninety Six formed the Salem Society "to endow and support a school and seminary of learning." One of the loudest complaints of the Scotch-Irish Regulators against the Low Country was its failure to give them public schools. Altogether, these and similar undertakings constitute a remarkable record for a new country and set the pace for post-colonial development.[84]

Cut off from aid from the Old World by the English colonial system, German immigrants could not expect much help, but they succeeded remarkably in providing elementary instruction for their children. They established parochial schools as soon as they could procure teachers, and through the efforts of the coetus of the Reformed Church at Philadelphia catechisms were printed and distributed. As early as 1747 an able master, Thomas Schley, conducted

[84] Va. Gaz. (Rind), Jan. 28, 1773; Aug. 4, 1774; Va. Gaz. (Purdie & Dixon), May 20, 1773; Aug. 4, 1775; Summers, "Botetourt Records," 109–10; Draper MSS (Wisconsin Historical Society), 2QQ141, 3QQ8, 4QQ31; Hart, Valley of Virginia, 29; Va. Mag., XXX (1921), 179; Charles L. Raper, The Church and Private Schools of North Carolina (Greensboro, 1898), 13, 32–37, 40, 50–51; Caruthers, David Caldwell, 29–31, 37, 40–41; Fulham Palace MSS, Nos. 62, 91; S.C. Gaz., Dec. 15, 1772.

a school for Maryland Germans at Frederick. St. John's Church in Mecklenburg, composed of Reformed and Lutherans, sent to Europe for teachers in 1772, and a year later Gottfried Arndt arrived to begin a notable career. The Moravians at Wachovia methodically arranged for schools as soon as they were needed: first they provided English lessons for the single brothers; then regular schooling as children came along. Outsiders willing to pay a fee could send their children to the Moravian schools. There were night classes for older boys learning trades, and in 1774 Brother Reuter found sufficient interest for a class in geometrical drawing. The Quakers appear to have been slower in starting schools, although they had several in Virginia and North Carolina in 1775. Having no great concern either for an educated ministry or for schooling in general, the Baptists entirely neglected this activity. More remarkable, however, was the failure of the Church of England to pursue missionary activities in the west by opening schools as the Society for the Propagation of the Gospel had done earlier in the century. Charles Woodmason's classes at Pine Tree Hill failed because the Presbyterians insisted upon the use of the Westminster Catechism and would not send their children to him, but he never gave up the conviction that schools would win souls for the Established Church, because tracts were of no use in an area where "very few can read, fewer write." [85]

In the thickly settled portions of the west that enjoyed local government, the English apprentice system and the custom of binding out orphans fostered education. Eliza-

[85] Cunz, *Maryland Germans*, 68, 117, 120; *Col. Recs. N.C.*, VIII, 731, 732; Fries (ed.), *Records of the Moravians*, I, 160, 181, 241, 331; *ibid.*, II, 657, 663–66, 774, 827, 828, 829; Bernheim, *History of the German Settlements*, 187, 257; Raper, *Church and Private Schools*, 61–63, 67–68, 70; Erwin, *Rowan County*, 50–51; *Hopewell Friends History*, 155; Weeks, *Southern Quakers*, 143; Woodmason, Journal, 4, 7, 37, 44, 52, 54; *S.C. Statutes*, VIII, 117–18.

beth Dixon of Rowan County was bound in 1754 to James Carter, who was ordered "to Learn the sd. orphan to read English." Ralph Smith's indenture to a cordwainer enjoined his master to "Educate him in Reading, Writing and Arithmetic as far as the five Common Rules." By this means many children acquired a minimum education, although an efficient apprentice system obtained in only a few communities in the South.[86]

The interest of the new and poor Back Country in schools and the determined efforts to establish them compare more than favorably with the accomplishment of the older and wealthier Tidewater and Low Country. In the matter of higher education, the interior set an enviable example, in particular to "so rich, so luxurious, so polite a People" as the Charlestonians. The Reverend Joseph Alexander started a little classical school at Sugar Creek, North Carolina, which Presbyterians and others of Mecklenburg County sought to expand into a college. In 1771 they persuaded the Assembly to charter it as "Queen's College," because boys graduating from "the several Grammar schools . . . long taught in the western parts" needed an institution where they "might imbibe the principles of Science and virtue" and "obtain under learned, pious and Exemplary Teachers in a collegiate and academic mode of instruction a regular and finished education." With Edmund Fanning, the most cultivated man in the province, as first president and with a board of Presbyterians, the future of the foundation appeared promising to interested people throughout the colonies. Students began to attend and tickets for a building lottery were sold as far away as Williamsburg. In spite of the announcement that the King-in-Council had disallowed the law of incorporation in 1773, "Queen's Museum," as it was then

[86] Rowan Co., Minutes, I, 39, 72, 382, 544, 550, 694; *ibid.*, II, 13, 39.

called, continued to instruct boys, of whom there were eighty in 1776, in the "languages and other literary attainments." Some Anglican and Presbyterian gentlemen of Prince Edward and other counties of the southern Virginia Piedmont combined to promote an academy at the courthouse in 1775 by donating "a valuable Library of the best Writers," and a philosophical apparatus. The Reverend Samuel Stanhope Smith and three masters, who expected shortly to be joined by two more, were ready to begin with a system of education like that of Nassau Hall. Hampden-Sydney accepted children of any communion when it opened on September 1, 1775, under the auspices of the Hanover Presbytery in the face of Anglican opposition from the Tidewater, its stated object being the training of "good men and good Citizens." [87]

Given the state of the Back Settlements one would not expect to find many signs of cultural development in these years, which required action rather than contemplation from everyone. Yet here and there in the rough, new country, little oases of dignity and culture could be found. A few men had books and they read them. At Stephensburg in 1775, delighted Philip Fithian spent a day in the office of Mr. Joseph Holmes among "many useful and amusing books—The Spectators, Pope's Works, Shakespear's Works, Gay's Works, and many single valuable Books." The Reverend Mr. Woodmason, formerly a bookseller, possessed many volumes at his quarters in Camden, and at Wachovia the Moravians assembled a variety of devotional and German literature for their

[87] Woodmason, Journal, 60; William H. Foote, *Sketches of North Carolina* (New York, 1846), 513–14; *Col. Recs. N.C.*, VIII, 486–90, 526; *ibid.*, IX, 249–50, 597, 665; *S.C. Gaz.*, May 23, 1771; *Boston News-Letter*, June 27, 1771, suppl.; *Va. Gaz.* (Purdie & Dixon), May 28, 1772; Dr. Joseph Clitherall, Diary (Typescript, S.C. Hist. Soc.), 1776; *Va. Gaz.* (Dixon & Hunter), Oct. 7, Nov. 18, Dec. 9, 1775; Feb. 3, 1776.

"Reading Meetings." South of Winchester at his 21,000-acre estate Marlboro, Isaac Zane, erstwhile member of the American Society for Promoting Useful Knowledge, accumulated a library of 400 books to which in 1778 he added "near 4,000 volumes" of the famous Westover Library purchased from Mary Willing Byrd for £2,000.[88]

These exceptions should not obscure the fact that many ordinary people owned a few religious books just as their fellows did in the eastern parts: Bibles were common everywhere, and not infrequently Virginia and North Carolina families displayed volumes published at Germantown by Christopher Saur, in addition to his *Geistliches Magazien* and German almanacs. Palatines imported Lutheran and Heidelberg catechisms in considerable quantities, and traveling Friends distributed Quaker journals and writings sent out from Philadelphia. When the Reverend Mr. Woodmason regretted that "Few or no Books are to be found in all this vast Country," he meant Anglican works, because he did find common among the Scotch-Irish the Assembly's *Catechism*, Watt's *Hymns*, and Bunyan's *Pilgrim's Progress*, as well as copies of Russell's, Whitefield's, and Erskine's sermons. The *Psalter, Book of Common Prayer*, and volumes of sermons could be found in the cabins of Episcopalians. The "Mecklenburg Library" was established at Charlotte in 1771 by Waightstill Avery and others with gifts from about forty men, plus a representative selection of current books and a selected list of works on Presbyterian divinity ordered from the British Isles. With the steady improvement of the highways, newspapers —especially Saur's *Pennsylvanische Berichte*, Henry Mil-

---

[88] Albion and Dodson (eds.), *Fithian Journal, 1775–1776*, 15; *S.C. Gaz.*, Aug. 10, 1752; Woodmason, Journal, 12, 14, 17, 32; *Tyler's Quarterly Historical Magazine*, XVI (1934–35), 107, 109; *Va. Mag.*, XXXVIII (1930), 52; Hart, *Valley of Virginia*, 25–26.

ler's *Der Wochentliche Philadelphische Staatsbote,* and
the important *South Carolina Gazette*—began to circulate
in the Back Country. In 1772 Adam Boyd of Wilmington
arranged for a rider to distribute his *Cape Fear Mercury*
as far inland as Hillsboro, Cross Creek, and Salisbury
fortnightly. Newspapers were read aloud at taverns, and
by this means many an illiterate at least learned the latest
advices. Notwithstanding such hopeful signs, I can take no
exception to Mr. Woodmason's strictures on the ignorance
and lack of intellectual curiosity of most of the back inhabitants: "Nor do they delight in Historical Books or
wish to have them read to them, as do our Vulgar in England, for here the people despise Knowledge, instead of
honouring a Learned Person, or any one of Wit or Knowledge be it in the Arts, Sciences, or Languages, they despise
and ill treat them." [89]

The natural wonders of the interior and men's attempts
to cope with the wilderness brought forth some writings,
which, if never intended to be regarded as literature,
treated native American themes and surpassed in importance and interest the pallid imitative effusions of the
eastern gentry. Unpretentious, these pieces had validity
because in them one could feel beating the pulse of the Back
Settlements. Such were Hermon Husband's *Some Remarks
on Religion* (1771), a recital of the spiritual wanderings
of a religious pioneer, and his spirited defenses of the
North Carolina Regulators: *An Impartial Relation*
(1770); Continuation of the Impartial Relation (n.p.);
and *A Fan for Fanning* (1771). In the great tradition of

[89] Meriwether, *Expansion of South Carolina,* 63; *Col. Recs. N.C.,* VIII,
731; *ibid.,* IX, 356; Fries (ed.), *Records of the Moravians,* II, 706; Philadelphia *Pennsylvania Journal,* Jan. 12, 1764; Weeks, *Southern Quakers,*
140, 143; Mecklenburg Library, F. L. Hawks MSS, North Carolina (N.Y.
Hist. Soc.), I; *S.C. Gaz.,* Aug. 25, 1764; *Cape Fear Mercury,* Sept. 22,
1773; May 11, 1774; Woodmason, Journal, 52–53.

English and Scottish popular balladry, Rednap Howell
clothed the Regulation with homespun epic qualities as he
set the whole Piedmont to singing:

> When Fanning first to Orange came
> He looked so pale and wan,
> An old patched coat upon his back
> An old mare he rode on.

> Both man and mare wan't worth five pounds
> As I've been often told
> But by his civil robberies
> He's laced his coat with gold.

Written among the "cheerful brave Chikkasah" between
1761 and 1768, Indian trader James Adair's *History of
the American Indians* (London, 1775) is an account of
the natives of the Cherokee and Muskhogean tribes of
the colonial Southwest. Called forth by a long and rich
experience, Adair's not only is a classic work on ethnology
but remains today one of the most enjoyable books on the
American Indian.[90]

Years of devoted translation and editing by the learned
and able late Adelaide L. Fries have placed in our hands
the most remarkable literary corpus of the colonial South
in the first two volumes of the *Records of the Moravians
in North Carolina*. Consisting of diaries, memorabilia,
reports, letters, memoirs, obituaries, hymns, occasional
verse, an herbal, and miscellaneous papers of the Wachovia
experiment, they are invested with a Biblical flavor and
vigor that captivate the reader. Notes of human sympathy
and compassion, so noble and so rare in the Back Country,

[90] Hudson, "Songs of the North Carolina Regulators," 470–84; Samuel
C. Williams (ed.), *Adair's History of the American Indians* (Johnson
City, 1930).

suffuse these community writings, depicting the Moravians as what they truly were—the brethren of all men. In these simple accounts of the wanderings of the faithful, of their work and worship, shot full of Teutonic humor or rather, irony, we sense the longing for a better world and richer spiritual experience that impelled so many humble folk to seek in the interior "L'Age d'Or" about which European philosophers merely dreamed.[91]

The Back Country's wild grandeur, its great expanse, its profusion of flora and fauna—all these inspired travelers to record their impressions of an amazing land. That first gentleman of Virginia the second William Byrd took as the theme of his fanciful writings the "Lubberland" of the Roanoke Valley after a journey to the "Land of Eden." Fithian and Cresswell penned absorbing journals of life in the Great Valley, as did John Bartram of his botanizing excursions in the far South. The latter's son William gave to his *Travels* through the interior, 1773–1777, an enchanting quality that made it one of the first American performances to attain the level of literary art. If John Singleton Copley was the colonial master of portraiture, William Bartram's still unpublished drawings of the flowers, birds, reptiles, and fishes made on the scene in the Carolinas, Georgia, and Florida represent the initial successful, and immensely significant, departure from traditional English modes of painting into what would become a truly American art form.[92]

Of all the arts music makes the greatest appeal to peasant peoples. The scraping of the fiddle belonged, with the ring of the ax, the songs of birds, and the calls of wild animals, among the most familiar sounds of the Back Set-

---

[91] Fries (ed.), *Records of the Moravians,* II, 758, *passim.*

[92] Albion and Dodson (eds.), *Fithian Journal, 1775–1776,* 15; Fries (ed.), *Records of the Moravians,* I, 250; *ibid.,* II, 557–87.

tlements. Folk songs of Old England were so widely sung as to have survived into our own day, but it was the muse of the sublime hymn rather than Erato with her lyre that inspired these people. One Sunday in May, 1767, the Reverend Mr. Woodmason read services at newly settled Rocky Mount to over four hundred people, many of them Presbyterians and Baptists. The "excellent singing" of the women, which he deemed better than that of the girls of London's Magdalen Chapel, caused the enraptured parson to marvel that they all came from Pennsylvania or Virginia, "not an English person or a Carolinian among them." The Palatines piously preserved in this raw country the most living element of German culture to survive the Thirty Years' War—the moving hymns of Luther and his followers. In all religious observances the United Brethren gave music a prominent part, and some of the members actually composed devotional music for use at Salem. Not only did they have a highly trained chorus for special occasions, but also daily *Singstunden.* Members received careful instruction on the organ, trombone, French horn, and violin, and the death of a Brother or Sister was announced with impressive solemnity by trombones at the instant of its occurrence. That the Moravians did not restrict their singing and playing to devotional music is evident from a decision of 1772, which decreed that the "musicians" not play "Minuets, Polonaises, Marches or other worldly music" on the Sabbath, "but rather confine themselves to Chorales." [93]

For too long have we been limited in our understanding of the Back Settlements by applying uncritically the concepts of the forest freedom of the Indian trader and the

[93] Reuben G. Thwaites and Louise P. Kellogg (eds.), *Documentary History of Lord Dunmore's War* (Madison, 1905), 433–39; Woodmason, Journal, 19; Fries (ed.), *Records of the Moravians,* I, 172, 353, 354–55, 369, 463; *ibid.,* II, 690, 709, 750, 764, 830–31, 838.

cattleman to those who endeavored to found permanent communities and succeeded. In this chapter I have tried to depict a backwoods existence that was constantly becoming rural in imitation or in extension of Pennsylvania and of the Chesapeake and Carolina societies. I have stressed that on the eve of Independence the Back Country was a land of sharp contrasts and amazing antitheses. The elements for a society were there, but fusion had not yet taken place because its exact form had still to be determined. The west had not as yet enunciated or even adumbrated a theory of American democracy. Conditions of landholding, the stage of economic development, and absence of a unified tradition did sustain a rough sort of equality among this human miscellany, which, however, thought not in terms of present but of future prospects. Charles Woodmason, who knew England and the Low Country as well as the Back Parts, voiced this sentiment in answer to John Rutledge's scornful remark that for people exhibiting the license of the upcountry to call themselves slaves was both "Impertinent and Invidious." With brutal directness the clergyman countered: "Are any of your Descents Greater, Nobler, ancienter, more reputable than ours? Have you more Virtue, more Religion, more goodness than us? Many, far less; Indeed you may be sd. to have more Learning, Politeness, Wealth, Slaves, and Lands, but we speak of Intrinsic Worth. All we wish is, that you had better Hearts than we can boast. But what hinders that we be not yr Equals in ev'ry Respect? . . . Will you pronounce that in 50 Years, our Posterity may not ride in their Chariots, while yours walk on foot? Or do you fear it? It seems so by your conduct toward us." [94]

That "Corruption and Jobbing" were "as well understood here, as in the Old Country," or to the eastward,

[94] Fulham Palace MSS, No. 60 (1771).

and that venality and moral dishonesty were all too evident, wise men admitted of the Back Parts. But what they were mattered less than what they might become. The future promised to bring manufactures and diversified farming, and to produce a well-balanced economy of small proprietors that augured an orderly, cultured society resembling that of Pennsylvania. But with time powerful provincial forces—land regulations, extension of county government, the arrival of the big planter with his slaves —these local forces narrowed the influence of distant Philadelphia and strengthened the bonds between east and west. Brother fought brother in the bitter partisan warfare of the Revolution, and when it was all over many miserable Tory back inhabitants had to flee to British dominions for safety. Times had changed profoundly. Not until 1790 was the Back Country ready to crystallize into a definite society, and by that time much of its old colonial character had been modified by the exigencies of the new age, or had disappeared forever.[95]

[95] Woodmason, Journal, 39.

Bibliographical Note

It was obviously impossible to make an exhaustive study of the materials relating to the social history of the eighteenth-century South in preparation for these lectures. I have, however, read every Southern newspaper and magazine published before 1776, a large part of the literature of the time, all printed records of the five colonies considered plus the manuscript records of South Carolina at Columbia. In addition, I have worked through all the publications of Southern local and state historical societies. I think it fair to state that I have consulted all of the relevant secondary literature on the subject. Over a period of years I have supplemented my studies of maps and photographs by personally inspecting much of the surviving remains of the civil and domestic architecture of the late colonial period as well as many of its paintings in private and public collections. Into the mass of unused manuscripts I have dipped freely, and have succeeded in turning up significant new evidence on several hitherto obscure matters.

In the footnotes to the foregoing pages I have supplied references with a dual purpose in mind: to indicate the sources of quotations or other data; and to provide prospective investigators with a quick guide to what I consider the best sources and secondary authorities on the topic treated in the text. To reduce the footnotes to a decent size and for ease of ready reference, I have dispensed with much of the customary bibliographical paraphernalia and used simple forms of short titles and abbreviations without, I think, in any way obscuring their identity. For this reason, it seems unnecessary to list all such materials here.

Although many old hands are familiar with the standard method of citing the *Virginia Gazette,* perhaps a word of explanation is due at this point. Up to 1765 there was but one *Virginia Gazette* published at Williamsburg; after that date there were two, and at times three, newspapers called the *Virginia Gazette*. In citing the issues after 1765, therefore, I always give the name of the printer (as Rind, Purdie & Dixon, etc.) to designate which *Virginia Gazette* I used. Further explanations of the trouble caused to posterity by this singular absence of originality in titles are given by Cappon and Duff in the *Virginia Gazette Index,* cited below.

The records of county courts constitute the great unworked manuscript source for the social and cultural life of the Southern colonies. There are rich materials in abundance which cry for exploitation, but which are virtually untouched. Some indication of their incalculable worth is the large amount of data the records of York County, Virginia, yielded to the researchers of Colonial Williamsburg. I was able to consult only five of these sets of records, but found them indispensable. The court records of North Carolina are nearly all available on film at the Historical Commission in Raleigh, while those of Virginia and Maryland may be consulted at the Virginia State Library in Richmond and the Hall of Records at Annapolis. For workers in the western part of the United States it should be pointed out that the Historical Society of the Mormon Church at Salt Lake City, Utah, is rapidly assembling on film the local records of all of the Atlantic Coast states, and will shortly have the most complete collection in the entire country. These films are open to qualified scholars.

Other manuscript collections, such as letters, diaries, commercial and plantation papers, and miscellaneous documents, very few of which have been systematically examined by historians, lie in the vaults of the Maryland Historical Society at Baltimore and the Hall of Records at Annapolis; of the Virginia Historical Society and the Virginia State Library in Richmond, the Alderman Library at Charlottesville, the College of William and Mary Library and the archives of Colonial Williamsburg, Inc., at Williamsburg; of the North Carolina Historical Commission at Raleigh and the great collections of the universities at Durham and Chapel Hill; of the Charleston Library Society and the South Carolina Historical Commission at Columbia; and in the Georgia Historical Society at Savannah. Repositories outside of the South, such as the New York Historical Society, the Historical Society of Pennsylvania, and the American Antiquarian Society, often contain rare items of great value to the investigator. Most of these institutions have publications which serve as useful guides to their resources and not infrequently contain documents drawn from them.

With the completion of the important *Virginia Gazette Index* (2 vols., Williamsburg, 1950) under the editorship of Lester J. Cappon and Stella F. Duff, Virginia now has the best and most complete bibliographical guides to its history of any state in the Union, and there should no longer be any excuse for neglect of its little-studied and less-understood eighteenth-century life and society.[1] Recently, too, J. H. Easterby has published a most useful *Guide to the Study and Reading of South Carolina History* (Columbia, 1950); and in its *Catalog of the Measured Drawings and Photographs of the Survey in the Library of Congress, March 1, 1941* (Washington, 1941) the Historic American Buildings Survey performed a notable service. That students in distant parts of the country are taking a renewed interest in the colonial South will soon be made evident when the distinguished agricultural economist, Paul S. Taylor of the University of California, publishes in the *William and Mary Quarterly* a remarkable study which will for the first time place the economy and social system of early Georgia on a sound and realistic basis.

No bibliographical statement on a subject such as this can henceforth be complete without a tribute to the great Historical Records Survey, which not only salvaged and gave purpose in life to much fine human material during the dark days of depression, but in a long series of guides, calendars, and listings provided the key to old hitherto unusable sources and uncovered vast collections whose existence was unknown. The best introduction to these surveys is ac-

---

[1] The other standard Virginia reference works are: Earl Gregg Swem, "A Bibliography of Virginia," Virginia State Library, *Bulletin,* VIII (1916); and the same compiler's monumental *Virginia Historical Index* (Roanoke, Va., 1934–1936).

quired at one of the repositories listed above, for their number is too great to be listed here. It is to be hoped that before it is too late an effort will be made to publish a bibliography of the Historical Records Survey and some account of the methods and aims of this significant undertaking to preserve the remains of the American spirit of the past.

Index

Adair, James, 192
Adams, John, 15
Agriculture, Back Country, 135, 140-43; in Carolina Society, 56, 57; in Chesapeake Society, 4-5
Alexander, Joseph, 186, 188
Allison, William, 168
Allston, Joseph, 68, 71
Allston, William, 82
American Company of Comedians, 28, 90, 92, 94
American Philosophical Society, 50, 107, 108
American Society for Promoting Useful Knowledge, 190
Anburey, Lt. Thomas, 148, 155
Ancient South River Club, 28
Anderson, Dr. Abraham, 177
Anderson, Hugh, 107
Architecture, Carolina Society, 109; Chesapeake Society, 47; *see also* Houses
Aristocracy, Back Country, 170-72; Carolina Society, 65-68, 75; Chesapeake Society, 10-18, 27; dress, 78; manner of life, 21, 24, 69-70, 72-74, 76-79; middle-class origins, 12, 20; patrons of art, 46; political privileges and powers, 11, 15, 16
Arndt, Gottfried, 187
Art collections, 111
Artisans, Back Country, 143, 148, 150, 152; Carolina Society, 62; Charles Town, 60
Artists and painting, Carolina Society, 110-11; Chesapeake Society, 48; preference for English, 48

Audubon, John James, 111
Augusta Academy, 185
Aust, Gottfried, 152
Avery, Waightstill, 186, 190

Back Country, 119-96; Americanization vs. national traits, 134; appraisal and review, 194-96; lands and boundaries, 120-21; regional variations, 136-37, 142-43; settlement, 122-28, 136
Bacon, Thomas, 32, 40
Ballads, 41, 192
Bartram, John, 58, 73, 107, 119, 193
Bartram, William, 107, 111, 119, 193
Baths and watering places, 95, 179-80
Beaufain, Hector Béranger de, 111
Bee, Thomas, 67
Benbridge, Henry, 111
Benbridge, Letitia Sage, 110, 111
Benfield, David, 7
Bethabara, N.C., 151
Bethania, N.C., 151
Beverley, William, 123
Blair, James, 31
Bond, Dr. Phineas, 50
Books and reading, Back Country, 189-91; Carolina Society, 103-105; Chesapeake Society, 40-42; *see also* Libraries, Printing and publishing
Bordley, John Beale, 48, 50
Boucher, Jonathan, 14, 18, 20, 31, 37, 40, 45
Bouquet, Col. Henry, 77
Boyd, Adam, 191
Braxton, Carter, 10